W9-AQR-474

The Ideologies of Theory
Volume 1

Theory and History of Literature
Edited by Wlad Godzich and Jochen Schulte-Sasse

For other books in the series, see p. xxx.

The Ideologies of Theory
Essays 1971-1986
Volume 1: Situations of Theory

Fredric Jameson
Foreword by Neil Larsen

Theory and History of Literature, Volume 48

PN 94 .J36 1988 v.1
Jameson, Fredric.
The ideologies of theory

University of Minnesota Press, Minneapolis

RITTER LIBRARY
BALDWIN-WALLACE COLLEGE

Copyright © 1988 by the University of Minnesota
All rights reserved. No part of this publication may be reproduced,
stored in a retrieval system, or transmitted, in any form or by any
means, electronic, mechanical, photocopying, recording, or
otherwise, without the prior written permission of the publisher.

Published by the University of Minnesota Press
2037 University Avenue Southeast, Minneapolis, MN 55414.
Published simultaneously in Canada
by Fitzhenry & Whiteside Limited, Markham.
Printed in the United States of America.

Library of Congress Cataloging-in-Publication Data
Jameson, Fredric.
  The ideologies of theory.

  (Theory and history of literature ; v. 48-   )
  Includes index.
  Contents: v. 1. Situations of theory.
  1. Criticism. 2. Marxist criticism. I. Title.
II. Series.
PN94.J36   1988   801'.95   88-4725
ISBN 0-8166-1577-2 (set)
ISBN 0-8166-1578-0 (pbk : set)
ISBN 0-8166-1558-6 (v.1)
ISBN 0-8166-1559-4 (pbk. : v. 1)

The following chapters are reprinted with permission of the
publishers: Chapter 1, "Metacommentary," from *PMLA*, 86, no. 1
(January 1971), pp. 9-18, copyright © 1971 by the Modern
Language Association of America; an earlier version of Chapter 2,
"The Ideology of the Text," from *Salmagundi*, 31-32 (Fall
1975-Winter 1976), pp. 204-46, copyright © 1975-76 by Skidmore
College, Saratoga Springs, N.Y.; Chapter 3, "Imaginary and
Symbolic in Lacan," from *Yale French Studies*, 55-56 (1977), pp.
338-95; Chapter 4, "Criticism in History," from *Weapons of
Criticism*, edited by Norman Rudich, pp. 31-50, copyright © 1976
by Ramparts Press, Palo Alto, Calif.; Chapter 5, "Symbolic
Inference; or, Kenneth Burke and Ideological Analysis," from
Critical Inquiry, 4 (Spring 1978), pp. 507-23, copyright © 1978 by
the University of Chicago Press; Chapter 6, "Figural Relativism; or,
The Poetics of Historiography," from *diacritics*, 6 (Spring 1976), pp.
2-9, copyright © 1976 by the Johns Hopkins University Press,
Baltimore, Md.; Chapter 7, "Modernism and Its Repressed; or,
Robbe-Grillet as Anti-Colonialist," from *diacritics*, 6 (Summer 1976),
pp. 7-14, copyright © 1976 by the Johns Hopkins University Press;
and Chapter 8, "Morality versus Ethical Substance; or, Aristotelian
Marxism in Alasdair MacIntyre," from *Social Text*, 8 (Winter
1983-84), pp. 151-54, © 1983 by Social Text.

The University of Minnesota
is an equal-opportunity
educator and employer.

An die Nachgeborenen:
Seth, Anne, Justin, Jenny

Wenn die Verknüpfung der Einzelphänomene zum
Kategorienproblem geworden ist, so wird durch
ebendenselben dialektischen Prozess jedes
Kategorienproblem wieder in ein geschichtliches Problem
verwandelt . . .

When the problem of connecting isolated phenomena has
become a problem of categories, by the same dialectical
process every problem of categories becomes transformed
into a historical problem . . .

Georg Lukács, *History and Class Consciousness*

Contents

Contents of Volume 2: Syntax of History

Foreword
Fredric Jameson and the Fate of Dialectical Criticism
Neil Larsen

The radical literary and cultural criticism of Fredric Jameson has today a currency among North American intellectuals in the humanities which no other Marxist criticism has enjoyed since the 1960s, and perhaps even since the pre-Cold War period. Jameson's book-length works, especially *Marxism and Form* (1971), *The Prison House of Language* (1972), and *The Political Unconscious* (1981), have achieved a virtual textbook status both as broadly appealing arguments for a Marxist, or dialectical, theory of literature and as themselves among the best practical guides to contemporary non-Marxist critical theories. One cannot dispute the historic importance of these works, especially *Marxism and Form*, in establishing the legitimacy of Marxist aesthetic theory among broad sectors of the literary critical profession—and in guaranteeing that the interest in precursors such as Lukács and the Frankfurt School theoreticians, rekindled during the student revolts of the 1960s, would survive to the present. Despite their considerable topical range, the many "occasional essays" collected in these volumes and punctuating the appearance of the longer works (the records, to use a phrase of Jameson's, of more "local skirmishes") all bear the marks of the same intellectual campaign. At almost no point in the varied pages herein contained does the particular argument cease to function as a general one *for* the method being applied. Jameson's occasional name for this method is "metacommentary," a term introduced in the opening essay and for which Jameson adduces mainly theoretical and even philosophical advantages. But surely the space across and beyond which commentary was and is to carry us has also been a historical space with its own set of coordinates.

How is this new legitimacy to be explained, particularly in view of our present ideological climate, which, if the standard wisdom holds true, shows a hostility to Marxism reminiscent of that seen during the depths of the Cold War? To be sure, "legitimacy" may be an overly generous word for a phenomenon limited to the academic circuits where books like Jameson's are read. But as evidenced by the publication in recent years of feature articles in newsweeklies on the subject of Marxist professors in the universities and by the formation of groups such as Accuracy in Academia, this phenomenon is significant enough to have rattled a few extra-academic cages. A partial answer may be sought in the theory of literature and the humanities as the "weakest link" in the chain of ideological workshops engaged in the reproduction of subjects required by contemporary bourgeois society. Jameson himself, writing with James H. Kavanagh, has invoked this notion in a contribution to the second volume of *The Left Academy*.[1] Then there is the familiar generational hypothesis, surmising that the entry into the professoriat of student radicals from the 60s has supplied the real base for a Marxist renaissance. Surely there is some truth in this as well, and the important concluding essay of *The Ideologies of Theory*, "Periodizing the 60s," may be read as in some ways Jameson's own testament to both a generation and a conjuncture preconditioning his own somewhat later discursive moment.

But there is a deeper anomaly in Jameson's success. This is the ironic and perhaps tragic condition of all "Western Marxism" diagnosed by Perry Anderson in his much read little book[2] as the divorce of Marxist theory, following on the defeats of proletarian revolution in Germany and Central Europe between the world wars, from mass revolutionary practice and its remarriage, or at any rate cohabitational relationship, to major bodies of bourgeois theory as a species of left critique and radical conscience. Whatever may ultimately be its 60s genealogy, Jamesonian Marxism can point to no current surge of broad, open class struggle for which it might serve as theoretical guide post or from which it might draw fresh dialectical insights. Jameson's, too, is a "theoretical practice" that makes no pretense to be anything else, at least for the present.

It is, in some measure, for this reason that, even as Jameson has achieved extraordinary success in gaining for Marxism a theoretical hearing among non-Marxist literary scholars, his own particular claim to a properly Marxian standpoint has, ironically, aroused suspicions among other avowedly Marxist and radical critics. A certain among of this can perhaps be attributed to what has often been a practice of distrusting theory itself, in preference for the more immediately "practical" questions of pedagogy. In its left version, such antitheoreticism typically regards the major theoretical questions as already solved, so that the task of Marxist scholars and intellectuals—questions of organizational type and affiliation aside—becomes one of "bringing theory to the masses" of literature students themselves by the more direct means of, for example, contesting and revising the established, ideologically dominant canon. Jameson, of course, would hardly be the one to oppose such pedagogical applications.³ Indeed, his books are likely to be included on the syllabus in the classroom struggle for radical interpretive positions. But Jameson's still primarily theoretical stance—which must begin by ascertaining "where the street *is* in the superstate"⁴—draws into question the very possibility of any local, micropolitical strategy of advancing against a late capitalist system of containment and domination which appears to have proved itself perfectly capable of adapting to the occasional critical encounters with its cultural manifestations. It is possible to invoke and perhaps even to remember historical situations in which the need to go beyond such a purely theoretical stance would require no argument other than events themselves. From a rhetorical standpoint at least, our own present seems not (yet) to be one of those. Sooner or later the debate about the authentically revolutionary character of a Marxist theory historically severed from what ought to be its corresponding revolutionary practice seems to find itself back on the same theoretical ground that it has called into question. Thus, whether or not one ultimately finds it possible to conform with Jameson's theoretical positions themselves, his theoretical posture as such cannot simply be refused.

What often passes for a "left" theoretical opposition to Jameson—"left" here referring to those dissenting positions that on some level identify themselves as either Marxist or sympathetic to a generally anticapitalist politics—has largely been taken up with Jameson's consistent allegiance, throughout his many and far-ranging forays into a variety of modern theoretical discourses, to a classical, Hegelian construction of the dialectic, with its notorious "imperative to totalize." Jameson is today to be counted as perhaps the most prominent among the small number of contemporary thinkers who continue to work within a tradition of Hegelian-Marxist philosophy and aesthetics stemming from the work of Georg Lukács. One work in particular—*History and Class Consciousness*—has been and remains *fons et origo* in this respect. To be sure, the Freudian moment—via Althusser—may assert a species of semiautonomy within the Jamesonian interpretive and theoretical apparatus, as much so here as in *The Political Unconscious*. But the very fact that it is, in Jameson's scheme of things, a *moment per se*, governing its own proper sphere within the mediated theoretical totality, confirms the Hegelian (via Lukács) perspective as ultimately authoritative and, in its own way, radical

To render a full account here of the intellectual "left" turn against Lukács and "Hegelian Marxism" is surely unnecessary for any reader who has been either a party or an onlooker to "Western" literary, methodological, and philosophical history in the last two to three decades. Beginning perhaps with the general turn of Western intellectual radicalism toward a Brechtian/Benjaminian left modernism over and against the realist aesthetic championed by

Lukács and a waning Marxist orthodoxy associated with the established Communist parties, the falling out with classical dialectic gathers momentum in the (still ambivalently Hegelian) defense of modernism of the late Adorno, until its great torrential spill into the left wing of structuralism and poststructuralism, as formulated first by Althusser and subsequently by the variety of Althusserian currents presently in circulation. In the course of this broadly ideological shift—with or without its accompanying, mass moment of praxis, depending on how you read the "60s"—the mantle of orthodoxy, though now largely conferred by academies rather than parties, comes to be placed on the shoulders of the onetime dissenters. Representative of this new left-modernist orthodoxy as it has lodged itself in the intellectual and political premises of what is perhaps its first generation of popularizing disseminators are recent works such as Eugene Lunn's *Marxism and Modernism* (1982), in which Lukács, while allowed his hearing as a singular historical player, is politely consigned to his "Stalinist" leanings. This latter term, always a fashion and a convenience among left intellectuals wary of their good academic standing, becomes increasingly useful as a means of conflating criticisms aimed at classical dialectic with those more mythological and reactionary broadsides against "totalitarianism," as if this connection were somehow self-evident. At some point Leninism too, though still formally upheld by old-line Althusserians, receives the stigmatizing stroke. Thus Lunn can, with serene condescension, contrast Lukács' adherence to Leninist party discipline with "Marx's insistence on the *self-emancipation* of the working class,"[5] as if the history of the last one hundred years and its practical lessons and problems were somehow unequivocal on this matter. In tracts like Michael Ryan's *Marxism and Deconstruction* (1982), one can still find honest theoretical arguments for such a position, but one wonders how long it will be before the newly authorized Marx of the Left Academy is himself found to be a "Stalinist," and the carefully drawn line that is supposed to separate the Lunns from the Lévys and Glucksmans can no longer be plotted.

In the face of repudiation of his philosophical allegiance as unorthodox and tainted by "totalitarian" affinities, Jameson has avoided the more characteristically Lukácsean and Leninist path of open polemics and has instead taken what is in effect the full rhetorical advantage of his methodological stance. Thus he slays his critics (actual and potential) not by exposing their thinking to what one might take to be its reactionary or nonrevolutionary essence, as measured by a "political equivalence" (as, e.g., in Lukács' equation of expressionist aesthetic doctrince with the ideology of the Independent Socialists[6]), but rather by gathering it directly onto the plane of metacommentary wherein its specific dissension from totalizing dialectic is itself rewritten as a reified and unreflecting aspect. In attempting to assert its own irreducible difference and refusal of mediation, the part expresses only what has become an unexpected movement of the whole itself, which is History. So, for example, in the course of assessing Hayden White's theory of historical tropes (see "Figural Relativism; or, The Poetics of Historiography"), Jameson expounds the practical interpretive advantages of *Metahistory* but only as conditional on an ultimate recognition of its antihistoricist standpoint as "not complete in itself and . . .intelligible concretely only at the price of its reintegration into the social history of culture as a whole."[7] The same sort of anticipatory historicizing has also served Jameson in confronting the more aggravated anti-Hegelianism of current left (and right) poststructuralisms, as in the remarkable feat of theoretical parrying whereby the "de-centered subject" and the "schizophrenic flux" are rethematized as reified presentiments of a new, utopian collective subject.[8] "An 'anti-Marxist' argument is only the apparent rejuvenation of a pre-Marxist idea. A so-called 'going beyond' Marxism will be at worst only a return to pre-Marxism; at best, only the rediscovery of a thought already contained in the philosophy one believes he has gone beyond."[9] The words here are Sartre's, but they could as well be Jameson's.

But whatever one may think of it, this endlessly adroit discursive maneuvering into positions that have Jameson *mediating* among the theoretical contestants as the very historical self-consciousness of their aporetic fix, far from vanishing into a restored sense of the whole, seems only to draw vexed attention to itself. The mediator, despite his broadly good intentions, is thought to be a meddler, whereas the appeal to a History in which all sides are expected to recognize their own reified frames emerges as the most suspect of notions. The contemporary bystander to this peculiar critical dispute may at length begin to consider whether the Jamesonian critical "moment," if it can be called that, does not reside in the (itself intensely historical) distrust that greets any attempt to invoke a common past, present, or future.

Perhaps the most thoughtful and explicit challenge to Jamesonian dialectic is to be found in Sam Weber's "Capitalizing History: The Political Unconscious,"[10] originally published as a review of Jameson's last major book-length work. Drawing on Louis Hartz' *The Liberal Tradition in America* (1955), Weber proposes to read in Jameson's view of Marxism as ultimate "horizon of interpretation" a covert repetition of paradigmatically North American liberal premises regarding the essentially abstract locus of conflict and difference. North American intellectuals, according to Hartz, inherited Locke without his aristocratic counterparts in questions of moral and political philosophy, and in thus decontextualizing what was a historically determined and relative critique of irrational social privilege, they ended up with a hypostatic model of political and intellectual "freedom" reflecting itself both in the institutions of North American capitalism (from legislatures to universities) and in their respective ideologies, e.g., pluralism. From its position of dominance among domestic intellectuals—including those in the literary critical profession—the liberal tradition has, according to Weber, reacted with characteristic anxiety at the prospect of rival, nonliberal theories of conflict and conflict resolution, notably orthodox Marxism and more recently poststructuralist theory. Both Marxist and poststructuralist theory are said to insist not only on the legitimacy and inevitability of conflict, but also on the fact that the institutional arenas are or should themselves be "conflictualized." But this challenge is then met with the predictable ruse, whereby the arbitrary authority of an interpretive claim on the meaning of a given text (the inherently conflictual nature of interpretation) is simply affirmed as conforming to a given "community of interpretation," which is itself not brought into question (Weber's example here is Stanley Fish's *Is There a Text in this Class?*). Or, if this is unsatisfactory, a theory is invoked that, while appearing to transcend the question of institutionally circumscribed consensus in the name of some authentically universal ground, in reality succeeds only in hypostasizing on a "higher" plane. This, in Weber's reading of *The Political Unconscious*, becomes Jameson's maneuver. Marxism, which for Weber is or ought to be "a theory not only of the necessity of conflict as an *object* of study, but also as the medium in which thought itself operates,"[11] becomes a radical sanction for existing liberal interpretive practice,[12] leaving everything "just as it was" in return for the acceptance of History as the invisible truth-giving Whole. In the end, says Weber, Jameson simply reinscribes at the center of interpretive practice that liberal fetish par excellence—the individual—that Marxism originally sought to undermine. For what is the individual if not the very myth of presence and self-identity that alone enables the totality itself to be thought without simultaneously calling into question the necessarily exterior and synchronic standpoint of the thinker?

What is—or would be—the Jamesonian rejoinder to the charge of a covert liberalism is something we will come to shortly. First, however, it is important to consider for a moment the "metanarrative" within which Weber's critique—with its claim to represent a postliberal, authentically radical and "conflictualized" politics—lodges itself. Central to Weber's critical exposure of Jamesonian dialectic is its effort to establish its uniquely "American" genealogy. "America" becomes, in this account of things, a kind of hybrid offshoot from the stalk of European history, synonymous with a form of capitalism cut off from its precapitalist origins and, as a result, unable to form an accurate, fully historical image of itself. We are lead to believe that the very *inorganicity* of capitalist society in the United States determines its hypostasis in the minds of its intellectuals. On the other hand, "Europe"— more particularly France—presents an instance of organic growth and development of capitalism out of its feudal "other" as well as an "intellectual tradition" stretching back to and perhaps beyond the bourgeois revolution itself. This fact apparently has prevented "European" intellectuals from absolutizing their own bourgeois-liberal phase and (by implication) has produced in them a greater propensity to see beyond the fetishes of the marketplace. For Weber this historical privilege is to be measured in the survival of "philosophy" in such ideologically immunized institutions as the Collège de France and the École Normale Superieure. Hegelian dialectic itself could presumably not have arisen but for this "conflictualized" environment, even if it ultimately sought to deny or erase difference in a final cancellation. Transplanted to the Lethean watered soil of "America," however, even this inadvertent memory is missing. "American" intellectuals must seek to absolutize and totalize their own standpoint, whether in the name of "consensus" or the "dialectic," because "American" history, owing to its amputated, grafted origins, can give them no sense of alterity, no standpoint within a differentiated whole which preexists them, thereby obviating the need to reinvent it. Like all colonial societies, "America" is a "people without history"—with Fredric Jameson as its hypostatizing pseudo-dialectician.

Many "American" intellectuals, Fredric Jameson no doubt among them, would not fail to perceive a certain partial truth in such a metanarrative. Quite apart form its curiously Romantic reversion to a nineteenth-century (and itself proto-Hegelian) discourse of the "history of people," (Weber speaks of the "genius of French society"), however, it seems a fact worth noting that in order to expose the Jamesonian dialectic as somehow generically "American," Weber's poststructuralist-inspired criticism falls back on the nondialectical and blatantly organicist idea of the Whole implied in the notion of European capitalism as somehow consciously relativized by its own precapitalist ground. What is perhaps suggested here is that in those rare instances in which poststructuralist thinking is actually caught in a position of having to argue for its own historical conditions of possibility—as in Weber's effort to out-historicize *The Political Unconscious*—the version of diachrony that emerges does little more than replace the Marxist account of present conditions as linked to an overriding and subsuming contradiction with the vulgar image of a historical immediacy in which national entities and their subsets (intellectual traditions, institutions, etc.) appear as the fundamental realities.

Not the least of the defects in such a historical mythology is its complete failure to consider the effects of imperialism/monopoly capitalism on the liberal paradigm: as both a reflection and an analogue of laissez-faire economics, the myth of a "free marketplace of ideas," with its own "invisible hand" guiding the conflicting claims of theory and interpretation along the paths of an ultimate and consensual truth, could at least boast a certain objectivity well founded in appearances so long as the marketplace itself did not cease to operate as the more or less effective nexus of social reproduction per se. But with the collapse of liberal, free-market capitalism in the protracted crisis of 1873-95 and the emergence of consolidated capitalist monopolies able, in partnership with the state, to increasingly assert control over the "free" movements of the market, the basis for even the objective illusion of truth as a spontaneous derivative of "unfettered" debate disappears. Social reproduction becomes more and more a process requiring the techniques of "marketing," a phenomenon that perhaps reaches its clearest cultural and political manifestation in fascism. Classical liberalism, whether "absolutized" or not, survives as little more than an apologia for a monopoly capitalist/imperialist power that can ill-afford even the limited scope of conflict allowed for under "free trade" policies and their intellectual and cultural analogues. Admittedly, the sheer untruth of the liberal paradigm may be harder to glimpse in the contemporary United States than in other more transparently centralized and statified societies—something no doubt linked to the extreme fragmentation of intellectual culture in the United States and the absence of any significant links between that culture and the masses, who remain largely unaffected by the debates, real or imagined, that grip the intellectual professions. But Weber's reduction of *The Political Unconscious* to the working out of some would-be *pensée sauvage* of the American intellectual tribe seems in many ways (as one might expect, given its odd redolence of a nineteenth-century European discourse of colonial exploration) to be based on a romanticized view of the United States as one huge barbaric marketplace. A more credible sociology of "metacommentary" and the "American" impulse to schemes of dialectical totalization might see here the drive to offset the effects of extreme intellectual fragmentation and atomization (a condition, unlike "conflict," that denotes an absence of connection between intellectual entities) through the elaboration of a new theoretical and interpretive division of labor. And whatever the ultimate validity of Jameson's particular division, it at least appears to constitute a discursive space, a kind of intellectual universe, in which one is not immediately forced to choose between one or another of the various methodological autisms. Weber mistakes for liberal accommodationism and the comfort of being on the winning side of the game what may be simply the relief experienced in the avoidance of self-willed isolation. Jameson's is after all a discourse that *talks* to the reader even as it cajoles, somehow suggesting the existence of a common predicament, rather than some absolute and inscrutable philosophical ban.

Despite the anachronism that frames his critique, Weber does raise the inevitable question with respect to the practice of Jamesonian "metacommentary": what accounts for the possibility of the stance of the metacommentarist as at once part of and exterior to the reified world s/he surveys? "As ideological criticism," Weber writes, "Marxism is 'simply' the place of the imperative to totalize, nothing more, nothing less. But is that place so simple to find, especially if its name can often be distorted or disguised by forms of Marxism that themselves must be subjected to the 'imperative to totalize'?"[13] And again,

> Viewed from a formal perspective ... Jameson's defense of marxism is caught in a doublebind: it criticizes its competitors as being ideological in the sense of practicing "strategies of containment," that is, of drawing lines and practicing exclusions that ultimately reflect the particularities—the partiality and partisanship—of special interests seeking to present themselves as the whole. But at the same time, its own claim to offer an alternative to such ideological containment is itself based on a strategy of containment, only one which seeks to identify itself with a whole more comprehensive than that of its rivals.[14]

Jameson's way out of this "doublebind," his discovery of a ground upon which the supervalidity of Marxian interpretation with its vision of the whole can be claimed to rest, is to appeal to the experience of History as sheer Necessity, History as—in Jameson's now memorable phrase—"what hurts," thus finally resisting all attempts to reclassify it as just another master narrative. Weber is quick to renew the charge of hypostasis at this final movement to arrest the proliferation of interpretive claims:

> The reader is thus led to reflect on the tension that pervades *The Political Unconscious*, between the "struggle" that is said to constitute the ultimate subject matter of texts and of their interpretations, on the one hand, and on the other, an essentially "constative" or "contemplative" conception of the process of interpretation itself."[15]

Here again, Weber's particular theoretical grounds for rejecting this appeal to History—itself an ahistorical hypostasis of "conflict" and nonidentity that rather slyly attempts to award itself Marxist credentials by redefining Marxism as a Nietzschean belief in the "necessity of conflict" (but *what* conflict, fought out by *what* opponents, and with *what* outcome?)—are a cure considerably worse than the disease. As with much of contemporary neo-Nietzschean thought, seeming left-wing goals rest on right-wing premises. Nevertheless, Weber's observation of the above-mentioned tension between the experience of History, which itself is fraught with struggles and the uncertainty of their outcomes, and the seemingly untroubled, self-warranting theoretical stance that pronounces all this as in accord with the laws of Necessity is undeniably acute.

Marx sought a solution to this tension or contradiction in the objective, historical existence of the proletariat. Reduced to the status of a commodity in a bourgeois society that is itself summed up in the internal contradiction of the commodity form, the proletariat becomes conscious of the whole of which it is a part by virtue of its own simultaneous precontainment of the whole. In contemplating itself, the proletariat views the social totality, as it were, from within. And yet the proletariat does not remain stationary and contemplative in this objective/self-knowledge, but "heralding the dissolution of the existing order of things, the proletariat merely announces the secret of its own existence because it *is* the *real* dissolution of this order."[16] Lukács, then, will build upon this fundamental principle of historical materialism an explicit epistemology, whereby the adoption of the "standpoint of the proletariat" as "identical subject/object of history" comes to constitute the material, historical ground from which the "knowledge of society as an historical totality"[17] becomes possible. Without entering into the various objections that have been raised against aspects of this particular "inversion" of Hegel, from the later self-critical Lukács himself to Althusser, it must still be observed that with it the problem of exteriority as raised by Weber is itself exposed as requiring a metaphysical solution to what is already revealed as a concrete, historical contradiction. The terms of Weber's critique become those of a "pre-Marxist" standpoint (recalling Sartre), seeing *aporias* where a materialist dialectic perceives the maturing contradiction of a capitalism that produces its own "gravediggers." It is surely a measure of Weber's poststructuralist Marxism (if that is what it is) that it never so much as entertains the question of the "standpoint of the proletariat," much less refutes its claim to supply an epistemological ground from which to build a dialectics of the whole.

But then so too is it a measure, albeit more ironic and contradictory, of Jameson's Marxism itself, which in a sense calls forth the charge of hypostasis for the very reason that it has often seemed unwilling to openly acknowledge the standpoint implicit in its claims as a methodology. In place of the dynamic, fully partisan, yet scientific impulse to dialectical thinking posited by historical materialism—the thesis that the proletariat is *driven* toward a dialectical thinking of its own situation by the very historical forces that have engendered it—Jameson falls back on an orthodox Hegelian notion of a second, self-conscious reflection. Thus in *Marxism and Form* Jameson characterizes dialectical thinking as

> a moment in which thought rectifies itself, in which the mind, suddenly drawing back and including itself in its new and widened apprehension, doubly restores and **regrounds** its earlier notions in a new glimpse of reality; first, through a coming to consciousness of the way in which our conceptual instruments themselves determine the shape and limits of the results arrived at (the Hegelian dialectic); and thereafter, in that second and more concrete movement of **reflection** which is the specifically Marxist form, in a **consciousness** of **ourselves** as at once the product and the producer of history, and of the profoundly historical character of our socio-economic situation as it informs both solutions and the problems which gave rise to them equally.[18] (emphasis added in bold face type)

From a descriptive standpoint there is certainly nothing to object to in this. But when the inevitable question is posed as to how this "dialectical and historical self-consciousness" that is Marxism is itself historically determined, one is left with the notion of some inexorable correction of nondialectical thought by a History that, in its very fateful and transcendent agency, seems to have severed itself from the real forces, agents, and events to which the concept is simultaneously held to refer.

Why this omission to claim for the dialectical method what Lenin once called the "partisanship of objectivity"? And what would the effect be on Jamesonian Marxism if the implications of the "standpoint of the proletariat" were to be worked back into its presuppositions? In answer to the first question, one may immediately point to the long prevailing view among sectors of both the North American and the European New Left that the proletariat—if indeed it any longer exists in anything like its industrial capitalist form in current "postindustrial" late capitalism—has shown itself unlikely to be, if not incapable of being, raised to a revolutionary class consciousness, and that in its place have arisen new revolutionary, or at least rebellious, social groupings (ethnic minorities, women, gays, and other countercultural and marginalized subjects) that cut across the now blurred lines of traditional class affiliation. Since publication of *Marxism and Form*, Jameson has consistently shown his affinities for this revised, essentially countercultural politics, although always carefully stipulating what may be its "exceptional" status as regards both past and (in "Periodizing the 60s") future struggles. Indeed, Jameson's writings, though classed formally as "theory," come as close as anyone's to being a general philosophy of the cultural and intellectual anticapitalism that grew out of the general social crisis of the "60s," and which, though diminished in scope and energy, still persists. Perhaps one could go even further and suggest, again along the lines of *History and Class Consciousness*, that the very tendency for the interconnectedness of capitalist relations to be revealed in sudden catastrophic form in conditions of economic crises accounts for the reemergence of a theoretical concern for totality in Jamesonian criticism. The apparent hypostasis of this dialectical consciousness, insofar as it can only account for its own historical genesis through the abstract postulate of a second reflection brought about through the seemingly fortuitous collison of thought with an absolute limit called History, might then be seen as a theoretical reflection of this catastrophic appearance of capitalist crisis (here the onset of the full-blown decline of United States imperialism) in the minds of intellectuals who, given the previous relative absence of any clear revolutionary analysis, are largely unprepared for its occurrence.

As its readers are well aware by now, Jameson's most recent work (not included in the present volumes) has sought to address the problem of "standpoint" by raising the question of third world literature and culture and their potentially critical impact on metropolitan theory and methodology. His 1986 essay, "Third World Literature in the Era of Multinational Capitalism," concludes by casting the contrastive "situational consciousness" of first and third worlds in terms of Hegel's master/slave dialectic: whereas the slave "knows what reality and the resistance of matter really are," the master "is condemned to idealism." "It strikes me," Jameson continues,

> that we Americans, we masters of the world, are in something of that very same position. The view from the top is epistemologically crippling, and reduces its subjects to the illusions of a host of fragmented subjectivities ... This placeless individuality, this structural idealism which affords us the luxury of the Sartrean blink, offers a welcome escape from the "nightmare of history," but at the same time it condemns our culture to psychologism and the "projections" of private subjectivity. All of this is denied to third world culture, which must be situational and materialist despite itself.[19]

The problem now, of course, remains to explain how the metacommentarist, as one who still presumably "views from the top," comes to occupy this epistemological ground which his/her "situation" would seem to withhold. And even if one knew precisely how a Jamesonian critical subject might incorporate its standpoint, there is still the problem of the "third world" itself as a category whose extreme generality and tendency to elevate nation over class makes it suspect. (Aijaz Ahmad, in a reply to Jameson, has proposed some salutary criticism on this score.[20]) But despite these very real difficulties, metacommentary at least demonstrates its general commitment to the idea of a historical and global praxis as, finally, the only genuine theoretical warrant. One is tempted to paraphrase the well-known Lukácsean defense of Mann and speak here of a class struggle whose "possibility" is still "glimpsed" at a time when postmodern dogmas assure us that classes themselves are no more than articulations within discourse. The third world may not be the place to look—if only because, if Ahmad is right, it isn't really a "place" at all. But Morazán, Managua, and Soweto are places—indeed, "situations"—that ought to mean the world to metropolitan-based theory.

But whether it is the "proletarianizing" or the "third world-izing" of metacommentary—the thrusting back into the actuality of class struggle (however "hidden") of the contemplative stasis of an abstract dialectical self-consciousness—it must be evident that we are here once again confronted in a general way with the dilemma of "revolutionary" theory severed from revolutionary practice, a dilemma that Jameson did not invent but, like the rest of us, inherited. Any criticism aimed at Jameson's "theoretical praxis" on this account must therefore, if it is not to fall into the facile groove of voluntarist projection, be embraced ipso facto as self-criticism without special exemptions. This condition being understood, we may be permitted a speculative observation regarding what might be the pressures exerted on

Jamesonian critical theory if and when, as intimated by Jameson himself in the final paragraph of "Periodizing the 60s," "traditional Marxism . . . become[s] true again."[21] For, this truth being recuperated, must one not thereby at least consider whether the various currents of non-Marxist theory with which Jameson has concluded a dialectical alliance "again" become false? With Marxism once again installed as the theory not only of the revolutionary proletariat but of the socialist transition and the advance to the classless society itself, will, say, the Kantian schemas of structuralism or the reified psyche posited in psychoanalysis still offer up to us their "moments of truth"? Or will they not, as in less exceptional days, justify the rather different assessment contained in the ascriptive category of *ideology?* This concept, while of significance to Jamesonian criticism and on occasion the object of both theoretical and methodological reflections, is nevertheless largely restricted by Jameson to the analysis of the literary and cultural text as such. The rival interpretive modes themselves, however, occupy a middle ground between ideology per se and the scientific, or at least fully critical and historically self-conscious, level of the dialectician—as, for example, in Jameson's account of the perennial Greimasian semantic rectangle as "the graphic embodiment of ideological closure as such [which] allows us to map out the inner limits of a given ideological formation."[22] Jameson's ingenious solution to what would otherwise be the problematic introduction of a theoretically undesirable and logically embarrassing third level wedged between a manifest ideological content and a latent historical and political content is of course to deploy the paradigm of reification. In this way Jameson is able to ascribe to the non-Marxist first reflection a fragmenting optic situated above the ideological object but also, so to speak, alongside it at a severe and distorting angle which is itself to be rectified by the second, fully dimensionalizing gaze of the dialectizing historical self-consciousness. This has been and remains the basic Jamesonian move, from *Marxism and Form* down to the more recent contributions to a theory of postmodernism.

What is canceled out by this maneuver, however—and what, we may speculate, the-becoming-true-again of traditional Marxism might again bring to the fore—is the classical theoretical configuration of ideology as *inversion.* As reemphasized most recently in the works of Jorge Larrain on Marx and Engels' theory of ideology,[23] the founders of historical materialism retained throughout the various phases of their theoretical production a critical and negative conception of ideology as the inverted consciousness of an itself literally inverted capitalist reality—as in the efforts of bourgeois political economy to naturalize a society in which exchange, which is originally no more than a means to consumption or use, ousts the latter to become the end of production itself. Jameson's method of rounding out and adding historical movement to the frozen, fragmentary thinking of non-Marxist theory—his particular concepton of ideology as a "strategy of containment"—is highly productive, but it omits this insight, suggesting a theoretically possible end to ideology in the sheer prevalence of a sufficiently broadened corrective consciousness. Symptomatic here perhaps is the rarity in the often brilliantly produced rhetorical fabric of Jameson's arguments of the discursive figure of inversion, so frequent in Marx.

The question is: can inverted consciousness be so corrected under the persistent conditions of an inverted capitalist reality? And is there not expressed in the figure of inversion what is already a vision of the whole characterized precisely by its total falsity, by an absolute mystification of the real which only a second inversion and not a second reflection—a "standing on its feet"—could possibly rectify?

That this attenuation in Jamesonian Marxism of the figure of inversion and its corresponding way of constructing the position of the scientific-critical subject over and against ideology has more than purely abstract, theoretical significance may be corroborated by turning once again to the question of poststructuralism—together, perhaps, with postmodernist culture, which Jameson has suggested as corresponding to it as its more immediate, nontheoretical, and aesthetic equivalent—and its peculiarly unstable orbit within the solar system of metacommentary. Jameson's refusal to be pinned down as to the politically progressive or reactionary character of these intellectual and aesthetic currents (see, e.g., "The Politics of Theory: Ideological Positions in the Postmodernism Debate" as well as "Periodizing the 60s," the concluding essay in *Ideologies of Theory)* in the name of a provisional dialectical suspension of all such "ethical" dualisms is premised on the notion that, like it or not, we are all *in*, as it were "coated" by a postcontemporary *Zeitgeist*, which poststructuralist theory and postmodernist aesthetics objectively, if distortedly, reflect. "The point is that we are *within* the culture of postmodernism to the point where its facile repudiation is as impossible as any equally facile celebration of it is complacent and corrupt."[24] It is thus not a matter of defining a political position somehow "for" or "against" what must, in good faith, be recognized as facets of our own cultural-historical present, but again of correcting the reified, ahistorical frame, and even, in the case of the poststructuralist rejection of "humanism" and the centered, self-identical subject, of uncovering the "seeds" of some collective, postindividual "future." Jameson echoes Marx's remark concerning the workers of the Paris Commune: they "have no ideals to realize" but only (in Jameson's words) "to disengage emergent forms of new social relations from the older capitalist social relations in which the former had begun to stir."[25]

The analogy drawn here between a proletariat bursting the past asunder through the sheer negative and at times unconscious force of its specific historical gravity (a force deriving from alterations in the base) and the political opacity of the superstructural trends which Jameson wishes, if not to defend outright, then to preemptively rescue from ideology, is a bold one indeed. And perhaps it is justified, at least insofar as it serves to remind us that "emergent" and "oppositional" culture (in Raymond Williams' sense) may crop up in the least expected places. The future is, after all, a somewhat dim prospect these days no matter where you look.

But it all depends on how you understand the present. Jameson fairly consistently holds to a view of late capitalism—emergent in the 60s—as a period of renewed capitalist expansion into the last redoubts of "Nature ... the third world and the unconscious."[26] His principal authority here is Ernest Mandel, although much the same analysis is developed by Immanuel Wallerstein, André Gunder Frank, Samir Amin, and other onetime "dependency" theorists. To be sure, the fact of such expansion itself is not to be disputed, but in the context of Jameson's cultural-historicism it suggests an underlying continuity on the level of the economic base, such that penetration of the social relations inscribed in capital preserves the former in an essentially identical configuration. The theory that contemporary bourgeois intellectual and cultural trends are the legitimate objects of historical materialist critique only insofar as they are cut off from the social-historical totality whose true features they nevertheless convey in negative hieroglyphic traces is thus ramified in the theory of capitalism per se as a whole that preserves its identity as it seeps into the farthest crevices of space and the psyche.

At least one theory of contemporary late capitalism, however, disputes this postulate of identity. In *Intellectual and Manual Labour*[27]—a work still largely unknown in the United States, although Jameson cites it in *The Political Unconscious*—the German Marxist sociologist and philosopher Alfred Sohn-Rethel argues, for example, that the introduction of techniques of "scientifically managed" flow production (Taylorism) at roughly the turn of the century—an intrinsic facet of the development of modern imperialism and monopoly—laid the basis for what he terms a new "social synthesis." The latter, unlike the market or exchange nexus which united classically capitalist society, derives from "the commensuration of labour in action."[28] It is the renewed "logic of production" implied in the resocialized labor of contemporary capitalist production which, according to Sohn-Rethel's quite literal application of the historical materialist guidelines set forth in Marx's famous preface, grounds the historical transition to a socialism (obviously to be distinguished from those "actually existing") characterized not only by the transfer of power and the socializing of the means of production, but by the actual disappearance of the old division of intellectual and manual labor erected upon and enabled by exchange-based social synthesis.

At the same time that this transition to what is in effect the earliest phase of communism becomes a real possibility, however, the capitalist monopolies themselves, in close coordination with the state, seek strategies of containing and arresting it. Principal among these is the creation of a caste of technical and bureaucratic managers (in German the *Betriebs-* or *Usurpatorenbürokratie)* charged with wresting the subjective control of the automated production process from the workers themselves. "Its activity and position," writes Sohn-Rethel in the second German edition of his work (see the section entitled "The Subject of Classless Societization"),

> presuppose the continuation of the capitalist market economy, indifferent to the fact that this economy is no longer able to effect social reproduction and instead tends toward the production of an increasing proportion of nonreproductive values.[29] (my translation)

This usurpatory agency—a precondition and perhaps the very "economic definition" of fascism[30]—becomes the source of a "managerial fetishism"[31] expressed in the spontaneous conviction that it is the sheer intellectual fact of "management," as a subject indifferent to all social aspects of production except its simple occurrence as an alienated process, that regulates society.

But meanwhile the truth of present-day society is precisely its *nonreproductive,* historically negative course, the result, in West as in East, of "dual social synthesis." We live temporarily enthralled to what may be the most inverted reality yet—one in which the very subjective faculty of socialized labor is laid prostrate before the pure fetish anonymity and subjectlessness of "scientific management." "The intellectual tasks vested in ... management are not seen as representing the worker's mind, but as deriving directly or indirectly from science and scientific technology."[32]

What are the forms of ideology (inverted consciousness) determined by such a real inversion? Beyond identifying the obvious instances of scientism and high-tech worship, Sohn-Rethel does not pursue his thesis to such lengths. But may we not ourselves speculate that they include the "theoretical" recourse to a poststructuralism characterized by Perry Anderson as "subjectivism without the subject,"[33] as well as, perhaps, the neo-Nietzschean doctrine of the ubiquity and "ambivalence" of power struggles? May not the "postindividual" future allegedly glimpsed by the vanguard sensibility of "postcontemporary" culture be, rather, the inverted, ideological images of what is already our substantive present?

It goes without saying that the conclusive discovery of any such ideological linkage remains to be carried out. Still, even its hypothetical possibility would seem to be canceled by the exclusive projection of current intellectual and cultural developments as integral if reified parts of a contemporaneity that informs our entire range of experience, so that we have no choice but to see the world through postmodern eyes. For it must still be asked: is it the world we thus see ... or the inverted image registered on a *camera obscura?*

Introduction

It does not seem to me particularly worthwhile to reconstruct the polemic contexts in which, over a number of years, the following essays were composed. Only the more theoretical interventions and statements have been retained here, literary critical essays and studies of mass culture being reserved for another place. The texts have mostly been reprinted without change; in only one instance ("The Ideology of the Text") have I experimented with a reconstruction, long after the fact, of the original plan of which the published section was a fragment.

Various ways might be imagined to frame such a collection or to confer a semblance of unity upon it: such as an intellectual autobiography, in which a certain number of themes are allegorized, in order to construct either a narrative of subjective development or a historical account of the tendencies of the period itself. This last, however, the reader will already find in the concluding chapter of this two-volume collection ("Periodizing the 60s"), an experiment in describing the tendencies of a historical period (along with a discussion of the theoretical and methodological problems involved in doing so), but framed at a level of abstraction that will do little to help position the specific topics of the essays themselves.

One might also have considered writing a general account of the preoccupations of literary criticism in the United States during those years. I must feel, however, that what we all experienced was less the logical (or dialectical) exploration of a *problematic* than the gradual emergence of one. Coherence in such an account, indeed, would seem above all to presuppose—even before the existence of an articulated field of conceptual problems—the very existence and social relations of groups of intellectuals, related by their very divisions and ideological oppositions, organized around institutions—most notably journals, and avant-garde movements (which play a function the university as such cannot sustain)—and, finally, active within a genuine public sphere. These conditions did not then (and perhaps can never) obtain for the superstate, although they may have been possible from time to time in national contexts in other parts of the world. Indeed, in my opinion, the "cultural envy" of the North American intellectual for imported (most often, but not exclusively, European) theoretical and cultural productions is to be explained primarily as a social, rather than a conceptual, matter: the longing for a public sphere in which intellectual work might again be felt as act and event, rather than as reified object and end product. Meanwhile, for Left intellectuals, the absence of mass political movement is notoriously debilitating and encourages compensatory sectarianism of a wholly personal nature, or else the free-floating vision of the isolated individual as the guardian of negativity and the place of the implacable "critique of what is."

My own intellectual trajectory is therefore as unrepresentative and as uncharacteristic as that of other North American intellectuals of my generation. I will mention only that feature of my situation which strikes me as the most positive, if not the most unusual. Sartre once observed that the happiest position for any writer to be in was to have to address two distinct publics (with their different codes and idiolects) at one and the same time. This proposition has always seemed to me to offer a very distant analogy with the contraints under which the essays here collected were mostly composed: the gap or tension between literary criticism (and its practice and theory) and the simultaneous vocation to explain and to popularize the Marxist intellectual tradition. I have rarely—in *writing*—been much interested in doing one of these things without the other; nor can I imagine that readers interested in one of them alone did not experience a certain frustration.

Times have changed since my initial experiment in this vein—an essay called "Metacommentary," which is included here for its substantive as well as for its formal interest—and literary criticism and Marxism alike have in the United States today a significance and a sophistication calculated to astonish the time traveler from the mid- or late 60s. This is to say that the situation has itself been historically modified; and in this respect I cannot feel that the problems posed by a historical account of the texts reprinted here are very different in kind from those posed by any attempt to transform disparate books and literary texts into that narrative we sometimes call literary history. What one writes, in doing such histories, is, in other words, the history of the *situations* of the texts, and not some "history" of the texts themselves, which, whatever they are considered to be—expressions, symptoms, symbolic acts, social and political events, subversive interventions, speech acts—are all profoundly discontinuous with each other.

Let me now briefly characterize the two types of changes I sought to help promote in the North American intellectual and cultural climate as I personally assessed it at the beginning of the work collected here. The first was to enlarge the conception of the literary text itself, so that its political, psychoanalytic, ideological, philosophical, and social resonances might become audible (and describable) *within* that experience of literary language and aesthetic form to which I remain committed. (The stereotypical characterization of such enlargement as *reductive* remains a never-ending source of hilarity.) To explain why this did not involve substituting for literature "some other thing," or why a commitment to the aesthetic never seemed at odds with a commitment to the political (but rather, indeed, *implied* it)—such explanations now seem to demand that very history of the period and of myself which I promised, at the outset, to avoid. But, of course, aestheticist traditions in other countries—for example, Latin America, in Russia, in many Third World cultures—have often been profoundly political in their conception of the nature of a cultural avant-garde; and perhaps even the North American 1950s—the Eisenhower era—will look a little different if one remembers that its aestheticism—in which I was formed—stood as a revulsion against an anticultural and antiintellectual business society. The 60s can then, just as easily, be seen as the ultimate confluence between culture and politics, as it can be interpreted as a reaction against the university system in which successful 50s aesthetes found their reconciliation with society at last.

The second impulse of my work—involving Marxism—I will try to characterize in a fashion designed to confuse those who think they know what this particular slogan means. For a second source of mirth—in this case, I have to confess, never altogether unmixed with exasperation—is afforded by the universal advance knowledge of your own positions shown by people who would probably be more careful in their "refutations" of the wearers of other labels—of Kantians, for example, or nuclear physicists, or Roman Catholics. Indeed, one of the satisfactions of our present intellectual situation is the greatly increased caution with which the ideologically hostile express their opinions on Marx, or Marxists, or Marxism, since they now face an intellectual public that has some minimal direct knowledge of the texts themselves. This does not yet, of course, amount to that "legitimation" of Marxism, that active presence of a Marxist intellectual culture and tradition in North American life, which seems desirable to many of us; but it is an improvement over the 50s and 60s.

I will, however, not now argue directly for Marxism, something that might be done by raising any number of very different but related topics: the power and extension of the commodity form, the peculiar dynamics of late capitalism, and the fate of culture (or of *postmodernism* within it), the comparative status of First-World technocrats and Third-World political and cultural intellectuals, the Utopian vision of socialism itself, the dynamics of ideology and of a properly political unconscious, the ongoing symbolic influence of social class and of class antagonism, the ontological difference between individualism and collective or group existence, and so on. In any case, any number of excellent introductions to Marxism now exist in English and, as with *Capital* itself, afford case histories in *Darstellung* or in "language experiments," which ought to be no less interesting for literary analysts than the incomparably better known texts of Freud.

I prefer, however, to speak of this second of my "themes" or "impulses" in another way here, in terms of the attraction of a Marxian worldview, or better still, of what J. F. Lyotard has called, in a wonderful phrase, "the desire called Marx." Here too, in my opinion, it is a matter of expansion rather than reduction, but of a different type. For my own intellectual formation was not merely aesthetic or aestheticizing ("style study" of the Romance philological kind, but also, let us say, the poetry of Ezra Pound)—but also existential, and very specifically Sartrean. I mention this final biographical fact to underscore the way in which (for me) a sense of the existential, of the unique and biological limits of personal existence, did not have the subjectivizing and psychologizing consequences often attributed to such philosophies.

On the contrary, it has always seemed to me that an intense awareness of one's individual existence serves to provoke and to exacerbate an equally strong and painful sense of what transcends it, in particular of what we call History.

The time of individual human biology is radically incommensurable with the time of nature or the time of social history (or indeed, in capitalism, the time of the great economic cycles); nor is this some easily adjustable matter of *durées*, but rather a vision of interlocking, yet somehow also alternate, worlds, in which beings of brief life spans are also the components of enormous and properly unimaginable totalities which develop according to vast and inhuman rhythms, and in a different temporality altogether. The units of individual life, whatever meaning we try to give them, are never the same as those of history, even when in rare and punctual convulsions—what we call revolutions—they briefly coincide. The "desire called Marx," then, is not the will to reduce one of these dimensions to the other (in any case an impossible matter), but rather the effort to develop organs of perception capable of enabling us fitfully to position ourselves in that other temporality, that other story, over which we also hope—but now as groups and collectives, rather than as individuals—to assert some influence and control. The "desire for Marx" can therefore also be called a desire for *narrative*, if by this we understand, not some vacuous concept of "linearity" or even *telos*, but rather the impossible attempt to give representation to the multiple and incommensurable temporalities in which each of us exists.

These essays do not, therefore, seek to convert their readers to Marxism; ideological commitment springs in any case from deeper sources and situations than those of discursive or rhetorical persuasion. But they do try to stage the attractiveness of a worldview—the only one, I think—for which those multiple dimensions and temporalities we sometimes crudely call the political, the history of forms, the dynamics of desire, the class texture of the social, the originality of the act, and geological rhythms of human history, all unimaginably coexist.

As for this collection, then, *its* story might now be told—if you like—as something like a shift from the vertical to the horizontal: from an interest in the multiple dimensions and levels of a text to the multiple interweavings of an only fitfully readable (or writable) narrative; from problems of interpretation to problems of historiography; from the attempt to talk about the *sentence* to the (equally impossible) attempt to talk about *modes of production*. This having been said, however, the formulation becomes one story among others, since the "author" no longer has any particularly privileged authority over these now printed texts.

Theory and History of Literature

I

Chapter 1
Metacommentary

In our time exegesis, interpretation, commentary have fallen into disrepute. Books like Susan Sontag's *Against Interpretation* emphasize a development no less central to modern literature than to modern philosophy, where all great twentieth-century schools—whether those of pragmatism or phenomenology, existentialism, logical positivism, or structuralism—share a renunciation of *content*, find their fulfillment in formalism, in the refusal of all presuppositions about substance and human nature, and in the substitution of method for metaphysical system.

What is felt to be content varies, of course, with the historical situation: thus the concept of a "symbol" once served a negative, critical function, as a wedge against an older Victorian moralizing criticism; now, however, along with the other basic components of the new-critical ideology such as irony and point of view, it all too often encourages the most irresponsible interpretation of an ethical or mythical and religious character. To name a symbol is to turn it into an allegory, to pronounce the word "irony" is to find that the thing itself, with all its impossible lived tension, has vanished into thin air. No wonder we feel symbolism in the novel to be such a lie; no wonder Williams' attack on metaphor came as a liberation to a whole generation of American poets!

The question about meaning, most frequently expressing perplexity before an object described as obscure, signals a fateful impatience with perception on the part of the reader, an increasing temptation to short-circuit

3

it with abstract thought. Yet just as every idea is true at the point at which we are able to reckon its conceptual situation, its ideological distortion, back into it, so also every work is clear, provided we locate the angle from which the blur becomes so natural as to pass unnoticed—provided, in other words, we determine and repeat that conceptual operation, often of a very specialized and limited type, in which the style itself originates. Thus the sentence of Gertrude Stein "A dog that you have never had has sighed" is transparent on a level of pure sentence formation, as paradigmatic as the operations of translation machines or transformational grammar. But I would hesitate to claim that it has a meaning, and indeed Gertrude Stein is a particularly good example of a writer whose characteristic materials—household odds and ends, string, boxes, lettuce leaves, cushions, buttons—disarm modern criticism in that they neither solicit visual perception nor haunt the mind with the symbolic investment of depth psychology. We cannot, therefore, interpret these sentences, but we can describe the distinctive mental operations of which they are a mark and which in the present case (distant relatives in that of Ionesco's mimicry of French middle-class conversation) consist in collages of American words designed to reveal in pure syntactical fashion, above and beyond any individual meanings, the peculiar flatness of the American idiom.

In matters of art, and particularly of artistic perception, in other words, it is wrong to want to *decide*, to want to *resolve* a difficulty. What is wanted is a kind of mental procedure that suddenly shifts gears, that throws everything in an inextricable tangle one floor higher and turns the very problem itself (the obscurity of this sentence) into its own solution (the varieties of Obscurity) by widening its frame in such a way that it now takes in its own mental processes as well as the object of those processes. In the earlier, naive state, we struggle with the object in question; in this heightened and self-conscious one, we observe our own struggles and patiently set about characterizing them.

Thus, very often the urge to interpret results from an optical illusion: it is no doubt a fairly natural first thought to imagine that there exists somewhere, ultimately attainable, some final and transparent reading of, say, a late sonnet of Mallarmé. But very often that ultimate reading, always just a hair beyond our own reach, turns out to be simply the reading of other people, the prestige of the printed word, a kind of ontological inferiority complex. Mallarmé's works exasperate this hopeless effect through their very structure, in that— wholly relational—nothing ever remains behind, even from the most exhaustive reading, from the most thoroughgoing familiarity. For the poet has devised his sentences in such a way that they contain no tangible substances or objects which we can substitute for the work itself, not even as a mnemonic device. All the apparent symbols dissolve back into sheer process, which lasts only as long as the reading lasts. Thus Mallarmé shows us how the reluctance to interpret, on the part of the critic, tends to veer around into an aesthetic on the part of the artist, tends to reappear in the work itself as the will to be *uninterpretable*. So form tends to glide imperceptibly into content; and Sontag's book is itself not exempt from the conceptual embarrassment of this position, which begins by denying the rights of *all* interpretation, of *all* content, only to end up defending a particular type of (modernistic) art that cannot be interpreted, that seems to have no determinate content in the older sense.

We must apply to the problem of interpretation itself the method I have suggested for the interpretation of individually problematic works: not a head-on, direct solution or resolution, but a commentary on the very conditions of existence of the problem itself. For we are all now in a position to judge the sterility of efforts to devise a coherent, positive, universally valid theory of literature, of attempts to work out some universal combination good for all times and places by weighing the various critical "methods": the illusion of Method has come to seem just as abstract and systematic an enterprise—in the bad sense—as the older theories of beauty that it replaced.[1] Far more useful for our purposes is Paul Ricoeur's distinction, in his monumental study of Freud, *De l'interpretation* (English title, *Freud and Philosophy*), between a negative and a positive hermeneutic: the latter aiming at the restoration of some original, forgotten meaning (which Ricoeur for his part can only conceive of in the form of access to the *sacred*), while the former has as its essential function demystification, and is in that at one with the most fundamental modern critiques of ideology and illusory consciousness associated with the names of Nietzsche, Marx, and Freud.

The starting point for any genuinely profitable discussion of interpretation therefore must be not the nature of interpretation, but the need for it in the first place. What initially needs explanation is, in other words, not how we go about interpreting a text properly, but rather why we should even have to do so. All thinking about interpretation must sink itself in the strangeness, the unnaturalness, of the hermeneutic situation; or to put it another way, every individual interpretation must include an interpretation of its own existence, must show its own credentials and justify itself: every commentary must be at the same time a metacommentary as well.

Thus genuine interpretation directs the attention back to history itself, and to the historical situation of the commentator as well as of the work. In this light, it becomes clear how the great traditional systems of hermeneutic—the Talmudic and the Alexandrian, the medieval and the abortive Romantic effort—sprang from cultural need and from the desperate attempt of the society in question to assimilate monuments of other times and places, whose original impulses were quite foreign to them and which required a kind of rewriting—through elaborate commentary and by means of the theory of figures—to take their place in the new scheme of things. Thus Homer was allegorized, and both pagan texts and the Old Testament itself were refashioned to bring them into consonance with the New.

It will, of course, be objected that such rewriting is discredited in our own time, and that if the invention of History means anything, it means respect for the intrinsic difference of the past itself and of other cultures. Yet as we become a single world system, as the other cultures die off, we alone inherit their pasts and assume the attempt to master that inheritance. *Finnegans Wake*, on the one hand, and Malraux's *Voices of Silence*, on the other, stand as two examples—the mythical and the conceptual—of the attempt to build a syncretistic Western system. In the socialist countries, where the feeling of a conscious elaboration of a universal world culture and world view is stronger than in our own, the problem of a Marxist hermeneutic poses itself with increasing intensity. Let the work of Ernst Bloch stand as an illustration of everything it has so far achieved. Yet our initial embarrassment remains: for in modern times what cries out for interpretation is not the art of other cultures so much as that of our own.

Thus it would seem that we are condemned to interpret at the same time that we feel an increasing repugnance to do so. Paradoxically, however, the rejection of interpretation does not necessarily result in anti-intellectualism, or in a mystique of the work; it has also, historically, been itself the source of a new method. I am referring to Russian Formalism, whose originality was precisely to have operated a crucial shift in the distance between the literary object and its "meaning," between form and content. For the Formalists carried the conventional notion of artistic technique to its logical conclusion; in Aristotelianism, this concept of technique had always led outside the work of art itself, toward the "end" or purpose for which it was constructed, toward its effect, toward psychology or anthropology or ethics.

The Formalists reversed this model and saw the aim of all technique simply as the production of the work of art itself. Now the meanings of a work, the effect it produces, the world view it embodies (such as Swift's misanthropy, Flaubert's ennui), become themselves technique: raw materials which are there in order to permit this particular work to come into being. With this inversion of priorities the work itself is turned inside out, seen now from the standpoint of the producer rather than that of the consumer, and a critical revolution is achieved that bears striking resemblance to what the "epoche" or setting of reality between parentheses does for Husserl's phenomenology. For now the referential values of the work (its meaning, the "reality" it presents, reflects, or imitates) are suspended, and for the first time the intrinsic structures of the work, in its autonomy as a construction, become visible to the naked eye.

At the same time, a host of false problems are disposed of. In his classic essay "The Making of Gogol's *Overcoat*," for instance, Boris Eichenbaum is able to adjourn permanently the vexing problem of whether Gogol is to be considered a "romantic" (the grotesques, the ghost at the end, the occasional pathos in tone) or a "realist" (the evocation of Saint Petersburg, of poverty, of the lives of little people). For Gogol's starting point is not a "vision of life," not a meaning, but rather a style, a particular type of sentence: he wishes to transpose to the level of the art-story the gestures and storytelling techniques characteristic of the traditional Russian *skaz*, or oral yarn (something on the order of the American tall tale or the stories of Mark Twain, as the Formalists were fond of pointing out). It is therefore a misconception to imagine that in Gogol form is adequate to content: on the contrary, it is because Gogol wishes to work in a particular kind of form, and to speak in the tone of voice of the *skaz*, that he casts about for raw materials appropriate to it, for anecdotes, names, piquant details, sudden shifts in manner. It now becomes clear why neither the grotesque nor the pathetic can be seen as the dominant mode of the story: for the *skaz* lives by their opposition, by their abrupt alternation with each other.[2]

In much the same way, Viktor Shklovsky undertook to prove that the meaning of character, the implications of apparently mythical figures, results from a similar kind of optical illusion: Don Quixote is not really a character at all, but rather an organizational device that permits Cervantes to write his book, serving as a thread that holds a number of different types of anecdotes together in a single form. (Thus Hamlet's madness permitted Shakespeare to piece together several heterogeneous plot sources, and Goethe's Faust is an excuse for the dramatization of many different moods; indeed, one begins to wonder whether there is not some deeper correlation between these Western "myth" figures and their technical function as a means of holding together and unifying large quantities of disparate raw material.)

Ultimately, of course, the implications of Formalist doctrine spill out the work into life itself: for clearly, if content exists in order to permit form, it follows that the lived sources of that content—the social experiences, the psychological obsessions and dispositions of the author—also come to be formally motivated, to be seen as means rather than ultimate ends or meanings. "Tout, au monde, existe pour aboutir à un livre" ("The function of the world is to serve as raw material for its own book"), said Mallarmé, and Formalism is a similarly radical aesthetization of life, but one of a relatively nonmystical, artisanal variety. In an essay entitled "Tolstoy's Crises," Eichenbaum shows how even Tolstoy's religious conversion itself can be considered a kind of "motivation of the device," in the sense that it provided new material for an artistic practice on the point of exhausting itself. Thus the writer becomes himself/herself only one more instrument toward the bringing into being of the work.

Formalism is thus, as we have suggested, the basic mode of interpretation of those who refuse interpretation: at the same time, it is important to stress the fact that this method finds its privileged objects in the smaller forms, in short stories or folktales, poems, anecdotes, in the decorative detail of larger works. For reasons to which we cannot do justice in the present context, the Formalistic model is essentially synchronic and cannot adequately deal with diachrony, either in literary history or in the form of the individual work, which is to say that Formalism as a method stops short at the point where the novel as a problem begins.

For the novel—no longer really a "genre" in the traditional sense—may be thought of as an attempt to come to terms with Time, and since it is a temporal process, and never fully present at any point, every effort to grasp it conceptually, to step back and think about it as an object, is of necessity interpretation before the fact. So that what cries out for explanation above all else is not so much that we interpret novels, but that we do not always feel the need to do so, that there are certain types of novels which, for whatever reasons of internal structure, somehow seem self-justifying and to dispense with external commentary. I am thinking, for example, of the classical well-made plot, the novel of intrigue and denouement, of which the model, no doubt, remains *Tom Jones.*

At this point, therefore, we reach a second basic principle of metacommentary: namely, that the absence of any need for interpretation is itself a fact that calls out for interpretation. In the novel of plot, in particular, the feeling of completeness is substituted for the feeling of meaning; there would seem to be something mutually exclusive about the type of attention required in apprehension of the various strands of plot, and the transformational process whereby for the sentences of the individual work is substituted a sudden global feeling of a vision of life of some kind. The processes of plot resolution tend to sink us ever more deeply into the empirical events themselves and find their intrinsic satisfaction in a logical immanent to the anecdotal. Indeed, the "philosophic" effect of the well-made plot, if I may term it that, is first and foremost to convince us that such a logic exists, that events have their own inner meaning along with their own development and do not have to be transformed into images. But such "philosophic content" is not a question of ideas or insights, but rather something more closely approximating what classical German philosophy would have called a formal Idea, one that works through sensible appearance only and cannot be abstracted out, cannot exist in the form of the general but only in its particular, sensory mode. Not as illustration to abstract thesis, therefore, but rather as experience to the very preconditions of experience itself, the novel of plot persuades us in concrete fashion that human action, human life, is somehow a complete, interlocking whole, a single, formed, meaningful substance.

In the long run, of course, the source of this lived unity lies not in metaphysics or religion, but in society itself, which may be judged, at any given moment of its development, from the fact that it does or does not offer raw materials such that plot can be constructed from them. Thus the appearance of a melodramatic strain in classical plots (particularly toward the middle of the nineteenth century) is a sign that events no longer cohere, that the author has had to appeal to Evil, to villains and conspiracies, to restore some of the unity he felt it beyond his power to convey in the events themselves.

For it is axiomatic that the existence of a determinate literary form always reflects a certain possibility of experience in the moment of social development in question. Our satisfaction with the completeness of plot is therefore a kind of satisfaction with society as well, which has through the very possibility of such an ordering of events revealed itself to be a coherent totality, and one with which, for the moment, the individual unit, the individual human life itself, is not in contradiction. That the possibility of plot may serve as something like a proof of the vitality of the social organism we may deduce, negatively, from our own time, where that possibility is no longer present, where the inner and the outer, the subjective and the objective, the individual and the social, have fallen apart so effectively that they stand as two incommensurable realities, two wholly different languages or codes, two separate equation systems for which no transformational mechanism has been found: on the one hand, the existential truth of individual life, which at its limit is incommunicable, and at its most universal turns out to be nothing more than the case history; and, on the other, the interpretive stereotype, most generally a sociological overview of collective institutions that deals in types of character when it is not frankly expressed in statistics or probabilities. But at the time of the classical novel, this is not yet so; and faced with such tangible demonstration of the way in which individual destinies interweave and are slowly, through the process of their interaction, transformed into the collective substance itself before our very eyes, we are not unwilling to limit ourselves for a time to the "realistic" mode of thinking about life. For the existential always excludes the symbolic, the interpretive: we cannot see the surface of life and see through it simultaneously.

Melodrama is, however, only a symptom of the breakdown of this reality. Far more significant, from the point of view of literary history, is the replacement of the novel of plot with something new, in the occurrence, with what we have come to call the psychological novel. This consists in the substitution of the unity of personality for the unity of action, at which point that essential "philosophical" satisfaction of which we spoke above is shifted from the feeling of completeness of events to the feeling of identity or permanence in time of the monad or point of view. But that shift is, of course, a qualitative leap, what Bachelard called a "coupure épistémologique," a kind of mutation in our distance from life and our thinking about it. What is relevant about the psychological novel for our present purposes is that in the novel of point of view, where little by little the action of the book comes to coincide with the consciousness of the hero, interpretation is once more interiorized, immanent to the work itself, for it is now the point-of-view figure who from within the book, reflecting on the meaning of his experiences, or hers, does the actual work of exegesis for us before our own eyes.

Point of view, therefore, is something a little more than sheer technique and expresses the increasing atomization of our societies, in which the privileged meeting places of collective life and of the intertwining of collective destinies—the tavern, the marketplace, the high road, the court, the paseo, the cathedral, yes, and even the city itself—have decayed, and with them, the vital sources of the anecdote. The essential formal problem of monadic storytelling is, of course, the location of the proper windows. In this sense, when Jean Rousset sees the very paradigm of the novel form in the act of *eavesdropping*—from *La Princesse de Clèves* to *Sodome et Gomorrhe*[3]—he thereby designates the essential narrative gesture of the psychological novel, rather than that of the novel in general, which can have no paradigm. Ultimately, the social reality that lies behind point of view—the isolation and juxtaposition of closed subjectivities—stands revealed in the very effort of the form to transcend itself: think of those *récits* through which Gide expressed the truth of individual existence, and then of his attempt, in his one *roman*, to "combine" them in additive fashion, as though to fashion a genuinely collective structure through an effort of the will.

With the death of the subject, of the consciousness that governed point of view, the novel, bereft of either unity of action or unity of character, becomes what we are henceforth agreed to call "plotless," and with the plotless novel, interpretation reasserts its claims with a vengeance. For once again it is a question of sheer reading time itself, sheer length. On every page a book like *Naked Lunch* approaches the hallucinatory intensity of the movies or the dream, a kind of narcosis of sensory perception. But over longer stretches the mind blows its fuses, and its abstract, pattern-making functions reappear underground: Reason, one is tempted to say, at work unconsciously, is unable to cease making those intricate cross-references and interconnections that the surface of the work seems to deny.

The plotless work thus stands before us as a kind of rebus in narrative language, a strange kind of code written in events or hieroglyphs, and analogous to primitive myth, or fairy tales. At this point, therefore, a new hermeneutic, developed precisely out of the study of such privileged objects, proposes itself, that of structuralism. For structuralism as a method or mode of research is formalistic in that it studies organization rather than content and assumes the primacy of the linguistic model, the predominance of language and of linguistic structures in the shaping of meaningful experiences. All the layers or levels of social life are ordered or systematic only insofar as they form languages of their own, in strictest analogy to the purely linguistic. Styles of clothing, economic relationships, table manners and national cuisines, kinship systems, the publicity apparatus of the capitalist countries, the cosmological legends of primitive tribes, even the mechanisms of the Freudian mental topology—all are systems of *signs*, based on differential perceptions and governed by categories of exchange and transformation.[4]

Structuralism may thus be seen as one of the most thoroughgoing reactions against substantialist thinking in general, proposing as it does to replace the substance (or the substantive) with relations and purely relational perceptions. This means, in our own terms, that it eschews interpretation in the older sense, which was essentially substantialistic: for just as Adam, naming the creatures, founded a poetry of nouns, so for the older forms of interpretation symbols are visual nouns, which you translate back into their meanings; and the attachment to content in general may be seen as a mark of belief in substance as such. But when, as in structuralism, substance is replaced by relationship, then the noun, the object, even the individual ego itself, become nothing but a locus of cross-references—not things, but differential perceptions. That is to say, a sense of the *identity* of a given element derives solely from our awareness of its *difference* from other elements, and ultimately from an implicit comparison of it with its own opposite. Thus the dominant category of structuralism as a method is the concept of the binary opposition, the notion that all meanings are organized, following the pattern of phonology, in pairs of oppositions or determinate differences.

The value of the binary opposition as an instrument of exegesis may be most strikingly demonstrated, perhaps, in Lévi-Strauss' henceforth classic analysis of the Oedipus legends,[5] the episodes of which he sorts out into paired groups of ever widening comprehensiveness. Thus, on the one hand, struggles with monsters (the Sphinx, Cadmus' dragon); on the other, physical deformity (as signaled etymologically by the names of Oedipus and of his forefathers); elsewhere an "unnatural" intimacy between kin, which stands in evident contrast to the murder of fathers and brothers. These groupings or categories are not, however, empirically derived, for they could scarcely have been formulated in the absence of the key methodological presupposition as to the essential structural organization of the material by pairs of opposites in the first place. In a different scheme of things, for instance, the Antigone episode might have been understood in contrast to the paternal incest, as the defense of natural law against the unnatural breaking of a taboo. Here, however, the two episodes are pronounced to entertain a structural relationship to each other; their classification together is preselected by the initial arrangement of the material into an opposition of the "overestimated kinship relations," of which they are the embodiment, with the "underestimated" ones of patricide and fratricide.

The interpretation by binary opposition depends, therefore, on a process of increasing abstraction, on the evolving of a concept "such that" otherwise unrelated episodes may be perceived in its light to be opposed to each other, a concept sufficiently general to allow two relatively heterogeneous and contingent phenomena to be subsumed beneath it as a positive to a negative.

Nowhere is this process more transparent than in the construction of the first pair of oppositions, where it is the category of the Inhuman in general that allows us to assimilate the Monstrous to the Deformed, that permits us therefore to correlate the slaying of the monsters (as a triumph of man over the dark forces) with that physical deformation of life which marks a partial defeat at their hands.

Binary opposition is, of course, only one of the heuristic instruments of structuralist analysis, just as it is only one aspect of the structure of language. It seems to me an exceedingly useful device for the exploration of enigmatic works, such as medieval romances, where a string of apparently arbitrary episodes must somehow be correlated together meaningfully. Yet when the structuralists come to deal with more conventional literary forms, we find that the concept of binary opposition is subsumed under the analogy of discourse in general, and that the standard procedure of such analysis is the attempt to determine the unity of a single work as though it were a single *sentence* or message. Here the most revealing paradigm, perhaps, is that of Freud in the *Interpretation of Dreams*, particularly as the unconscious mechanisms described in it have been reworked by Jacques Lacan into a series of rhetorical figures.[6] And let us also mention here, for the sake of completeness, that ultimate linguistic opposition of metaphor to metonymy, codified by Roman Jakobson, and similarly adopted by Lacan to describe the psychic forces. The work is therefore analyzable as a communication elaborated according to these mechanisms, which are the basic mechanisms of language and of all language systems or systems of signs.

But a sentence, of course, also has a *meaning;* and to return to Lévi-Strauss' treatment of the Oedipus myth, we may there surprise an imperceptible slippage from form into content, which is one way or another characteristic of all the other types of structuralist analysis as well. For having worked out his essential pattern of oppositions, Lévi-Strauss then proceeds to *interpret* it. The monsters are Earth deities, or symbols of Nature; the human figures either possessed by them or liberating themselves from them are consequently images of consciousness or better still of Culture in general: "the overevaluation of blood relationship is to the underevaluation of the latter as the effort to escape autochthony is to the impossibility of doing so."[7] The myth becomes a meditation on the mystery of the opposition between Nature and Culture; becomes a statement about the aims of Culture (the creation of the kinship system and the incest taboo) and about its ultimate contradiction by the natural itself, which it fails in the long run to organize and to subdue. But what I would like to stress is not so much the overemphasis on knowledge (for Lévi-Strauss, as is well known, so-called primitive thought is a type of perceptual science as worthy of respect as, although quite different from, our own), but rather the way in which the myth is ultimately given a content that is none other than the very creation of the myth (Culture) itself. "Myths," he says elsewhere,[8] "signify the spirit which elaborates them by means of the world of which it is itself a part." Thus a method that began by seeing myths or artworks as language systems or codes in their own right ends up passing over into the view that the very subject matter of such works or myths is the emergence of Language or of Communication, ends up interpreting the work as a statement *about* language.

As a pure formalism, therefore, structuralism yields us an analysis of the work of art as an equation the variables of which we are free to fill in with whatever type of content happens to appeal to us—Freudian, Marxist, religious, or indeed the secondary and, as it were, involuntary content of structuralism itself as a statement about language. The distinction would seem to be that described by Hirsch[9] (following Frege and Carnap) as the meaning, or *Sinn*, of the work, its essential and unchanging formal organization, and its significance, or *Bedeutung*, the changing evaluations and uses to which it is put by its generations of readers, or indeed, what we have called the giving of a type of content, *interpretation* in the more traditional sense. But I cannot think that this literary agnosticism offers anything more than a temporary and pragmatic solution to the deeper theoretical problems involved.

It seems to me that a genuine transcendence of structuralism (which means a completion, rather than a repudiation, of it) is possible only on condition we transform the basic structuralist categories (metaphor and metonymy, the rhetorical figures, binary oppositions)—conceived by the structuralists to be ultimate and rather Kantian forms of the mind, fixed and universal modes of organizing and perceiving experience—into *historical* ones. For structuralism necessarily falls short of genuine metacommentary in that it thus forbids itself all comment on itself and on its own conceptual instruments, which are taken to be eternal. For us, however, it is a matter not only of solving the riddle of the sphinx, that is, of comprehending it as a locus of oppositions, but also, once that is done, of standing back in such a way as to apprehend the very form of the riddle itself as a literary genre and the very categories of our understanding as reflections of a particular and determinate moment of history.

Metacommentary therefore implies a model not unlike the Freudian hermeneutic (divested, to be sure, of its own specific content, of the topology of the unconscious, the nature of libido, and so forth), one based on the distinction between symptom and repressed idea, between manifest and latent content, between the disguise and the message disguised. This initial distinction already answers our basic question, Why does the work require interpretation in the first place? by posing it forthrightly from the outset, by implying the presence of some type of Censor which the message must slip past. For traditional hermeneutic, that Censor was ultimately History itself, or cultural Difference, insofar as the latter deflected the original force and sullied the original transparency of Revelation.

But before we can identify the place of censorship in our own time, we must first come to terms with the message itself, which may very loosely be described as a type of *Erlebnis*, or *expérience vécue*, a lived experience of some sort, no matter how minimal or specialized. The essential characteristic of such raw material or latent content is that it is never initially formless, never, like the unshaped substances of the other arts, initially contingent, but rather is itself already meaningful from the outset, being nothing more nor less than the very components of our concrete social life: words, thoughts, objects, desires, people, places, activities. The work does not confer meaning on these elements, but rather transforms their initial meanings into a new and heightened construction of meaning; and that transformation can hardly be an arbitrary process. I do not mean by that that it must be realistic, but only that all stylization, all abstraction in the form, ultimately expresses some profound inner logic in its content and is ultimately dependent for its existence on the structures of the raw materials themselves.

At this point, therefore, we touch on the most basic justification for the attack on "interpretation," and for the resolute formalism of a metacommentary or a metacriticism. *Content does not need to be treated or interpreted because it is itself already essentially and immediately meaningful,* meaningful as gestures in situation are meaningful, as sentences in a conversation. Content is already concrete, in that it is essentially social and historical experience, and we may say of it what Michelangelo said of his stone, that it sufficed to remove all extraneous portions for the statue to appear, already latent in the marble block. Thus, the process of criticism is not so much an interpretation of content as it is a revealing of it, a laying bare, a restoration of the original message, the original experience, from beneath the distortions of the censor: and this revelation takes the form of an explanation why the content was so distorted; it is inseparable from a description of the mechanism of censorship itself.

And since I have mentioned Susan Sontag above, let me take as a demonstration of this process her essay on science fiction, "The Imagination of Disaster," in which she reconstructs the basic paradigm of the science-fiction movie, seeing in it an expression of "the deepest anxieties about contemporary existence . . . about physical disaster, the prospect of universal mutilation and even annihilation . . . [but more particularly] about the condition of the individual psyche."[10] All of this is so, and her essay provides a thorough working through of the materials of science fiction *taken on its own terms.* But what if those terms were themselves but a disguise, but the "manifest content" that served to mask and distract us from some more basic satisfaction at work in the form?

For beneath the surface diversion of these entertainments, beneath the surface preoccupation of our minds as we watch them, introspection reveals a secondary motivation quite different from the one described above. For one thing, these works, particularly in the period atmosphere of their heyday after the war and in the 1950s, rather openly express the mystique of the scientist. And by that I do not refer to external prestige or social function, but rather to a kind of collective folk dream about the condition of the scientist himself—he does not do *real* work, yet he has power and crucial significance; his remuneration is not monetary, or at the very least money seems no object; there is something fascinating about his laboratory (the home workshop magnified into institutional status, a combination of factory and clinic), about the way he works nights (he is not bound by routine or by the eight-hour day); his very intellectual operations themselves are caricatures of the way the nonintellectual imagines brainwork and book knowledge to be. There is, moreover, the suggestion of a return to older modes of work organization, to the more personal and psychologically satisfying world of the guilds, in which the older scientist is the master and the younger one the apprentice, in which the daughter of the older man becomes "naturally enough" the symbol of the transfer of functions. And so forth: these traits may be indefinitely enumerated and enriched. What I want to convey is that ultimately none of this has anything to do with science itself but is simply a distorted reflection of 1950s male feelings and dreams about *work*, alienated and nonalienated: it is a wish fulfillment that takes as its object a vision of ideal work, or what Herbert Marcuse would call "libidinally gratifying" work. But it is a wish fulfillment of a peculiar type (and it is this structure that I wish also to insist on); for we do not deal here with the kind of direct and open psychic identification and wish fulfillment that might be illustrated (for the subject matter of scientists) through the works of C. P. Snow, for instance. Rather, this is a symbolic gratification that wishes to conceal its own presence: the identification with the scientist is not here the mainspring of the plot, but rather its pre-condition only, and it is as though, in a rather Kantian way, this symbolic gratification attached itself, not to the events of the story, but to that framework (the universe of science, the splitting of the atom, the astronomer's gaze into outer space, and also, no doubt, some patriarchal guild system) without which the story could not have come into being in the first place. Thus, in this perspective, all the cataclysmic violence of the science-fiction narrative—the toppling buildings, the monsters rising out of Tokyo Bay, the state of siege or martial law—is but a pretext, which serves to divert the mind from its deepest operations and fantasies, and to motivate those fantasies themselves. (In this fashion, metacommentary adopts, if not the ideology, then at least the operative techniques of Russian Formalism, in its absolute inversion of the priorities of the work itself.)

No doubt we could go on and show that alongside the fantasy about work there is present yet another, which deals with collective life, and which uses the cosmic emergencies of science fiction as a way of reliving a kind of war-time togetherness and morale, a kind of drawing together among survivors, which is itself merely a distorted dream of a more humane collectivity and social organization. In this sense, the surface violence of the work is doubly motivated, for it can now be seen as a breaking of the routine boredom of middle-class existence as well, and may contain within itself impulses of resentment and vengeance at the nonrealization of the unconscious fantasy thus awakened.

But the key to the disguises of such deep content, of such positive but unconscious fantasy, lies in the very nature of that fantasy itself: we have attached it thematically to the idea of work satisfaction, and it is certain that experience has as its most fundamental structure *work* itself, as the production of value and the transformation of the world. Yet the content of such experience can never be determined in advance, and varies from the most grandiose forms of action to the most minute and limited feelings and perceptions in which consciousness can be specialized. It is easier to express the properties of this phenomenon negatively, by saying that the idea of Experience always presupposes its own opposite, that is, a kind of life that is mere vegetation, that is routine, emptiness, passage of time. The work of art therefore proves to unite a lived experience of some kind, as its content, with an implied question as to the very possibilities of Experience itself, as its form.

It thereby obeys a double impulse. On the one hand, it preserves the subject's fitful contact with genuine life and serves as the repository for that mutilated fragment of Experience which is her treasure, or his. Meanwhile, its mechanisms function as a censorship, which secures the subject against awareness of the resulting impoverishment, while preventing him/her from identifying connections between that impoverishment and mutilation and the social system itself.

When we pass from a collective product like science fiction to the products of what might be called official literature or official culture, this situation changes only in degree and in complexity, and not in its basic structure. For one thing, there is now to be reckoned into it the value of writing itself, of the elaboration of style or of the individual sentences of the work; but as we have already suggested, this value (which makes the Formalist inversion of the work possible, and which justifies stylistics as a way into the work) may at once be converted into terms of work satisfaction, for it is precisely in the form of the sentence that the modernist writer conceives of concrete work in the first place. For another, the work now shows a far greater degree of conscious and unconscious artistic *elaboration* on the basis of its primitive element or original content; but it is this elaboration and its mechanisms that form the object of the methods described above. Metacommentary, however, aims at tracing the logic of the censorship itself and of the situation from which it springs: a language that hides what it displays beneath its own reality as language, a glance that designates, through the very process of avoiding, the object forbidden.

January 1971

Chapter 2
The Ideology of the Text

All the straws in the wind seem to confirm the widespread feeling that "modern times are now over" and that some fundamental divide, some basic *coupure*, or qualitative leap, now separates us decisively from what used to be the new world of the early or mid-twentieth century, of triumphant modernism and the revolt against positivism and Victorian or Third Republic bourgeois culture. MacLuhanism, theories of the *sociéte de consommation* and of postindustrial society, postmodernism in literature and art, the shift from physics to biology as the prototype of the hard sciences, the influence of the computer and information theory, the end of the Cold War and the ratification of a Soviet-American world system of "peaceful coexistence," the New Left and the countercultural instinctual politics, the primacy of the linguistic model with its ideological expression in structuralism as a new movement— all of these phenomena testify to some irrevocable distance from the immediate past (itself reconfirmed by the surge of 30s, 40s, and 50s nostalgia everywhere in the advanced countries) at the same time that each offers something like an apologetics for its own version of the transformation. So the awareness that a change has taken place is subtly converted into a prophetic affirmation that the change is good, or, in the terminology we follow in the present essay, the theory of the change becomes at length, through a process of inner momentum, the latter's *ideology*. This apparently unavoidable slippage from what are essentially historical perceptions into the ideologizing of those perceptions is a function of an incomplete historical view and of the failure to make connections between what are basically local or "superstructural transformations" and ongoing concrete modifications of the social order as a whole, the failure—indeed, the unwillingness—to put all of these observations together and see them in terms of the long-range destiny of our particular socioeconomic system, in other words, monopoly capitalism.

Even in the local regions enumerated above, however, this particular "great transformation"—grasped idealistically in terms of transformations in our modes of *thinking* rather than in those of more concrete structures or situations—has rarely been the object of a systematic anatomy. Rather, the new conceptuality has been enthusiastically developed and applied in the absence of a measured and diagnostic investigation of what Collingwood would have called its "absolute presuppositions" or what more recent historians of ideas have called its "basic paradigms" (Kuhn) or its "underlying epistémé" (Foucault). Such an investigation would perhaps better be realized in individual probes rather than by way of some inconceivable global system; such is at any rate the strategy of the following pages, in which a few recent critical works have provided the occasion for more general reflections on one of the more fundamental of the new conceptual categories, namely the idea of textuality.

Textuality may rapidly be described as a methodological hypothesis whereby the objects of study of the human sciences (but not only of the human ones: witness the genetic "code" of DNA!) are considered to constitute so many texts that we *decipher* and *interpret*, as distinguished from the older views of those objects as realities or existants or substances that we in one way or another attempt to *know*. The advantages of such a model are perhaps most clearly visible in the nonliterary disciplines, where it seems to afford a more adequate "solution" to the dilemmas of positivism than the more provisory one of phenomenological bracketing. The latter merely suspends the ontological problem and postpones the ultimate epistemological decisions, while in some ways actually reinforcing the old subject/object dichotomy that was at the root of the contradictions of classical epistemology. The notion of textuality, whatever fundamental objections may be made to it, has at least the advantage as a strategy, of cutting across both epistemology and the subject/object antithesis in such a way as to neutralize both, and of focusing the attention of the analyst on her own position as a *reader* and on her own mental operations as *interpretation*. At once, then, she finds herself obliged to give an account of the nature of her object of study *qua* text: she is thus no longer tempted to view it as some kind of empirically existing reality in its own right (think, for instance, of the false problems to which the optical illusion of society, or even of the various social "institutions," has given rise), but must rather reconstitute it in such a way as to resolve her "facts" back into so many semantic or syntactic components of the text she is about to decipher. In fields like anthropology or sociology, in the lingering atmosphere of an older referential or "realistic" positivism, this requirement to "textualize" data serves the function of restoring the concrete contexts in which the so-called data were gathered, at the same time that it extends the interpretive situation to the totality of social life itself. This is the spirit in which the ethnomethodologists replace the events of social life with our accounts and interpretations of those events, and in which the newer anthropology seeks to dissolve the practices, habits, and rituals that used to be thought of as so many "institutions" and to grasp them, in a new transparency, as so many types of discourse a social group holds about itself.[1] Meanwhile, in linguistics itself, the concept of the text provides the means of breaking out of the artificial confinement of smaller and more abstract units of study like the sentence and evolving in the direction of pragmatics and text grammars, which try to reincorporate the concrete context and positions of the participants back into purely verbal phenomena, which are, taken alone, a mere hypostasis of langauge as such.

It is possible, of course, to see the new textual model as a reflex of the changes wrought by the media, and the information explosion, in our experience of society and of the world. It is tempting, indeed, to associate the illusions of a traditional Aristotelian realism (reality existing calmly "out there," truth nothing but the adequation of the ideas in our head with the things themselves of which they are the pictures) with a world poor in messages, in which the shimmering heat waves of a swarm of signs and codes are not present to blur our limpid gaze across the distance that separates us from the realm of things. And it is certain that the sensitivity of recent times for problems of language, models, communication, and the like, is closely linked with the emergence of these phenomena as relatively autonomous and opaque objects in their own right in the new distribution mechanisms of industrial capitalism.

At any rate, it would seem that the relevance of the concept of textuality is most problematic there, paradoxically, where it would seem the least metaphorical, namely, in the realm of literary study itself. The paradox indeed is simply this: why and how the analysis of literary works can be transformed by a reminder of what it must have known all along, namely, that its objects of study are "nothing but" verbal texts. A whole range of newer theories reorient the interpretive process around the hypothesis— generally borrowed from Chomsky in a metaphorical way—that the empirical text we see before us is only the end-result and product or effect of some deeper absent linguistic or textual structure which must be reconstituted, a deep-textual machinery whose characterization ranges from systems of tropes (Hayden White, Lotman, DeMan) to the narrative apparatus of Greimassian semiotics. An interpretation, however, is generally effective only when it visibly or even violently rewrites the surface appearance of the text, that is, when the restoration of the "deep structure" alters our initial reception of the sentences themselves. Such interpretive intervention generally requires the added presupposition that the logic of the deeper structure is somehow in conflict or in contradiction with the surface appearance, something posited most dramatically in Kristeva's notion that the "genotext"—the forces of Desire or the unconscious—erupts into the surface or "phenotext" to subvert it in ways the interpreter seeks to make visible.

Yet the concept of textuality can also modify our approach to the literary text in a different way, which I am tempted to call horizontal, in distinction to this deep-structural "vertical" model. Here the model of textual production makes for an intensified sense of the emergence of individual sentences in isolation, which stands in marked contrast to the more traditional valorization of the aesthetic whole (of which all the parts are hierarchically organized components and expressions). The view of the literary text as a perpetual production of sentences, indeed, now seems to exclude traditional emphasis on the organic unity of literary form. It is precisely because its very mode of presentation dramatizes this opposition that Roland Barthes' S/Z^2—a lengthy line-by-line commentary on a little known and romantically melodramatic novella of Balzac, "Sarrasine"—seems preeminently symptomatic for our present purposes, which involve the assessment of the results of textuality as a framework for literary analysis just as much as an account of the ideological service into which it may be pressed.

I

S/Z is also symptomatic of the intellectual itinerary of Roland Barthes himself, of all the foxes of modern criticism (Lukács may be said in retrospect to have been the latter's most stubborn hedgehog) surely the most exemplary. Like Lukács, indeed, had he never existed in the first place, someone like Barthes would have had to have been invented, for his virtuoso practice of critical methods was contemporaneous with a methodological explosion in the human sciences, and what is generalizable about his work is precisely his solution to the dilemma of methodological proliferation, which may be characterized, following Adorno's terminology in the *Philosophy of New Music*, as the valorization of "pastiche." For the crisis in modern criticism is surely closely linked to that more fundamental crisis in modern literature and art, which is the proliferation of styles and private languages; and Adorno had argued, in the Stravinsky section of his book, that the Russian composer's composition of music about other music was a characteristic and virtually textbook illustration of one of the two basic strategies of modern artists, faced with a crushing accumulation of dead styles in a situation in which it seems unjustifiable to invest still newer ones. (The hedgehog panel of Adorno's diptych was then represented by Arnold Schoenberg, who eschewed pastiche in favor of a relentless and sometimes forbiddingly inhuman totalization—a strategy that no doubt has its equivalent in modern literary criticism as well.)

Of the first, eclectic, parody- or pastiche-oriented strategy (of which he himself offered the defense in his pamphlet *Critique et vérité),* Barthes' work is the monument, constituting a veritable fever-chart of all the significant intellectual and critical tendencies since World War II: Bachelardian phenomenology (in his book on Michelet), Sartrean Marxism (in *Writing Degree Zero),* Hjelmslevian linguistics, but also Brechtean *Verfremdung* (in *Mythologies),* orthodox Freudianism (in *On Racine),* hard-core semiotics (in *Système de la mode), Tel Quel* textual productivity, as well as Lacanian psychoanalysis (in *S/Z* itself), poststructuralism (in *Le Plaisir du texte),* and finally, a return to origins, in that ultimate squaring of the circle that is his recent commentary on himself (*Roland Barthes par lui-même),* a work that, as he himself observes, reminds one of nothing quite so much as the subject of his own first published essay, namely the *Journals* of André Gide. Such a trajectory suggests that it is less productive to read Barthes as a theorist than as the intuitive and idiosyncratic practitioner of a host of different methods, whose perspicacity, shot through with sudden fits of boredom, makes the ultimate *yield* of such methods clearer than any theoretical disquisition. What happened to Barthes was, I think, that he became too conscious of what he himself calls the "precritical" or presystematic nature of his own observations, too lucid about the process of formation of his own sentences: this is the ultimate implication of his notion of the *scriptible*—sentences whose *gestus* arouses the desire to emulate it, sentences that make you want to write sentences of your own. (Meanwhile, the emphasis on the expressive and gestural capacities of the individual sentence tends with time to result in a virtual canonization of the fragment, although Barthes' increasing predilection for brief notes and glosses is perhaps evident in *S/Z,* where it is motivated and "covered" by the traditional requirements of the exegesis or line-by-line commentary.)

Still, it is evidently only a self-conscious sentence that can provoke such emulation, and this accounts for Barthes' need, in *S/Z,* to devise another category, namely the *lisible,* or "legible," to designate the dull and rusty lack of finish of the so-called realistic or representational kind. For *S/Z* is also, as we shall see, something like a replay of the realism/modernism controversy, although its force certainly springs in part from Barthes' own ambivalence in the matter: *"Things I Like:* lettuce, cinnamon, cheese, spices, frangipan, newly mown hay (I'd like some 'taster' to make a scent out of it), roses, peonies, lavender, champagne, political *désinvolture,* Glenn Gould, ice-cold beer, flat pillows, toast, Havana cigars, Handel, measured walks, pears, white peaches, cherries, colors, pocket watches, ball-point pens, quill pens, main courses, coarse salt, realistic novels, the piano, coffee, Pollock, Twombly, romantic music."[3]

It should be added, however, that the view of "realism" that emerges from *S/Z* is generally implied rather than directly stated, in a study whose object, an early work of Balzac and a throwback—like so much high-Romantic storytelling—to the older Renaissance-type novella, is distant enough from Balzacian realism, let alone the triumphant realistic discourse of the nineteenth-century novel as its apogee. The essentials of Barthes' conception of realism are more succinctly exposed in a short essay, "L'Effet de réel," in which, as the title suggests, realistic narrative is defined less as a structure of discourse in its own right than as a kind of optical illusion, the production of a so-called reality-effect by means of a certain number of key *details* that function as *signals*. So it is with Michelet's observation that when Charlotte Corday's final portrait was being painted in her death cell, "after an hour and a half, someone tapped softly at a little door behind her": the detail is without any genuine function, in the sense that it might easily have been omitted without damage to the narrative. What is more important is that in the strict sense it has no *meaning*—in contrast, let us say, to the expressivity of a "timorous" knock on a door or a "feeble" rapping on a wall, which would have converted this "sign" into a genuine *symbol*. Thus we can say that for Barthes the vehicle of a reality-effect is relatively indifferent: any number of other, analogous details would have done just as well; in other words, unlike the canonical theorists of realism, Barthes' analysis suggests that the *content* of the Michelet passage is what is least important in it, serving merely as a kind of pro forma credentials for the accreditation of the "referential illusion" on which such discourse depends. "The truth of this illusion is as follows: suppressed from realistic enunciation *qua* denotative signified, the 'real' returns to inhabit it as a signified of connotation; for in the very moment in which these details are supposed to denote reality directly, they do little else—without saying so—than to signify it: Flaubert's barometer, Michelet's little rear door finally have nothing to say but this: *we are the real*; it is the category of the 'real' itself (and not its contingent content) which is thereby signified; in other words, it is the very deficiency of signified as opposed to referent which becomes itself the signified of realism: a 'reality-effect' is produced, the basis of that unspoken category of verisimilitude which makes up the aesthetic of all of the standard works of modern times."[4]

It would be wrong, however, to conclude that this analysis, which so radically devalues the importance of content in realistic discourse, is for all that an example of some incorrigibly formalistic practice either; for the reality-effect would appear to be something more closely resembling a *by-product* of realistic discourse than a mark of its fundamental linguistic structure. And while Barthes does not go so far as to say that *any* type of discourse can on occasion, and as it were laterally, in passing, generate the *effet de réel*, it would seem implicit in his description that what has hitherto passed under the name of "realistic narrative" is at least a mirage to the degree that it has nothing structurally to distinguish it from narrative discourse in general.

A key term in the passage quoted above suggests the specificity of Barthes' approach here and explains how it can do the seemingly impossible and avoid categorization in either the formalistic camp or that of content-oriented analyses: this is the word "connotation," which may be said to designate the fundamental method of the early Barthes, a method that persists on into more recent books like S/Z, where, as we shall see, it coexists uneasily with the later methodology of semiotics proper. The connotative method, indeed—derived from the work of the Danish linguist Hjelmslev and most fully codified by Barthes himself in the long theoretical conclusion to his Mythologies—differs from current semiotic practice in that, where the latter takes as its object of study the mechanisms by which signs function, the former is resolutely "semioclastic" (Barthes' own term) and finds its vocation in a denunciation of the ideological uses of signs, which is irreconcilable with the "scientific" character of semiotics itself. Thus the analysis of the reality-effect outlined above is precisely an ideological one in its exposure of the illusion the realistic detail is designed to produce (the ideological purpose of such an illusion—the propagation of a belief in the "referent" or in nature—is considered later in the present essay). The transcendence of form and content both can meanwhile be explained by a brief account of what Hjelmslev meant by connotation in the first place: to follow Barthes' helpful simplification, it is a kind of second-degree construction in which a complete previous sign (the combination signifier/signified) is pressed into service in the edification of a new and more complex sign of which it becomes itself the signifier. Thus the words of an individual sentence bear their own intrinsic meaning within the "frame" that is proper to them (denotation), while at the same time the sentence as a complete sign in its own right (the words plus the meaning, or the signifier plus the signified) may be used to convey a supplementary meaning of a more stylistic type, such as elegance or social distinction in a dialogue, for instance, or a value of some kind, as when the sentences of a Flaubert or a Joyce proclaim, above and beyond their own denotative content, "I am Literature."

The dissatisfaction of orthodox semiotics with this conception of a supplementary meaning or message which is the idea of connotation may be accounted for by the global character of the designation, which does not seem to allow much room for the more minute work of syntactic or semantic dissection. In effect, the connotative method seizes on the entire sentence or the entire sign as the vehicle for a supplementary meaning, thus virtually cutting itself off from the possibility of further analysis. The semiotic abandonment of the concept, however, has the signal disadvantage (it is of course a positive benefit for a discipline that wishes to flee the political into an untroubled realm of scientific research) of shutting down one of the few powerful instruments available to register the ideological. I would argue that there is a profound incompatibility between a "scientific" method, which seeks to restrict its work to pure positivities, and a dialectical one, which, thrusting its hands into the strange and paradoxical element of the negative, is alone capable of doing justice to "mixed" phenomena such as ideology, false consciousness, repression, and in all likelihood, connotation itself: one of the secondary interests of *S/Z*, indeed, will be precisely this tension between the two approaches, which runs throughout the work. In the present instance, however, the relatively spatial character of Barthes' objects of study in *Mythologies* (images, photographs, relatively visual oppositions, faces, and so forth) suggests a means of correcting the imbalance noted above, which would involve the *temporalization* of the concept of connotation and the reintroduction into it of process and of reading time. Such an approach would entitle us to speak now of a "connotation-effect," which is produced at a particular moment in the reception of a sign, and which can be described as a kind of ninety-degree rotation in which form is momentarily transformed into a new type of content in its own right, without losing its older properties; so, not the detail itself, not the little rear door, but rather the very form of the narrative sentence itself at that point suddenly begins to emit a secondary message about historiographic discourse in general. And such a view, linking autoreferentiality and connotation, by making of the latter a textual *event* in its own right, would then permit this method to be reabsorbed into a more complex, yet still ideology-oriented, investigation of the text in question.

At any rate, the tension between semiotic and semioclastic aims in *S/Z* reappears in a somewhat different register as a tension between text and form, or, more precisely, between modernism and realism, in Barthes' view of the Balzacian novella itself. Such a coexistence between the two modes is of course itself a feature of the theory:

> Thus the theory of the text tends to favor modernistic texts (from Lautréamont to Philippe Sollers) for a two-fold reason: such texts are exemplary because they manifest (to a degree hitherto unattained) "the operation of *semiosis* in language and with the subject," and because they constitute a de facto protest against the constraints of the traditional ideology of meaning. . . . Yet, by virtue of the very fact that texts are massive (rather than cumulative), and that they do not necessarily coincide with the works themselves, it is possible to discover textuality [*du texte*], although to a lesser degree, even in older productions; a classical work (Flaubert, Proust, why not even Bossuet?) may well include layers or fragments of *écriture.*[5]

Therewith the fundamental purpose of *S/Z* is set: to track and uncover "*du texte*" in Balzac, to expose layers and traces of textuality in what seems otherwise a traditional or even relatively conventional narrative. This is why it would be unwise to expect the kind of systematic attention to the plot of

"Sarrasine" that we have learned from other types of narrative analysis, such as those of Lévi-Strauss, Propp, and Greimas, whose effort is directed toward reading the events of the plot as a complete message of some kind; or traditional Anglo-American studies of fiction, which remain stubbornly committed to the principle that all the elements of a masterwork—style, images, episodes, etc.—cohere in some harmonious ethical or thematic statement, which it is the business of the critic to recover. The latter is indeed generally stigmatized by the theorists of the text as *interpretation* in the bad sense, while even the relatively "value-free" decipherment of the former remains holistic and demands a kind of distance, a kind of speculative leap in the grasping and positing of narrative wholes, which the minute and microscopic focus of Barthes' commentary can scarcely accommodate. This also results, it should be observed in passing, in the repression of one whole area of historical reality, namely that of the evolution of narrative form itself; for, ironically, the Barthes of *S/Z* is in no position to convey the purely formal *connotations* that result from Balzac's adaptation of older storytelling conventions to the newer reified and quantified narrative and social materials of his own time, a perspective to which we will return at the end of this essay.

Still, it would be a mistake to think such considerations have been completely eliminated from Barthes' commentary. In fact, *S/Z*, like the novella of which it is a study, may be said to be very much a mixed or hybrid object, and just as "Sarrasine" will include elements of textuality within an older "classical" or traditional form, so we may suggest that *S/Z* itself combines both realistic and modernistic features. For within the "modernistic" text-oriented structure of the commentary form, we may also from time to time detect elements of some older "realistic" or "representational" critical essay on Balzac, to which an earlier Barthes, one less addicted to the fragment, might well have lent the lapidary and elliptical form familiar to readers of *Writing Degree Zero* or of his *Collected Essays*. This more conventional study might then have been resumed as a thesis about the relationship between castration and artistic production in Balzac's tale (which involves the passion of a sculptor for a *castrato*), an anecdote then transformed by the "frame" of the novella into an exchangeable commodity in such a way as to make a statement about the relationship between classical storytelling and capitalism.

We will return to this "realistic kernel" of *S/Z* later; for the moment, we are concerned with what I will call Barthes' textualization of Balzac's story. It is, of course, Barthes' disentanglement of the *codes of* "Sarrasine" that is the most dramatic embodiment of the new textual methods. The structure of narrativity is here rewritten in language that will not be unfamiliar to the reader of Pound: "The text, in its mass, is comparable to a sky at once flat and smooth, deep, without edges and without landmarks; like the soothsayer drawing on it with the tip of his staff an imaginary rectangle wherein to consult, according to certain principles, the flight of birds, the commentator traces through the text certain zones of reading, in order to observe therein the migration of meanings, the outcroppings of codes, the passage of citations" (*S/Z*, pp. 14/20-21). The notion of the musical score, which will not be long in following this one, introduces, however, as we will see, the phenomenon of temporal succession into this splendidly spatial image, whose counterpart may be found in the very etymology of text itself, literally a *tissue* woven together by those fundamental molecular components of narrativity that are for Barthes the codes: "In their interweaving, these voices (whose origin is 'lost' in the vast perspective of the *already-written*) de-originate the utterance: the convergence of the voices (of the codes) becomes *writing*, a stereographic space where the five codes, the five voices, intersect: the Voice of Empirical Realities (the proairetisms), the Voice of the Person (the semes), the Voice of Knowledge (the cultural codes), the Voice of Truth (the hermeneutic codes), the Voice of Symbol" (*S/Z*, p. 21/28).[6]

What is tempting for that part of our minds that is still under the spell of an optical illusion of scientific rigor, what may be termed a kind of Cartesian idol in its own right, is the notion that the text may thereby be broken up into its minimal unities and the latter carefully and in businesslike scientific fashion analyzed one by one. From this point of view, of course, all interpretation of the other type, described above, is inadmissible precisely because it is speculative and seems to grasp intuitively at wholes, which are nothing but imaginary objects from the point of view of the patient and minute dissection of the text by its painstakingly scientific analyst. Unfortunately, perception does not work in this additive fashion, neither in storytelling nor in the visual arts, where the Gestalt refutations of the notion of some atomistic combination of small sensations into unified perceptions are the most striking reply to the Cartesian procedure. Hence the very real dangers of the commentary form as practiced here, which encourages a laborious enumeration of detail through which the essentials tend to slip (Barthes himself, in another context, mentioned that game described in a novel of Agatha Christie in which the more experienced player chooses a place name that marches so boldly across the map—for example, E U R O P E—that the other participants do not even notice it).

Barthes' five codes fall into two groups, and the distinction is not without its symptomatic value. The first group—those of the semes ("Code of the Person"), of cultural commonplaces ("Knowledge"), and of the symbol— are essentially batches of what he elsewhere calls *indexes*, that is, shorthand supplementary messages drawn from some more basic pool of shared cultural attitudes that permit us to decipher them (so, in a well-known example, Barthes reads the four telephones on James Bond's desk as an index of "advanced bureaucratic technology"; here the index might be seen as something like a nonideological connotation). This is perhaps the moment to remind the reader that the term "code," drawn from information theory, has little more than metaphorical value when applied, not to first-degree communications, but rather to those "secondary modeling systems" that are verbal representations. There are, it would seem, two relatively distinct uses of the term that both serve in different ways to articulate or underscore linguistic realities that might otherwise pass unnoticed. In the first use the word code, in the singular, is coupled with the notion of a message, so that the term forces the analyst to work more diligently at defining the structural affinities between the type of message emitted and the sign system or code through which it is conveyed. The other use is distinct from this, inasmuch as it stresses the multiplicity of different codes, or subcodes, at work in a given communicational act: thus, I convey a verbal statement, but accompany it by facial expressions that derive from an organized expressive system of their own, as well as gestures of the hand and shoulder that stem possibly from a different sign system (as when I imitate the gestural sign system of European speakers). In this usage, the emphasis has shifted to the contradictions, or at least imbalances, of the various codes among each other; and it is in this sense that, characterizing the cultural situation of the modern *Gesellschaft*, we speak of the proliferation or the explosion of codes as a symptom of the breakdown of the older social groups, which were relatively unified linguistically as well as institutionally (a perception which makes its literary appearance for the first time in Flaubert). In this sense, our own use of the term "code," drawn from a relatively technical and specialized discipline and applied to the quite unrelated one of literary study, is itself an example of code-switching. Still, one would think that these two approaches require either, for the first, that we show the unity of the sign system or code utilized in the transmission of a given message, or, for the second, that we reveal the contradictions and inconsistencies between the multiple codes in such a way as to make those contradictions and that multiplicity available to us as a phenomenon for analysis in its own right. But essentially Barthes does neither of these things, and for this reason one so often has the feeling that the commentary form, or the fragmented discourse, of *S/Z* tends to suggest that problems have been solved at the very moment in which they are becoming interesting.

Thus, to take up Barthes' semes, or "Code of the Person," one can certainly, as he does, make an inventory of the various indexes that a writer marshals as a kind of characterological shorthand (thus, the description of Sarrasine's peremptory entry into Bouchardon's studio, besides conveying a fact that accounts for his subsequent development as a painter, functions as a manifestation of the underlying character trait Obstinacy). Yet such an inventory would seem to have a merely lexical interest, even when certain semes are isolated as culturally idiosyncratic (only a nineteenth-century Frenchman would take this gesture as a sign of this attribute) or as personally and stylistically determined (only Balzac would have tried to convey this particular nature through this kind of action). The larger issue at stake here is raised only incidentally when, in one of those splendid asides that are, of course, the whole reason for being of *S/Z*, Barthes passes from the semes or indexes of the individual character to what holds the entire character together as a substantive unity, namely, the proper name itself: "To call characters, as Furetière does, *Javotte, Nicodème, Belastre* is (without keeping completely aloof from a certain half-bourgeois, half-classicist code) to emphasize the structural function of the Name, to state its arbitrary nature, to depersonalize it, to accept the currency of the Name as pure convention. To say *Sarrasine, Rochefide, Lanty, Zambinella* (not to mention *Bouchardon,* who really existed) is to maintain that the patronymic substitute is *filled* with a person (civic, national, social); it is to insist that appellative currency be in gold (and not left to be decided arbitrarily). All subversion, or all novelistic submission, thus begins with the Proper Name" (*S/Z,* pp. 95/101-2). With such an observation (echoing the classic chapter on naming systems in Lévi-Strauss' *Pensée sauvage),* we are on the threshold of one of the fundamental problems of narrative analysis, namely, the relationship between the category of a "character" and the cognitive content (traits, ideas, symbolism) that makes up a given character. The structural analysis of narrative has developed out of a refusal of the surface phenomena of narrative itself, substituting for them its own terminology in much the same way that chemistry or physics substitute the language and categories of atomic particles for the common-sense experiential data of physical substances like mud, rust, stones, wood, and the like. Yet the concept of character alone has proved recalcitrant to this kind of analytic translation, and it is hard to see how the structural analysis of narrative can make any further theoretical progress without attacking this particular problem, which may be described as that of the stubbornly anthropomorphic nature of our present categories of character. At this point, clearly, the problem intersects with the vaster philosophic one of the historical nature of the Subject itself, but characteristically, Barthes takes his own observation as a vehicle for sounding his own fundamental theme of naturalization (for example, the proper name gives a natural appearance to what is essentially a historical determination of the person), to which we will return later.

The cultural code is something like a storehouse of proverbial wisdom or commonplace knowledge about acts, events, and life in general, and will be articulated whenever a given detail needs motivation. In a sense, therefore, this code is the locus of ideology, albeit of a relatively inactive, nonfunctional type; one is tempted, indeed, to see it, not so much as a system in its own right, as any living ideology might be supposed to be, but rather as a kind of storehouse of older ideological fragments that can be appealed to now and then for a digression or an acceptable justification for some necessary move in narrative strategy. The basic object of study here would therefore be the various forms of what the Russian Formalists called "motivation," that is to say, what has to be pressed into service to make a given detail pass unquestioned by the reader, or, to use what will presently become an ideologically charged term, to make it seem "natural" to him. Indeed, in an interesting article, Gerard Genette has suggested that verisimilitude—*le vraisemblable*—is itself nothing but the degree zero of just such motivation, something like a cultural code that is able to dispense with its content.[7]

These considerations, of course, lead directly back to literary history insofar as a text of Balzac is a good deal more self-indulgent in this respect than would be any post-Flaubertian narrative. Indeed, one of the new and self-imposed constraints of the latter is precisely to reinvent something like Genette's notion of the *vraisemblable* by eliminating all recourse to such cultural codes and motivations that are so common to Balzac. At the same time, it should be observed that Barthes' Cartesian method, his pursuit of nothing but the minimal unities, obscures another fundamental role played by just such cultural codes, namely the overall organization of narrative ironies, as when, in the cumulative disasters of some naturalist novel, we sense the active informing presence of a commonplace of the proverbial type (waste not, want not; pride goeth before a fall). The relationship between the global structure of a long narrative and such ideational or conceptual elements has never been adequately studied, and this is all the more surprising in view of the fact that one of the deepest vocations of the twentieth-century novel has been its attempt to expunge just such elements, which are rightly thought to be vestiges of older and more superstitious thought-ways. We will return to this problem shortly in connection with another of Barthes' codes.

The enigmatically designated "Code of the Symbol" proves to designate bodily and sexual realities in a fashion preeminently characteristic of Barthes, who has always insisted on the body as the locus of a particular kind of nonuniversalizable private dimension of language. And as in his own work, the materials of this code range from the Bachelardian psychoanalysis of the elements to the Lacanian motifs of castration and phallic signifiers. Paradoxically, it is in this private and relatively ahistorical realm more than elsewhere that the lack of genuine historical reference proves limiting; for one would want to find these observations grounded in some sense of the incomparably poorer physiological reality of Balzac's style when compared with the later instrumental registers of Flaubert or of Zola.

On the whole, however, it would seem clear that the purpose of these three ("reversible") codes is to probe for the roots of the intelligible detail (the seme)—on the one hand in the socially conventional or ideological (the Code of Knowledge), and on the other in the psychoanalytic (that of the Symbol). Here, then, concealed beneath a scheme of code classifications, we once again touch on that fundamental option of contemporary criticism (sociology versus psychoanalysis), which is itself a prime symptom of the fundamental split in modern life between the public and the private, the political and the sexual, between the untotalizably collective and the alienated experience of the individual. We may wonder, however, whether the procedure of assigning each of these dimensions to a different code really helps clarify this dilemma (in fact, it would seem to presuppose that each dimension of being had found *adequate* expression in a full code or sign-system of its own), or whether the concept of various codes here merely forestalls the problem and prevents it from being adequately explored. Certainly, in the case of the ideological materials, it is clear that Barthes is concerned, in his later, semiotic period, to defuse this material and to reduce it to data as inert and malleable as possible (and we have seen how the conceptualization of ideology as mere cultural and proverbial knowledge achieves precisely this aim).

The other two codes are clearly, and by Barthes' own admission, of a quite different structure, in his term "irreversible," inasmuch as they are *forms in time*, and thus, passing now into musical figures, far more akin to melodic structures than to the harmonies of the previous "reversible" types:

> The readerly text is a *tonal* text (for which habit creates a reading process just as conditioned as our hearing: one might say there is a *reading eye* just as there is a tonal ear, so that to unlearn the readerly would be the same as to unlearn the tonal), and its tonal unity is basically dependent on two sequential codes: the revelation of truth [hermeneutic code] and the coordination of the actions represented [proairetic code]: there is the same constraint in the gradual order of melody and in the equally gradual order of the narrative sequence. . . . The five codes mentioned, frequently heard simultaneously, in fact endow the text with a kind of plural quality (the text is actually polyphonic), but of the five codes, only three establish permutable, reversible connections, outside the constraint of time (the semic, cultural and symbolic codes); the other two impose their terms according to an irreversible order (the hermeneutic and proairetic codes). (*S/Z*, p. 30/37)

It should be observed, however, that to name a thing does not always suffice to explain it: in particular, in *Morphology of the Folktale*, the structural analysis of narrative from Propp's on, an unjustifiable use has been made of the term "irreversibility," as though it did any more than to designate the basic problem to be accounted for, namely, that of the diachrony or sequentiality of narrative discourse.

In many ways, it is the proairetic code—that of empirical realities, or of the ordinary gestural and circumstantial unities of everyday life—which raises the most interesting issues for future study. What Barthes describes here is something like a dialectic of names, and of the realities—he calls them the "folds"—designated by those names:

> What is a series of actions: the unfolding of a name. To *enter?* I can

unfold it into 'to appear' and 'to come inside.' To *leave?* I can unfold it into 'to want to,' 'to break off,' 'to go on my way.' To *give?:*
'to present the opportunity,' 'to hand over,' 'to accept.' Inversely, to
establish the sequence is to find the name: the sequence is the currency, the *exchange value* of the name. By what divisions is this exchange established? What is there in 'Farewell,' 'Door,' 'Gift'?
What subsequent, constitutive actions? Along what folds can we
close the fan of the sequence? . . . The proairetic sequence is indeed
a series, i.e., 'a multiplicity possessing a rule of order' (Leibnitz),
but the rule of order here is cultural (*habit*, in short), and linguistic
(the possibility of the word, the word pregnant with its possibilities)
. . . . Thus to read . . . is to proceed from name to name, from fold
to fold; it is to fold the text according to one name and then to unfold it along the new folds of this name. This is proairetism: an artifice (or art) of reading that seeks out names, that tends towards
them: an act of lexical transcendence, a labor of classification carried
out on the basis of the classification of language. (*S/Z*, pp.
82–83/88–89)

At this point, indeed, we may glimpse an exploration of the proairetic code
that leads in a direction different from that explored by Barthes, and that
would be comparable to his observations here only as a kind of X ray of the
molecular structure of the textual substance might be juxtaposed with
something on the order of a psychology of perception in which the activity of
reading, like that of visual perception, is seen as the construction of meaningful wholes, or Gestalts, out of the initial raw material of verbal stimuli.
Here the most suggestive methodological discussion is furnished by Gombrich's classic *Art and Illusion* (1960): drawing independently on Roman
Jakobson's views of language, this work has protostructuralist credentials of
its own, and its more orthodox account of the nature and function of an artistic code has interesting implications for the whole realism/modernism controversy, quite different from those implied by Barthes himself.

Gombrich is of course arguing *for* representationality just as strongly as
Barthes is arguing against it; yet his apologia of the realistic mode does not
take the path of the more traditional valorization of the object—of "reality,"
historical, social, or natural—against mere artistic formalisms. It is not an
apologia based on mimesis, but rather it seeks to insert between subject and
object that third and more properly structuralist realm of artistic and perceptual codes that is the painter's essential medium: thus the latter does not
paint images that look like things, but rather works out and sharpens a set of
relationships (the classic binary oppositions, in this instance between figure
and ground, light and shade, and the like), which may then be perceived to
be analogous to the relationships that make up our perception of the object. It
is the binary pairs that are matched, not the objects themselves; the *parole* of
the various visual styles, of the languages of painting itself, that is

then—sometimes naively and unconsciously—read as an artistic equivalent for a complex of nonlinguistic perceptions.[8]

It is not, however, this aspect of Gombrich's account of the psychology of artistic perception that is comparable to Barthes' codes, for the latter is not really interested in the binary oppositions that organize narrative perception, and we would have to go to Lévi-Strauss' studies of myth for something analogous in the literary realm. It is at a somewhat later step in his reasoning that Gombrich will have something suggestive to tell us about the problems raised by S/Z. The art historian is indeed involved in a battle on two fronts: on the one hand, through his assertion of an intermediary realm—that of the artistic code—between the subject and his object in the real world, he seeks to dispel the illusions of a naive realism, in particular what might be called the Whorfian hypothesis about the relationship between artistic style and actual perception. Whorf's name is of course associated with the idea that the structure and inner limits of a given language may be at once translated into propositions about the structure and inner limits of its speaker's thinking. Applied to the languages of art, this suggests that readers whose minds have been enlarged by the complex perspectives of narrative realism as Auerbach showed them to have been developed over a number of centuries will necessarily have a more adequate instrument at their disposal for deciphering external reality than would have been the case for earlier generations. We will return to this hypothesis later; suffice it to say that Gombrich's attempt radically to dissociate style and perception—based on the reductio ad absurdum of a view that would finally suggest that only post-Renaissance Europeans have ever seen a three-dimensional world!—is not altogether satisfying either.

But his other conceptual adversary is something like the reverse of this one, and is constituted by the very psychologists whose work Gombrich had seemed to draw in making his first point. Here the target is what he considers to be the imaginary entity of those atomistic "sensations" on which, according to the psychologists, perception is itself constructed: the meaningless data of the various visual stimuli, which are then ultimately, through some mysterious process of transformation, metamorphosed into the recognizable objects of a familiar external world. For Gombrich, indeed, the existential reality of such a fictive entity as the visual sensation is simply the painted canvas itself, as, particularly since impressionism, it has seemed to offer the evidence of a host of unrelated and fragmented colors and brush strokes, which magically, as we step away from it, reorganize themselves into, say, the Mont Sainte Victoire. Still, the existence of phenomena like caricature—a few bare lines that cannot be read in any other way than as some well-known face—suggests what will be Gombrich's basic hypothesis in this area, namely that the visual raw materials are reordered into a meaningful "parole" or artistic representation by means of the intervening agency of what he calls "schemata"—a storehouse of ideas of things trigger our recognition of them in the language of art—in other words, precisely what Barthes means by pro-airetisms, or the "Code of Empirical Realities" (la Voix de l'Empirie).

The Gombrich version of this concept strikes me as more suggestive than that of Barthes, however, precisely because it seems to open up a whole realm of conceptual categories to our exploration, a realm in principle extending all the way from the isolated individual gesture to that of some overall generic comprehension itself. To be sure, for both writers, the immediate examples tend to be relatively local ones: thus, for Gombrich, the various recognizable natural phenomena that make up a Constable landscape, and, for Barthes, the various acts (coming and going), the various emotions (anger or sadness), the various gestures (a curious glance, a sudden look of bewilderment), whose conventional *names* provide our means of organizing the necessarily sketchy indications furnished by the narrative sentences themselves. And to be sure, the proof a contrario—the various examples of a pre-Brechtian estrangement-effect of which, for instance, we find so many in *Tristram Shandy*, those lengthy anatomies of a given physical gesture that force us to search for the identifying name that has been withheld—has also tended to find its privileged objects in the smaller unities of gesture and individual act. Yet I would suggest that such schemata have a much vaster functional role, particularly in more traditional narratives, one that is customarily assimilated to an illicit didacticism and moralism and that the present view for the first time puts us in a position to explore properly. This is the whole area of a kind of conventionalized identification of human experience itself, one that finds linguistic codification not so much in *names*—the experiences are a little too complex for that—as in *proverbs* and conventionalized poetic "ironies" of all kinds. The proverbial wisdom, however—"pride goeth before a fall"—is not so much a lesson to be taught by the events of a given narrative as it is rather the *name* of a recognizable destiny and of a single overall meaningful unity of human experience, and the reader uses it as a schema in precisely Gombrich's sense, a way of organizing the various, still fragmented events furnished by the narrative into a *Gestalt* whose form *is* its meaning. This is the way in which something like a psychology of perception might be developed for narrative analysis itself, yet it is conceivable only at the price of breaking with the kind of Cartesian attachment to visible analytic minimal unities that is reinforced by Barthes' commentary method in *S/Z*; for the most interesting narrative schemata lie on the most distant circumference of the hermeneutic circle, and, like the distance that alone permits us to identify the object in a landscape of Cézanne, are never present as positivities at any moment of the text itself, their existence deducible only by inference, from the forms into which its events slowly arrange themselves.

Such an approach would then allow something like an inventory of the various conventional concepts of human experience operative at a given

RITTER LIBRARY
BALDWIN-WALLACE COLLEGE

historical moment, in a given social formation, and in the narratives that find currency within it. What is more interesting in the present context is that it is precisely as a break with such narrative schemata that literary modernism can be understood, and here again, the analogy with the history of painting is revealing. For surely nothing has been considered quite so illicit and unjustifiable by modernist aesthetics as the operation of just such tacit and subterranean, even *ideological*, messages of the type described above: modern literature's break with plot is in reality far better understood as a break with the older narrative schemata, which are felt—rightly—to be indefensible conventional presuppositions about the nature of life and experience. The dilemma of the plotless novel, then, emerges only when it becomes clear to what degree plot is itself structurally inseparable from just such conventionalized schemata, which alone permit the reader to grasp a long series of events and pages in the unity of some larger form.

What happened in painting may serve as a dramatic object lesson in such a process, where description fatally overturns into prescription, and the new "scientific" descriptions of the process of perception are themselves transformed into a program for the production of a perceptual art of a wholly new type. This is of course what happened in impressionism when the psychological accounts of the organization of atomistic sensations into larger perceptual wholes were enlisted in an attempt to make painting reflect this psychology "more truthfully" than did the older classical type: clearly, contemporaries of such a scientific "truth" were unable to presevere calmly in the conviction that their world of *appearance*—that of the ordinary recognizable perceptions of everyday life—was stubbornly accompanied by some ghostly realm of *reality*—in other words, the stimuli and sensations supposedly at work in the retina of the eye, "objectively," and before any transformation into the merely subjective impressions of perception. They therefore itched to turn their own appearances back into realities, and much the same may be said for Barthes' revelation of the "textuality" at work within Balzacian narrative, that it can only be seen, no matter what the formal disclaimers, as a kind of manifesto urging the substitution, henceforth, in the literature of the future, of the most uncompromising textuality for all such older pretextual narrative forms: so difficult is it to identify something like this so-called proairetic code without at the same time calling for its abolition.

When we turn, finally, to the last of Barthes' five codes, the "hermeneutic" one, it does not seem superfluous to object to the confusion that is bound to arise when, for what might more properly be called the "Code of Enigma," Barthes revives the ancient term for the very science of interpretation itself. He no doubt wishes thereby to stigmatize this concept of critical activity in the process; what he has in mind descriptively, however, is the emphasis of the classical storyteller on sensational disclosures and his consequent misuse of all the rhetorical mannerisms that hold the reader in suspense and whet his appetite for melodramatic satisfactions. And it is clear that in its overall plan just as much as its sentence-by-sentence detail, Balzac's tale of the horrible secret behind the Lanty fortune is profoundly ideological in its projection of a whole series of tacit presuppositions about the nature of time and events, the role of origins, the relationship of past to present, and so forth. It has become conventional to associate these presuppositions with the so-called closed form of the traditional novella or storytelling plot, and Sartre is no doubt perfectly justified in suggesting in *What Is Literature?* that the frame novella, with its comfortable after-dinner audience taking in an anecdote along with their cigars and brandy, projects human action as "a brief disorder which is suppressed . . . told from the point of view of order. Order triumphs, order is everywhere, and contemplates an ancient abolished disorder as though the motionless water of a summer day preserved the ripples that once crossed it."[9] What is new in Barthes' denunciation of such classical plots (besides the relationship he established in this particular one between castration, storytelling, and the commodity) is the assimilation of the classical reader's desire for plot *resolution* to that more fundamental commitment of bourgeois ideology to a conception of objectivity and absolute truth that had already been the object of the critique of the *Tel Quel* group. The solution to the enigmas of plot, indeed, the kind of reading that attaches itself to finding out how everything turns out in the end, thus become profoundly ideological activities in their own right, and something like the aesthetic equivalent of the quasi-theological need for certainty of bourgeois thinking in general. Here also, one would like to distinguish between the practice of something like an empty form—those "irreversible" sequences opened and closed by the so-called hermeneutic code (the mysterious wizened figure of the opening pages, whose identity is revealed in the concluding ones)—and the supplementary ideological message for which this particular form is then used. And it is clear that here, once again, we find ourselves in the presence of that peculiar operatory overdetermination for which early Barthes reserved the term "connotation."

Still, the issue is a good deal broader than that of melodrama and of the code with which Barthes associates it. In its more general form, it concerns a literary phenomenon—irony (now understood in a more local and stylistic sense than we used the term above)—in which Balzac's text is relatively poor. Before evaluating the ultimate premises of *S/Z*, it therefore seems worthwhile to turn to another recent work in this tradition, namely, Jonathan Culler's study of Flaubert, whose title, *The Uses of Uncertainty*,[10] suggests its affinity with the French positions, the need for "certainty" in this context designating something very much like that mirage of absolute truth denounced by *Tel Quel* and tracked by Barthes into the most minute folds and articulations of the hermeneutic code.

II

Flaubert is in any case the historical fountainhead of an aesthetics of textuality, and, unlike the Balzac of Barthes, may be said for Culler to represent the
first genuinely *scriptible* novelist in terms of which the older "legible" and
traditional ones are explicitly or implicitly condemned. But Culler's book is
not only a study of Flaubert, but a study of Flaubert's interpreters as well,
and where Barthes, faced with the apparent formal unity of the older novella,
set out to pulverize the text and to shatter it into its multiple codes, Culler's
"metacommentary" makes its point by a series of snapshots gleefully arresting the various Flaubertians in the act of desperately trying to put their
master back together again.

So Culler has a field day detecting the nostalgia for meaning in a host of
Flaubert commentaries, beginning with Charles Bovary's hideous cap and all
of the attempts uncomfortable critics have made to transform it into a symbol
of one kind or another, that is to say, into a fully meaningful literary or verbal
object. Yet the cap solicits interpretation: "its mute ugliness has the depths
of expressiveness of an imbecile's face"; the critics have done no more than
to rise to the occasion, and the resultant readings, which range from the
psychological (Charles' personality) to the social and historical (the layers on
the cap representing the strata of French society), become, in the present
context, and like anyone's comments in front of the paintings in a museum,
so many candidates for an enlarged *sottisier*. This is no doubt appropriate for
those with temerity enough to pronounce themselves in public about a writer
whose fondest hope, in collecting his file of clichés, was to make people afraid
to open their mouths in the first place for fear of uttering one of them. The
point is, of course, that Flaubert's terrorism aims not only at stupid remarks
but also, and above all, at intelligent ones and at the secretly imbecilic face of
all sentences that aim at finality, or, as Culler would put it, at certainty.
("There are a whole crowd of such topics," Flaubert confided in a letter,
"which annoy me just as much whatever way they are approached. . . .
Whether one speak good or ill of them I am equally irritated. Most of the
time conclusions seem to be acts of stupidity.") So the critic of Flaubert's
critics plays fair and chooses as his targets not the worst of the latter but the
best: still, it remains an open question whether they could have done otherwise faced with a text that demands interpretation at the same time that it
undermines it: "It is as if the exuberant narrator, still characterized as a
youth engaged in mocking the new boy, had set out to reveal 'depths of expressiveness' and been defeated by his run-away prose, and the critic who
seeks the comfort of a world in which everything signifies must avert his eyes
from this defeat and treat the object as a sign whose *signifié* is Charles"
(Culler, p. 93).

But is not this simply to say that Flaubert—or his putative narrator in this passage—*writes badly?* We have of course long seen Flaubert's revolution in terms of a destruction of *rhetoric* in the name of *style* (see Barthes, *Writing Degree Zero*): what can this mean but that the systematic machinery of the rhetorical conventions, variously pressed into the service of oratorical ends or of such late effects as that of the "sublime," are here thoroughly subverted? For Culler, however, the resultant "style" is only incidentally, in Barthes' sense, a vehicle for private physiological expression; the principal function of such "bad writing" is rather the discrediting of the previous reading norms, and a stray description of Yonville, in *Madame Bovary*, allows us to witness the remarkable process whereby description of the older rhetorical type (*ekphrasis* in the terminology of the ancients) undergoes a sea-change into what can henceforth only be known as a "text": "It is not simply that each sentence appears to fritter itself away, as it runs down towards the minute and trivial; that is almost a by-product of the spectacle mounted by a prose style determined to show how grammatical devices enable it to link together a set of disparate and trivial facts. . . . The particularity suggests a single scene, but the mode is one of generalization; and the result is simply that we do not know who speaks or from where. The narrator is depersonalized, in that we cannot give him a character which would explain and hold together the moments of his discourse. We have, in short, a written text, which stands before us cut off from a speaker" (Culler, pp. 76–77).

Thus the text is organized neither objectively (according to the proportions of its object, which its various clauses and subclauses might imitate in some harmonious way), nor subjectively (through the consecutive experiences of a viewer that it might "render"), but is rather simply held together by "grammatical devices." The materials themselves are inert and fragmented, but it is as though the writer had discovered some new principle of order in the process by which the sentences are made to succeed each other across the page, the object of the game now being to marshal all the resources of syntax to prevent the reader from noticing how illogical is such a succession on the level of the content. (Mallarmé will then not long after this erect Syntax itself into the very narrative substance of his poems.)

The kind of coherent meaning thereby discredited on the level of the sentences is now shown by Culler to be analogous to that sought by critics on the level of the plot itself. Here the principal exhibit is that climactic final meeting between Frédéric and Mme Arnoux, in *L'Education sentimentale*, whose "irony" is for him as self-contradictory as the clauses in those humble descriptive sentences in *Madame Bovary* to which we have already alluded: "Flaubert must be either deflating, with consummate irony, the illusions of the characters and revealing their supposed love as false posturing or he must be defending, in a deeply touching scene, the ideal nature of this transcending love" (Culler, p. 152). The fact that neither of these mutually exclusive alternatives works may be taken as a symptom of the beginning crisis in the relationship between narrative and those proairestisms, or schemata, of which we spoke in the previous section: the latter are beginning to become unstuck, to wobble; they no longer function unequivocally as means of organizing narrative perception, yet the reader still gropes blindly for them, now applying the lens of the one, now the other, with imperfect and unsatisfactory results.

Under those conditions, it is the characters themselves who must attempt to reorder their pasts: "since Flaubert will not oblige they must attempt for themselves to organize their lives as a nineteenth-century novel told from the point of view of order." But their own, preeminently romantic reading is patently unsatisfactory: "If we accept this reading of the penultimate scene [in other words, that devised by Frédéric and Mme Arnoux themselves] we find we have made nonsense of our earlier perceptions and indeed of the explicit contrasts in terms of which the rest of the book appears to be constructed. . . . This penultimate scene, which overcomes oppositions and produces a fragile romantic triumph, seems to step outside the line of development adumbrated by earlier scenes. It is not, that is to say, the logical culmination of an experience, which enables us to see what Frédéric learned about love; it is rather an affirmation that while life must be lived and while this will entail disappointment and failure, nevertheless one can, if one proceeds with care, create a purified fiction which remains disconnected from one's experience. Instead of conferring meaning on earlier episodes and pointing to their lesson, it seems to empty the sentimental education, which is the ostensible subject of the book, of the content which it appeared to have" (Culler, p. 155).

Such a reading, or an antireading, suggests that Culler's principal theoretical adversary—although he is nowhere mentioned here—is Wayne Booth, whose own work has been concerned to denounce precisely such "irresponsible ironies" as are here offered as textual models. A careful rereading of the *Rhetoric of Fiction* shows that the "immorality" and lack of narrative perspective of a Céline merely provide Booth with a particularly striking scapegoat; the real villain, as it should be, although identified with only the greatest of tact, is evidently Flaubert himself:

> Henry James talks of Flaubert's "two refuges" from the need to
> look at humanity squarely. One was the exotic, as in *Salammbo* and
> *The Temptation of Saint Anthony*, the "getting away from the
> human" altogether. The other was irony, which enabled him to deal
> with the human without having to commit himself about it directly.
> But, James asks, "when all was said and done was he absolutely and
> exclusively condemned to irony?" Might he "not after all have
> fought out his case a little more on the spot?" Coming from James,
> this is a powerful question. One cannot help feeling, as one reads
> many of the "objective" yet corrosive portraits that have been given
> us since James, that the author is using irony to protect himself

rather than to reveal his subject. If the author's characters reveal themselves as fools and knaves when we cast a cold eye upon them, how about the author himself? How would he look if his true opinions were served up cold? Or does he have no opinions?[11]

In reality, Booth and Culler have surprisingly similar views on the "meaninglessness" of Flaubertian narrative; only what the one rejoices in, the other repudiates. And it is useful, in drawing the consequences of an "ideology of the text," to juxtapose a critic whose attachment to the formal completeness of the individual work and the coherent messages it will convey has led him to draw the final logical conclusions of his own position, whether these be of an unpopular or old-fashioned moralizing kind, or, as in *A Rhetoric of Irony,* a plea for a restriction of the play of literary meanings to what he calls "stable ironies," that is, those that permit coherent interpretations, or, in other words, what Culler would call "certainties": "The serious loss comes when readers, barraged with critical talk hailing the discovery of ambiguities as a major achievement, learn to live with blurred senses and dulled attention, and deprive themselves of the delights of precise and subtle communication that skillful stable ironists provide."[12] And it is certain that what Booth calls "irresponsible irony," that is, an irony that takes its own ironies ironically, engages me in a process of infinite regression to which I must ultimately put an end by confessing that I no longer know what is meant by the term "irony" in the first place. Clearly, then, it is for readers like myself that Booth's new book is intended, suggesting as it does that the term can only recover its function when restricted to its narrowest and most manageable sense: unfortunately, I do not really know what to do with this recommendation either, since the texts in question already exist in history and cannot be wished out of being again.

So it would seem that Culler has the last word, inasmuch as the climactic interview between Frédéric and Mme Arnoux exists in writing, as a text, in spite of its "theoretical impossibility" (Culler, p. 152) and against all attempts to assign it a coherent meaning. Nothing is indeed more irresponsible, from Booth's point of view, than a scene like this, which cannot be made to tell us something unambiguous about life; and Culler's examination of such self-unraveling mechanisms goes a long way toward explaining why this novel is one of the most fascinating and exasperating of world literature, at one and the same time the richest and the emptiest of books, one immense failure and at one and the same time—perhaps precisely *because* we are never able to make final sense of it—one of the rare novels to which one can return endlessly without exhausting it, a veritable summa of sentences, an encyclopedia of everything it is interesting to see narrative language do.

Still, we must take into account the possibility that Culler's victory may be a Pyrrhic one; for we cannot accept the implication that Flaubert is a kind of proto-existentialist, inventing diabolically meaningless objects—like Donald Barthelme's immense balloon that one day sags down upon Manhattan, or the indecipherable sentient ocean of Stanisław Lem's *Solaris*—that have as their ultimate purpose the therapeutic humiliation of the pretensions of the human mind to understanding. Clearly, Charles' cap is not yet an object of this kind, and indeed, Culler distances himself from such an extreme position, testily characterizing as "arrant nonsense" the description by Nathalie Sarraute of Flaubert's works as "books about nothing, almost devoid of subject, rid of characters, plots and all the old accessories" (Culler, p. 134).

Yet to say so puts his denunciation of Flaubertian "interpretation" in a somewhat different light, so it does not seem quite right to dismiss, as he does, Victor Brombert's reading of the landscape in Fontainebleau, through which Frédéric and Rosanette wander during the June massacre of 1848. ("There is irony in those trees which, on the one hand, join each other high up in the air like immense triumphal arches, and on the other seem to be 'falling columns.'. . .The political revolution is measured against the geological 'revolutions.' The 'immobolized Titans' remind us, in their angry pose, of the revolutionary fervour," and so on. Quoted in Culler, p. 101.) To be sure, once the drive to interpret gets out of hand and we transform all of these natural objects into *symbols* of history or nature or whatever, then all of Culler's strictures become applicable; yet Culler's own observations would themselves be impossible were we not precisely *tempted* by just such a longing for complete meaning. So, quoting other remarks by Brombert on the "feeling of numbness and torpor" aroused by this scene in *L'Éducation sentimentale,* Culler goes on to say: "It is as if he had responded to the scene in ways which seem wholly appropriate but had no other critical procedures for dealing with the text except those of symbolic interpretation. But it is not difficult to show that it is precisely through its resistance to the critical operations Brombert applies that the text produces the effects which he discerns." Resistance, yet invitation as well—for if, persuaded by Culler's reasoning, we decide to read Flaubert without any interpretive efforts whatsoever, the stuffing goes out of the novel in a different, but equally irremediable, way. It seems more adequate to say that such passages are *haunted* by a symbolic meaning that never completely coheres with them, and that our practice of Flaubert's text—which can be neither interpretation itself nor some outright indifference to the interpretive process—is very much a matter of "transgression" in the self-contradictory sense in which Bataille applied that term to a certain kind of sexual gratification, which must reaffirm the norm in whose infraction it finds its own pleasure.

To put it this way, however, is to wish to reexamine the unique structure of the Flaubertian text, and indeed the more general theory of the text that emerges from it, in terms of their contradictions and within a framework that

Culler does not really supply, namely, that of history itself; yet it is appropriate, before doing so, to glance at the twist-ending with which he transforms his formal observations into considerations about the deeper content of these works. The mechanism is indeed that of Russian Formalism, in which content is at length seen as the projection of sheer technique; and Culler's account of the two major themes of Flaubert, his rage before the bourgeois "stupidity" of the present and his nostalgia for a sacred that is for the most part projected into the distant past (the exception is Félicite's parrot in *Un Coeur simple*), ingeniously converts both into thematizations of the peculiar type of reading demanded by the text. Thus, stupidity becomes "the operation which reduces [the world] to a surface and makes it a series of signs without meaning [thereby leaving] the subject free before it" (Culler, p. 179). And if stupidity thereby stands as the condition of possibility of the text as such, the sacred is then seen as the hypostasis of some ultimate yet impossible *parole pleine*, or full interpretive certainty: "The Zaimph [the enigmatic sacred veil of Tanit in *Salammbo*] remains a symbol for a possible narrative integration which the text denies us."[13]

It is to designate this process of autoreferentiality that Culler then usefully revives the term "allegory," now used in a hermeneutic rather than a pejorative sense. For to say that such symbolic, or meaning-projective, elements of a text are to be grasped as allegories of the reading process itself, in other words, as figures for the very attempt to interpret and to assign textual meanings, is, it seems to me, quite a different type of hypothesis from the rather static and now somewhat conventionalized allegorical interpretations of the Derrida school, which, for example, by seeing Charles' cap as a figure of *écriture* and textual productivity, result in "certainties" no less unjustifiable and peremptory than the other kinds of interpretations Culler denounces. The advantage of his own approach is not only to make visible a whole range of autoreferential phenomena of this kind in traditional literature (one might, for instance, wish to see the preoccupation of a Proust or a Thackeray with memory as just such a disguised commentary on the sheer duration of the reader's reception of their own pages), but also to make possible a dialogue with that quite different, phenomenologically oriented, hermeneutic school of criticism referred to above, whose methods have not hitherto seemed compatible with those of the French or structuralizing tendency. And it is certain that we need a more adequate account of autoreferentiality in literary history than any that has previously been given; yet as Culler's demonstration of it in Flaubert alone suggests, without some more adequate historical framework, this particular phenomenon—with its suggestion of a kind of self-consciousness of the text—is only too easily pressed back into the service of the old modernism/realism antinomy, to which we therefore return in our conclusion.

III

"Sarrasine" was published in November, 1830, a few weeks before the appearance of Balzac's first "signed" novel (and first great success)—*La Peau de chagrin*—and a few months after the "three glorious days" of June, which saw the fall of the Bourbon dynasty. The moment is therefore a crucial one for Balzac, in which his "general ideology" (or political system) will be definitively formed, and in which his "aesthetic ideology" (his attempts to construct a distinctive form of his own) is ambitiously and energetically projected, in what will turn out to be something of a false step. For "Sarrasine" is only one of a cycle of what we would call "fantastic tales" (the influence of Hoffman is often adduced), which will very shortly be collected and republished in a three-volume edition called *Romans et contes philosophiques* along with *La Peau de chagrin* itself, of which the new collection is thus a second printing, drawing the *cortège* of the fantastic tales along behind it. The title of the collection will live on into the definitive classification scheme of *La Comédie humaine* of 1842, where it is modified as "Études philosophiques." A few additional (and very important) texts are added under this particular classification to the contents of the original collection, but none of them is written later than 1835, at which point Balzac's interest in this particular narrative form seems exhausted. Significantly, however, in 1835 Balzac will remove "Sarrasine" from the rubric of "philosophical tales" and reprint it as part of another subset entirely, the "scènes de la vie parisienne."

The subclassifications of *La Comédie humaine* often serve (particularly for the shorter texts) to focalize and thematize our reading and to orient it toward the production of a specific *Gestalt*, something of which the interpretive options of "Sarrasine" are virtually a paradigm case. Read as a "scene of Parisian life," the story organizes itself into an opposition between Italian and Parisian (or French) life which is relatively conventional throughout this period (and dramatized most forcefully in the works of Stendhal)—a world of passion versus a world of money and gossip. The dominant image or emblem of the tale, then, the opposition between the skeleton and the living woman's body, between death and life, on this reading becomes the retroactive interpretant of that essentially social and historical content, which we might reformulate as the radical difference between capitalism and precapitalist society, and which also governs the formal division of the tale into its two sections: the Parisian frame, the interpolated anecdote set in the Rome of the *ancien régime*.

When we replace "Sarrasine" in its first classification, however, that of the "étude philosophique" or fantastic tale, this reading or perceptual organization is with one stroke tangibly and dramatically restructured. To appreciate the extent of this reorganization, however, we must now observe that Balzac's category—the "étude philosophique" or philosophical tale—is at least in its ambitions and its concept broader than what we now designate as "fantastic" literature, since it specifically includes narratives set in earlier historical periods (*Sur Catherine de Médicis*) as well as texts with overtly philosophical, metaphysical, or mystical pretensions (*Louis Lambert, Séraphita*). The first of these features now far more strongly foregrounds the historical (and foreign) setting of the interpolated narrative of "Sarrasine," which ceases to function in opposition to the contemporary frame and becomes a kind of autonomous vision in its own right. We may indeed note in passing something like a definitive settling of accounts here with Sir Walter Scott, whose deeper historicist perspective has now so deeply penetrated the contemporary (or nineteenth-century) narratives that make up the bulk of the *Comédie humaine* that the antiquarian husk and trappings of Scott's romance can be discarded, and its Balzacian remnants gathered under the rather marginalizing and eccentric rubric of the "étude philosophique."

Meanwhile, the overtly "philosophical" focus captures the allegory of life and death and transforms it into an outright metaphysical theme, in the process transforming the historical opposition of the first interpretive option into a more existential sense of the withering of beauty and the passage of time.

On this second reading (chronologically the prior one), the "fantastic" component of the story is expressed through the "uncanny" repulsion/fascination of the aged Zambinella (younger people literally feel a chill in her proximity) and turns on the trick or secret of the castration itself, which in a wholly conventional way allows you to read the tale twice, first in all the ominous mysteries of ignorance, and then, in the light of disclosure, full of admiration for the storyteller's calculated ambiguities. This double reading, or inverted reading structure, is obviously what Barthes designates as the operation of the "hermeneutic code"; what is not yet clear is the way in which this rather limited narrative sleight of hand will be transformed by our other, more social and historical, interpretive option. But this is also the moment to read Barthes' own "interpretation" into the record, as I have summarized it elsewhere:

Balzac's novella speaks to us at once of itself and of its subject-matter, of art and of desire, both of which are present, with reversed emphasis, in the frame and in the actual tale alike. In the frame, the narrator tells a tale in order to seduce his listener; while within the tale itself an artist is destroyed by his desire, leaving only its representation—a statue and a portrait of Zambinella—behind in the catastrophe. This passion is narcissism and castration: the infatuated artist in reality sees his own image in the castrato with whom he falls in love, so that the gesture of symbolic castration or sexual renunciation is here given to be the very source of artistic productivity, just as it turns out elsewhere in the story to be the very source of the Lanty family's mysterious fortune (Zambinella as prima donna). The fable thus has something to say about the origins of classical art and the origins of capitalism and their relationship to each other; yet it does not leave the frame within which it is told intact. Rather, it contaminates teller and listener alike, who separate at its close, in the desexualized and desexualizing atmosphere, without having consummated their desire.[14]

It should be added that this resume is in the nature of an artificial reconstruction of Barthes' reading after the fact: the commentary form precludes the synthesis into any such general proposition of its local elements and punctual observations (all of which are to be found here and there in *S/Z*). But the invocation of historical material with which this section began, as well as the memory of the legendary Barthes-Picard debate on the former's rewriting of Racine along the lines of *Totem and Taboo*, should not lead us to the overhasty conclusion that Barthes has here willfully and arbitrarily "modernized" Balzac. On the contrary, all the elements enumerated in our summary are present in the text itself, and it is rather our "modern" sense that Balzac could not possibly have meant such things, or thought such "modern" thoughts, which is anachronistic. In fact, one cannot insist strongly enough on the "modernity" of Balzac's tactful but explicit (and no doubt rather daring) designations of a whole range of sexual peculiarities. In the text that concerns us here, for example, the narrator observes, to his listener: "L'aventure a des passages dangereux pour le narrateur" (Some parts of this adventure are dangerous for the storyteller) (*S/Z*, p. 234—trans. modified/p. 239). It is hard to see what this might mean unless one adopts Barthes' reading, which is also confirmed by the ending of the story ("Vous m'avez dégoutée de la vie et des passions pour longtemps. . . . Laissez-moi seule" [You have given me a disgust for life and for passions that will last a long time] [*S/Z*, p. 253/257]).

But this *aphanisis* (Ernest Jones' word, systematically recovered by Lacan, for the sudden extinction of sexual desire and the aimlessness in which the subject is left by its unexpected disappearance) marks a fundamental permutation in the earlier reading of the hermeneutic code: now the trick or the secret is a little more than a trick; it is no longer neutral, no longer a matter of possessing a crucial piece of information. Now, like the aged mummy himself, it sends a chill through the narrative itself and actively contaminates what we have read. We are, therefore, no longer in the fantastic, but rather very much in the "uncanny" in Freud's sense. What remains to be seen is the relationship between this effect and what must be called the ideological terminology or conceptuality of Desire evoked by Barthes to convey its meaning.

Metacommentary, as I sought to lay its groundwork in the preceding essay, should not be misunderstood as a refutation of other critical positions; if one insists on using that language, it would be better to say that it seeks to refute the interpretive code in which a given analysis is staged and articulated, while preserving the content of the analysis in question. Metacommentary demands, among other things, that we also account for Barthes' errors (to continue to use an older language); that is, that we have an obligation, not merely to endorse his insights and perceptions, or to denounce the faults and vices of his conceptualizations, but also to explain where these last came from in the first place (if not, indeed, to show historical necessity itself: why he had to think all of this as he did, why he could not have thought it otherwise). That second and more perplexing obligation can only be acquitted, I must feel, by showing that Barthes' conceptualizations are also projections of his content, afterimages of his object of study, mistaken for universal truths. In this, therefore, the movement of metacommentary replicates and reproduces the movement of dialectical thinking in general as it confronts its object and seeks to grasp, for example, the form of a work as the articulation of the deeper logic of the work's concrete content (in Hjelmslev's terminology, the determination of the dimension of form by that of *substance*). Only where in Balzac that content or substance is an untextualized history, a class, psychic, political, and aesthetic situation that must be reconstructed after the fact, for Barthes (besides being all of these things!) it is simply the historical object or text, "Sarrasine," whose historical peculiarities imperceptibly govern the thinking that takes it for its occasion and its pretext.

S/Z is in effect Barthes' return upon his moment of semiotic orthodoxy (embodied most notably in the classic "Structural Analysis of Narrative"): his farewell to the attempt "scientifically" to disengage from the infinite variety of human stories and tales some ultimate abstract narrative structure from which they are all generated. The shift in optical machinery, the exclusion of overall narrative form and its replacement by a line-by-line attention (which rewrites "Sarrasine" into a very different kind of aesthetic object), seems at once to banish the older ambitions (which Greimas' *Maupassant: la Sémiotique du texte*—an explicit reply to *S/Z*—demandingly reinstates by giving attention to the structures of narrative memory—anaphora, cataphora— within the text's individual sentences). Nonetheless it would seem that Barthes' "semic code" or "voice of the person" constitutes something of a survival of the older narrative perspective, insofar as it is still obliged to retain the stubbornly anthropomorphic category of the "character" on which to string its indexes. The other codes effectively explode the text, as Barthes intended them to do; this one—despite all "good intentions"—reintegrates it at least distantly into what still looks like an old-fashioned narrative about "people."

As for the cultural code, which seems to draw *doxa*, the "sagesse des nations," the broken pieces of stereotypes and dead proverbs, behind it with an inertia that forbids genuinely historical—that is to say, *situational*—analysis, it can readily be shown that Balzac's text deconstructs it in the very moment it is invoked and pressed into service. To limit ourselves only to Balzac's most annoying mannerism—the authoritative appeal to older works of art ("Et joignez à ces détails qui eussent ravi, un peintre, toutes les merveilles de Venus révérées et rendues par le ciseaudes Grecs" [And along with these details, which would have enraptured a painter, were all the wonders of those images of Venus revered and rendered by the chisels of the Greeks] [S/Z, p. 238/243])—it is clear that the interpretive regression that leads from Vien's - painting to Sarrasine's "original" statue, and beyond that to the ambiguous "real-life" model itself, now transformed from a fascinating young woman into a repulsive old man, retroactively undermines the legitimacy and the authority of such acts of reference by causing the "referent" itself to vanish in a sleight of hand. Meanwhile, the dual structure of the tale, its capacity to generate the two distinct and incompatible kinds of readings we have already mentioned—the historical one, appropriate to a "scène de la vie parisienne," the metaphysical one, appropriate to an "étude philosophique"—here finds its source: everything depends, indeed, on the nature of the question to which the interpolated story or anecdote—the adventure of the unhappy Sarrasine—is the answer. If the story is told in order to reveal the identity of the aged mummy, we have a fantastic tale that liberates a whole spectrum of "metaphysical" impulses and investments (specifically including Barthes' own Lacanian fantasies); yet at the same time something peculiar happens to what seemed to be the very center of the narrative, namely the story of Sarrasine himself, who is no longer essential in any way to the destiny of the famous singer, in whose career he will have been but a very brief episode, without any particular relevance for the solution to this particular enigma. We will return to this odd structural discontinuity in the text in a moment. That the "revelation" feels like the climax of the narrative every reader of the story can judge; a closer look at the text, however, shows this to be a misreading, since Sarrasine's story is in fact told in response to a question about the "identity" of the *painting*, and it is only in the context of that rather different question that it has any point.

This Gestalt-like shift in reading perspectives determines other fundamental changes as well, for example in Barthes' "symbolic code" in which the dynamics of what begin by tropes are ultimately grounded in the experience of the body itself, in that unnameable prelinguistic carnal existence to which, most notably, the central theme of gender and sexual identity will be linked. But if one sets contemporary *doxa* (including our own obsessions with sexuality and gender and Desire) aside, it seems to me by no means irrefutable that such an ultimate "code of the body" constitutes the interpretive bottom line of Balzac's story. An inspection of the narrative of Sarrasine's youth, indeed, discloses a movement from the male to the female subject, from the heroic materials of war and glory to the intimate or "sentimental" materials of love, which can historically be decoded in a very different way, as a displacement in formal paradigms, a shift in artistic styles, an *embourgeoise-ment* and interiorization of older aristocratic traditions, a displacement of categories of Line by those of Color, about which the art historians have had much to tell us in recent years. It seems to me at least plausible that the thematics of castration and desire metaphorize and express this historical situation, rather than, on our contemporary reading, the other way round. Meanwhile, this concrete but specialized historical topic—the emergence of bourgeois painting thematized as a transformation of masculine into feminine content—is itself overdetermined by a political anxiety specific to the period when Balzac wrote the story and to the generation of writers and intellectuals to which he belonged: namely the well-known sense of *Epigonentum* felt by this entire generation and most programmatically expressed in Musset's *Confessions d'un enfant du siècle*, where the shift from war to love, from public to private, is articulated as the disappearance of the great Napoleonic occasion and the melancholy of the latecomer whom History has passed by. Read from this perspective, in which the diachrony of the eighteenth century and Mediterranean material is grasped as a projection of Balzac's synchronic situation at the inaugural moment of the bourgeois monarchy of Louis Philippe, "Sarrasine" sheds its Lacanian overtones and comes to look a little like Virginia Woolf's *Orlando*. In the process, however, Barthes' Symbolic Code has disappeared.

We have not yet, however, confronted the formal specificity (and the historical peculiarity) of this *novella*, which bears little relationship to the modern short story and may rather be seen as an anachronism, an artificial revival of the older form of the classical or Renaissance framed tale in conditions that no longer have anything to do with that kind of cultural production, which is far more archaic and regressive than Scott's "romance." That the story's fantastic content (Freud analyzes such content and such effects in "The Uncanny" as the marks and the consequence of a "return" of psychically regressive materials) is related to the "return" of an archaizing form I will try to show in a moment. First, however, it is necessary to disentangle several distinct approaches to the historicity of a text, approaches which it would be simplistic to sort out in terms of a stereotypical opposition between form and content. I have found it more adequate, elsewhere, to suggest that each of the three approaches or methodological perspectives in question in effect reconstructs its object or text in a distinct way from the others (and in a way in which, for each reconstruction, specific relationships between form and content—or form and substance—obtain).

"Sarrasine" may thus be inserted into what I will call a specifically *political* rhythm and temporality of the events and chronological agitation of the momentous year 1830, to which it can then be seen as an elaborate and complex, mediated, symbolic reaction: the contemporary satire of a fallen commercial society being now accompanied by a nostalgic image of that society's precapitalist other which must be displaced onto another culture and another time, insofar as the palpable vacuousness and debility of the Bourbon Restoration block any recourse to that immediate historical material and indeed, at least for the moment, paralyze the conservative capacity to imagine history (a paralysis which Balzac will later overcome in interesting ways). Sarrasine's doomed obsession, therefore, which leaves only an absent work of art behind it, may here be taken as a figure for this imaginative and ideological contradiction, the difficulty of maintaining a satiric repudiation of the present in the absence of energizing visions of either a radically different past or a radically different future.

A second perspective or horizon takes the place of this one, and is accompanied by a thoroughgoing restructuration of the text or object, when "Sarrasine" becomes an episode in the larger crisis of bourgeois ideology that emerges after the triumph of this class in the Revolution of 1789, when its essentially negative and critical values and ideological instruments become hegemonic and universal or "positive" ones. This is something like a *social* level, or realm of class discourse and class struggle, which can be textualized and articulated only by the identification of a whole play or specific "ideologemes," and demands, as I have suggested above, the translation of Barthes' "cultural code," but also his "symbolic" one, into local lexical moves, in which general "themes" are invested with a specific ideological significance which may be lost on a later readership which has forgotten the meaning of those tacitly but universally understood ideological vocabulary words. The French literature of the early middle-class period (to limit ourselves only to that) tended to express and to confront its class antinomies and general ideological dilemmas by way of the figuration of the role of the artist, who thus comes to "represent" the situation of the bourgeois intellectual with something of the obsessive force and concentration of symptom-formation. From this perspective, then, "Sarrasine" will no longer be read as a political allegory, but rather as that seemingly more limited thing, the story of the artist, which, however, symbolically vehiculates larger issues of class and ideology (of which our remarks on heroic and sentimental painting, on line and color, are to be taken as one "coding" among others). The thematics of castration are here, then, something more than a punctual difficulty in "thinking" the Revolution of 1830; they express the more general problem of forging a new ideology (in Balzac's case, a new conservatism) in the historical situation that emerges from that revolution.

But there remains a final level or interpretive horizon that is historically vaster than either of these (and which I have therefore felt it appropriate to designate as *historical* in the most general sense), insofar as it opens onto the realm of modes of production as such and the transitions from one form of human society to another. Paradoxically, it is at this most general level of interpretation that literary form in its more specialized sense becomes visible as an ideologically charged move, as a socially symbolic strategy. It is therefore within this final perspective that we must return to the issue of Balzac's revival of an archaic form of storytelling, with a view toward some ultimate settling of accounts with Barthes' conception of a "hermeneutic code."

This will also, however, present the occasion for the reevaluation of another enormously influential contemporary critical text, which we have found it necessary to mention from time to time in this discussion, namely Freud's essay on "The Uncanny," whose object of study, E. T. A. Hoffmann's "Der Sandmann" (1816), has at least some distant kinship with Balzac's romantic tale. Indeed, the most obscure and least discussed section of Freud's essay—offered with uncharacteristic diffidence and hesitation—deals with the relationship between "uncanny" effects and the formal structures of narrative in ways that seem relevant to the dual structure or Gestalt of Balzac's novella noted above. Freud here shrewdly suggests that the formal articulation of uncanny or repressed materials may be organized as a kind of shell game (my image) in which the reader's attention is diverted to the empty receptacle in such a way as to preclude the psychic effect the filled one would inevitably have determined: "In the Herodotus story our thoughts are concentrated much more on the superior cunning of the master-thief than on the feelings of the princess. The princess may very well have had an uncanny feeling, indeed she probably fell into a swoon; but *we* have no such sensations, for we put ourselves in the thief's place, not in hers."[15] At this point, Freud unaccountably breaks off, having demonstrated only the first of the two points he intended to develop:

> The somewhat paradoxical result is that in the first place a great deal that is not uncanny in fiction would be so if it happened in real life; and in the second place that there are many more means of creating uncanny effects in fiction than there are in real life.[16]

Yet Hoffmann's story allows us to reestablish this second proposition in such a way as to shed light on "Sarrasine" as well, by raising the whole issue of the narrative *frame* as the fundamental mechanism in the shifting of Gestalt perceptions, and as the locus of that trick whereby, in the shell game of fiction, an uncanny effect can be produced by the unexpected appearance of the fateful token under a receptacle thought to be empty.

I use the terminology of framing here by way of analogy with off-camera space in film, where a peculiar *lateral* effect is possible in the insertion, as it were, of images between the camera apparatus and the eye, images that have nothing of the density of the objects before the camera but rather hover, divested of their object-world or background, and thereby of their normal materiality, with something of the free-floating quality of hallucinations that move across the perceptual field without belonging to it. Something like this has always disturbed me in the reading of the opening pages of Hoffmann's story, arousing the suspicion that Freud's topic had more to do with form than the conventional interpretation of this essay in terms of content (castration, regression, images of the double or the simulacrum) suggested. I will not go so far as to identify this connection with epistolary narrative as such (although it is a very peculiar form indeed); but it seems to me obvious that the strangeness of the Hoffmann text has a good deal to do with the inexplicable shift from the epistolary mode to conventional third-person narrative, something Freud does not mention but which Hoffmann himself awkwardly and unsuccessfully devotes a few pages to motivating.

The reader cannot help feeling a nagging skepticism about the improbability of these opening pages. It is a skepticism readily enough repressed in the name of literary convention (since by definition the fantastic is not supposed to be governed by verisimilitude), but which on the other hand does not really attach to the events themselves (the villainy of Coppelius, the secret experiments, the "significance" of the eyes); rather it is a skepticism that involves the initial narrative contract, and it bears on the unlikeliness of a situation in which the protagonist could grow up in the company of those who will become his betrothed and his best friend without their ever hearing anything about his traumatic childhood experiences. They cannot *not* have known; or, if we must have it this way, the reader's skepticism reverses itself and comes to focus on the peculiarity of the protagonist's confession at this point, at this *now* of the epistolary experience—so convenient for the storyteller, one thinks absurdly, as though it were not the chance appearance of Coppelius' double, the lens-grinder Coppola, which motivated the revelation in question. Only in the reading experience this follows that; and one has the sense of some simple but thoroughgoing and inadmissible narrative fraud, as when for the purposes of the denouement a novelist endows a long-familiar character with a hitherto concealed and quite preposterous and unexpected life history. But that is not quite the right way to put it either, since the conventional reversal of the detective story repeatedly does this without arousing anything of the feeling of protest and scandal I am trying to register here. It would be better to say, therefore, that what is "familiar" about the character to whom this unexpected past is somehow "spuriously" attributed is his first-person status, or at least his formal status as the protagonist, with whom, therefore, what is often loosely called "identification" is solicited. It is this contract, then, which is summarily broken and disregarded in the unexpected revelation itself, which abruptly separates us from the former protagonist, brutally shifting from first to third person, and stamping him as Other to us in all respects, no longer capable of sustaining our identification, indeed repelling it. The peculiarity of the situation may be conveyed by analogous (but structurally inverted) and equally artificial experiments in "first-person" film where we are asked to watch the contents of the screen through the hero's eyes. I have dwelt on it in such length not merely because it seems to me to hold the structural key to "the uncanny" itself (Freud's account shows us becoming *other* to ourselves), but also and above all because it characterizes the major literary and formal achievement of Balzac's "fantastic" period, namely the novel *La Peau de chagrin*, rigorously contemporaneous with "Sarrasine." Critics have not often been willing to admit, let alone discuss or theorize, the outrageous way in which—analogous in that to the introduction of the childhood memory in "Der Sandmann," but on a much more enormous scale—Raphael's autobiographical reminiscences (including a childhood evocation of the father very much in the spirit of the Freudian generic convention) drive a wedge between reader and protagonist, such that this last is moved inexorably and irrevocably into a third-person position in which, at the close of the novel, we observe him coldly and remorselessly in the throes of the absolute otherness of possession by what, in one characteristic period language, was then called "the demonic" and, in another, "frenzy." Indeed, in the psychological ideology of the period, "frenzy" is the specific ideologeme that designates a certain kind of otherness, or, more precisely, a certain kind of impotent rage and irredeemable agitation into which the "Other" who has been split off from the self is precipitated: the Nathanael of "Der Sandmann" undergoes the same formal metamorphosis, as does the eponymous sculptor in Balzac's short story (although here one is tempted to say that the moment of frenzy, radically foreshortened in its second- or third-hand retelling, is prolonged under another form in the phenomenon of *aphanisis* in which the frame story concludes).

It seems to me at least plausible that Freud's own interest in the Hoffmann variant of this peculiar structure was awakened by its analogy to the analytic situation itself, and to the dialectic of identification and otherness generated by a first-person frame which, violated, necessarily gives way to the more disinterested detachment of third-person observation. In our present context, however, it seems appropriate to evaluate these psychological but also textual peculiarities in terms of the history of form, and in particular in terms of the survival and readaptation of a form developed within one mode of production within the very different environment and ecosystem of a later one. This is already, as I have suggested, something of a return of the repressed in its own right, an unexpected repetition, a recurrence of the archaic; the Romantic revival of the Renaissance art-story or novella therefore already bears within itself formally the powers of the uncanny, irrespective of the content of this or that Romantic tale.

But I now want to suggest more than that, and to relate the form of the various kinds of narratives in question here to the structure of the psychic subject as it is variously constructed in distinct modes of production (or, as in capitalism, in distinct moments of a single mode of production). The art-novella, however, whose revival we are considering here, cannot be said to express the cultural dominant of the mode of production that precedes capitalism. Feudal art—whatever its dialectical transformations over a very long historical period—articulates the *ethos* of its twin ruling classes, a *samurai* nobility, obsessed with fate, death and glory, and a church whose function is to devise an essentially agricultural or peasant theology; and in the process must address, reconcile, or resolve the contradictions between those two ideologies. Art historians, however, have often remarked about the simultaneity, in many distinct cultures, between the emergence of "realistic" or "naturalistic" forms of representation and the growth of commerce or the development of a money economy and a system of cash exchange. It seems plausible, then, to posit some general relationship between the "realism" of the art-novella (Boccaccio, the *Novelas ejemplares* of Cervantes, Marguerite de Navarre) and commercial activity, provided this last is grasped as a limited enclave within a radically different economic system, an activity structurally subordinate to this last and assigned specific spatial and temporal boundaries (the city, the trade fair), within which it is "free" to develop in a semi-autonomous way. Such a qualification suggests that we must also grasp the specific cultural production associated with the art-novella in a similarly restricted and subordinate fashion: as a specific kind of narrative production that takes place within the pores and interstices, the intermundia, of a feudal narrative production that is organized on very different principles. The art-novella, then, will be governed by the experience of money, but of money at a specific moment of its historical development: the stage of commerce rather than the stage of capital proper. This is the stage Marx describes as exchange on the frontiers between two modes of production, which have not yet been subsumed under a single standard of value; so great fortunes can be made and lost overnight, ships sink or against all expectation appear in the harbor, heroic travelers reappear with cheap goods whose scarcity in the home society lends them extraordinary worth. This is therefore an experience of money which marks the form rather than the content of narratives; these last may include rudimentary commodities and coins incidentally, but nascent Value organizes them around a conception of the Event which is formed by categories of Fortune and Providence, the wheel that turns, bringing great good luck and then dashing it, the sense of what is not yet an invisible hand guiding human destinies and endowing them with what is not yet "success" or "failure," but rather the irreversibility of an unprecedented fate, which makes its bearer into the protagonist of a unique and "memorable" story. In this cultural production, then, the individual subject is still considered to be the locus of events and can only be articulated by way of nonpsychological narrative.

The bourgeois world, however, the life world of a now properly capitalist exchange system, is one in which the individual subject—now an economic and juridical unit within a matrix of equivalencies—begins to develop that rich, monadic, properly psychological autonomy which is thought to be the spiritual property of the West and has been celebrated (or denounced) in any number of familiar ways. In the formal context of the present discussion, it will be useful to mark its full narrative codification by means of the shorthand of the Jamesian conception of "point of view," whose function will be, among other things, to exclude the kinds of peculiar first/third person dysfunctionality we have glimpsed in Hoffmann and Balzac, and to regulate our distance from the protagonist in a more stable alternation of identification and irony. Looking back from this triumphant moment of narrative and psychic stabilization, then, it is clear that the texts we have dealt with here can be little more than oddities and curiosities, historical eccentricities.

Reestablished in its own historical situation, however, which is that of the setting in place of the new market system, but also of its provisionsl coexistence with institutions and ideologies that, incompletely liquidated, still survive from an older mode of production, the uncanny tale will take on a rather different historical and symptomatic significance—that of something like an interference or a contamination between two distinct cultural principles, which are structurally incompatible, but whose forced conjunction yields a text to be thought of less in terms of hybridization than of anamorphosis. Indeed, the uncanny tale presents some of the properties of a two-dimensional geometrical plane projected into a three-dimensional system: in it, a narrative governed by categories of the Event must now be represented by means of the very different representational categories of a narrative process organized around the Person or Subject. The uncanny tale is by no means the only formal symptom of this immence systemic transformation, in which the properties of an older cultural system survive, bereft of their function, within the emergent force-field of a new one. It is appropriate to inscribe here, without exploring it further now, the very different, yet equally anomalous, peculiarities of the *reading play,* as it comes into being in the Walpurgisnacht scene of Goethe's *Faust* and is bequeathed, via Flaubert's *Temptation of Saint Anthony,* all the way down to the Nighttown section of *Ulysses.* Here the representational paradoxes of the frame are mobilized, not around categories of event, but rather in terms of perception and description, by way of the interference between printed space and the properties of a spectacle now merely remembered or conceptualized.

Barthes' "hermeneutic code" can now at any rate be seen to be either excessively or insufficiently theorized, insofar as its specific object of study or raw material (what happened? when will we learn what happened?) is a historical form, the art-novella, on the point of artificial revival, and also extinction. Yet its inadequacies as a purely analytic instrument recover a certain use and functionality on a dialectical level, where this concept can serve to direct our attention to the presence or survival of more archiac narrative features within texts organized by different principles—provided we remember that this "code" governs, not all narrative as such (let alone "realism," or "the scriptible text"), but merely and very specifically this historical form of narrative as such.

As for Barthes' "proairetic code," it can now be seen to locate with unerring precision the places at which the new cultural logic eats away at archaic figures of the event and the act and undermines or decodes them. This is why it would be a mistake to consider S/Z as a contribution to the analysis of the short story as such; for the modern short story, as it emerges in Chekhov, bears no genetic relationship to the archaic tale revived in Balzac's text—or rather, if there is some distant genetic or evolutionary relationship between the two, it would be better to imagine it according to the ec-centric model of filiation proposed by the Russian Formalists—the "knight's gambit," not an inheritance from father to son, but at best one from uncle to nephew. Indeed, the modern short story emerges, not from the narrative system of the classical tale, but from what disintegrates it, that is to say, very precisely from the "proairetic code" itself, whose "unfoldings" of the older conventional names for events and actions open up a space for the writing of new kinds of texts. Paradoxically these texts—the modern short story—disclose an immediate and unexpected affiliation with another emergent form, namely the novel itself—but not the so-called realistic or classical nineteenth-century novel, rather its "modernist" successor (whose act of succession is equally to be grasped according to the Formalists' discontinuous model of development). That *Ulysses* should have first begun life as the project for a short story on the dimensions of *Dubliners*, that *The Magic Mountain* should equally have been first conceived as a novella not much more ambitious than "Death in Venice"—these otherwise peculiar facts are testimony to the corrosive power of the "proairetic code," which it was Barthes' supreme achievement to have formulated in S/Z but whose richness and suggestiveness we can explore only by grasping it, not as yet another analytic category in the "structural analysis of narrative," but rather as a historical force in its own right, as that active logic of disjuncture, separation, disaggregation, and abstraction which in other areas of study bears the name reification.

Such are, then, some of the ways in which Barthes' own critical categories are secretly informed by the "logic of content" of his texts, thereby cleaving to history and to the difference and resistance of the past despite his brilliant and Nietzschean "forgetfulness" of traditional literary history. That in this, however, such concepts also cleave to History in the present it will be the task of a final section to demonstrate.

IV

Returning in a very different way to the question of frames, it seems useful to pursue a hypothesis I have proposed elsewhere, namely that all apparently synchronic or ahistorical analysis depends on and presupposes (for the most part covertly) a diachronic scheme, a vision or "philosophy" of history, a historical "master-narrative," in terms of which its evaluations are processed. In an intellectual climate, however, in which such abstractions as the older "universal" histories with their broad periodizing schemes (along with any other diachronic patterns or "teleological" or evolutionary narratives that seem to have affinities with them) have fallen into disrepute and opprobrium, this structurally indispensable diachronic frame tends to be repressed, and at best to return in the form of a dualism or binary opposition. In the case of S/Z, this dualistic framing structure is articulated as that opposition between the "legible" and the "scriptible" which both generates Barthes' analytic categories in the first place (the five codes) and is then invoked for a more ambiguous evaluation of the findings they produce (Balzac's manifestly "legible" text turning imperceptibly into a "scriptible" one).

That this dualistic framing process in S/Z is by no means an isolated instance or an idiosyncracy can be appreciated by a random checklist of other such binary schemes at work in the most influential currents of contemporary thought: in the omnipresent Heideggerian story about "Western metaphysics," for example, but also in the Frankfurt School's conception of "enlightenment" (their word for "reification," accompanied by an ever-receding initial moment of the archaic, or of pre-Enlightenment); in the various anarchist (or Foucauldian or Weberian) conceptions of Power (always preceded by a moment before which "power" was formed); in various aesthetic forms of value or the absolute, such as "indeterminacy" or New Critical paradox or irony (both preceded by kinds of texts that had not yet self-consciously become aware of those essences of literariness); representation and the "centered subject" versus whatever is taken to be the opposite of those things; and so forth and so on—the list, clearly, might be extended indefinitely.

The objection to such dualisms is complicated, and involves a little more than the suspicion that all this makes for bad history (which it may well do). I want to say, first, that such diachronic frames are not in themselves objectionable; they are in fact indispensable, so that the vices of the various kinds of thinking enumerated above do not lie in the existence of such a frame but rather in the way it has been constructed. Second, it is clearly the binary structure of the frame that demands critical and negative attention, since in all these cases the very presence of a dualistic structure makes it quite inevitable for the mind to assimilate that opposition to the fundamental ethical one, and to sort the opposing terms out into a good one and a bad one. It is, then, this often imperceptible contamination by ethical thinking or moralizing which deprives such perceptions and formulations of trends and processes of their historical validity.

It is, however, the third qualification that may be the most unexpected: namely, that, as I have tried to show locally for Barthes' text, the defectiveness of what I have been calling the diachronic frame need not invalidate the work done within it (and in a moment I will add a fourth qualification: "on the contrary"). It is, indeed, with the relationship and the articulation of these two kinds of structures—a diachronic frame and a synchronic analysis—a little like the problem of the relationship of propositions and subordinate clauses in Frege, where the falsity or fictionality of the one need not necessarily entail the falsity of the other. But in this case, the priorities of Freud's joke (which has been adduced to dramatize this dilemma) may well be reversed: "Is this the place where the Duke of Wellington spoke those words?—Yes, this is the place; but he never spoke the words." There would seem to be something in the dynamics of contemporary theory that makes for a situation in which the Duke spoke the words, but not in this place at all.

I have introduced the question of the nature of contemporary "theoretical discourse" at this point to historicize the whole issue and to allow for at least the possibility that my fourth qualification may have some more general applicability: namely that for some reason what we call "theory" today seems to require a dualistic or binary frame in order to "produce" its "concepts." This will not, however, be a meaningful proposition unless "theoretical discourse" is grasped as a historical form of language production in its own right, a discursive phenomenon or genre developed in the last few decades, with only the most distant structural affinities to apparently related forms of writing associated with traditional philosophy or other disciplines. Indeed, one of the sub-themes of the essays collected here can be identified as the attempt to position "theory" historically and to formulate its status as a discourse, something that is undertaken more formally in the study of the 1960s that completes this collection, but whose essentials will also begin to emerge in the course of the present discussion. For the moment, it will be enough to retain this preliminary hypothesis on the structure of theoretical discourse as such: a binary diachronic frame within which "new" concepts or neologisms are generated for essentially synchronic operations of a linguistic nature.

This said, we may again take up the Barthesian opposition between the legible and the scriptible with a view toward determining its relationship to the older realism/modernism dispute, of which the newer "textual" issues often seem a contemporary replay. Indeed, the new terminology may be understood as the result of a French situation in which—paradoxically enough for the place in which it originated—modernism has borne no particular name as such (the word *modernité*, traditionally used in the sense of "modern times" in general or in what social scientists call *modernization*, is only now coming to take on this meaning). I want to suggest that this opposition is unsatisfactory, from a historical point of view, and that the premature ideological but also ethical judgments that are made in its name must be seen as *compensations* for its structural incapacity to do justice to diachronic phenomena.

But of course, from another point of view, the realism/modernism opposition is useful precisely in the kind of covert diachronic or genetic thinking it enables without declaring itself as such. Thus, we may observe that the division of literature into these two starkly antithetical tendencies (form-oriented versus content-oriented, artistic play versus imitation of the real, etc.) is dictated by the attempt to deal adequately with modernism, rather than the other way round (in this sense, even Lukács' accounts of realism are defensive and reflect his own "conversion" to the earlier artistic style). The concept of realism that thereby emerges is always that with which modernism has had to break, that norm from which modernism is the deviation, and so forth. It is as though, in spite of everything, only a historical and genetic approach to modernism, which leans fully as much on the story of the emergence of the new phenomenon as on some ahistorical or synchronic description of its structure, could provide the proper account, for which, therefore, the straw man of "realism" was formally necessary.

The proof of this assertion may be found in the peculiar fact that whenever you search for "realism" somewhere it vanishes, for it was nothing but punctuation, a mere marker or a "before" that permitted the phenomenon of modernism to come into focus properly. So as long as the latter holds the center of the field of vision, and the so-called traditional novel or classical novel or realistic novel or whatever constitutes a "ground" or blurred periphery, the illusion of adequate literary history may be maintained. But as soon as our critical interest itself shifts to these last, we become astonished to discover that, as though by magic, they also have every one of them been transformed if not all into modernists, at least into precursors of the modern—symbolists, stylists, psychopathologists, and formalists to a man! That this should happen, in Culler's hands, to Flaubert is hardly surprising, for the historical peculiarity of Flaubert is that he can be read either way, as old-fashioned realism (now perfected!) or as sheer text. But it is more surprising to find Genette, in the article referred to above, fall victim to this optical illusion: "Thus the predominance of the storytelling function itself proves to be, if not challenged, at least menaced, in a work that however passes for the very epitome of the 'traditional novel.' Another step, and the dramatic action will pass into the background, and the storyline lose its signifying primacy to the discourse itself: in a prelude to the dissolution of the novelistic form and the emergence of *literature* in the modern sense of the word. From Balzac to Proust, for instance, it is not so far as one might think," and so forth.[17] Barthes cannot himself go quite this far, since he picked Balzac as an example of the "traditional" in the first place; yet his anatomy makes it clear just how much of the modern "text" is already flesh and bone of the older novella, and on the point of separating itself from it. It is with the modernists, indeed, a little like Goering and the Jews (*"I* decide who's Jewish!"'): they are the ones who decide what is modern and what is not, and the privative term of realism is reserved for books they do not happen to be interested in at that moment (the minute they become interested, the modernity of the writer in question will not be long in disclosing itself). The reason for this is not hard to determine: like so many oppositions of this kind, to the negative or straw term has been attributed everything that is error, illusion, and the like. The "realists," in other words, are supposed to believe in representationality and the like, it being understood that such a belief is itself a superstition. Thus, it can be attributed to them only if, like the primitives of *participation mystique,* one does not really believe in their existence, and as long as they are held to be, simply, the Other. When they begin to affirm themselves as our equals, categories of otherness are no longer adequate.

It is therefore essential to remove the ethical content from this opposition, and insofar as the human mind seems particularly inclined—in spite of itself—to invest binary oppositions with a moral evaluation, this can often best be done, and the binary opposition historicized, by adding a third (and perhaps even, as we will see, a fourth) term, and restoring the apparently exclusive alternative of realism versus modernism to a whole series of historical terms and forms. Everything changes, indeed, the moment we envisage a "before" to realism itself: indeed, we have already suggested that "Sarrasine" cannot be fully evaluated formally without some feeling for its value as a kind of pastiche or revival of the older Florentine or Renaissance novella-form (a practice of the "art-novella," which will then be extensively developed through the nineteenth century up to Chekhov's decisive break with it). If to this we add a perspective in which the storytelling forms of the feudal age come into view, not to speak of those of primitive or tribal societies, then it becomes difficult to think of nineteenth-century realism as anything but a uniquely historical product, one unthinkable at any other moment in human history; but by the same token, this particular expression of a historical bourgeoisie forfeits its apparent claim to some permanent fulfillment of the categories of bourgeois thinking.

I would want, however, to distinguish this view from the traditional antiquarian type of literary history: for a Marxist historicism, indeed, the presupposition is that none of these forms of the past are of antiquarian interest alone, and that their actuality for us may be demonstrated—indeed, can only be demonstrated—by an analysis that juxtaposes the limits and the potentialities of our own socioeconomic moment with those realized or imposed by the systems of the past, in short, by other *modes of production.* Each moment of the past (or of other cultures) has a very special sentence or judgment to pass on the uniquely reified world in which we ourselves live; and the privilege of artistic experience is to furnish something like a more immediate channel through which we may experience such implicit judgments and attain a fleeting glimpse of other modes of life.

What would such a new historical perspective now do to the ideological judgments the theorists of the text believed themselves able to pass on the older type of "realistic" narrative? For one thing, it allows us to observe such judgments a little more clearly at work in the light of day, and to distinguish between genuine analysis and a kind of knee-jerk application of ready-made categories. One of the most frequent of the latter is indeed the notion of the open work, to which corresponds a similarly moralizing valorization of critical pluralism: "Let us first posit the image of a triumphant plural, unimpoverished by any constraint of representation (of imitation). In this ideal text, the networks are many and interact, without any one of them being able to surpass the rest; this text is a galaxy of signifiers, not a structure of signifieds; it has no beginning; it is reversible; we gain access to it by several entrances, none of which can be authoritatively declared to be the main one," and so forth (Barthes, pp. 5/11-12). Such pluralism is at best a refusal to go about the principal critical business of our time, which is to forge a kind of methodological synthesis from the multiplicity of critical codes; at worst, it is just one more veiled assault on the nonpluralistic (read, "totalitarian") critical systems—Marxism, for example.

The principal ideological judgments passed by the "ideology of the text" on its counterpart, the "ideology of realism," reflect two separate themes and preoccupations of Barthes' own work, older and newer motifs that coexist in *S/Z*. The first of these, which finds its fullest expression in the Brechtean estrangement-effects of *Mythologies*, is what in a characteristic neologism Barthes will denounce as "naturality," associating it with one of the most characteristic strategies of the bourgeois thought process and of the whole bourgeois way of rewriting the world after its own social and political victory. Hjelmslev's connotative method proves an apt instrument to detect the tendency everywhere in bourgeois society—from its ads to its works of art—to transform culture into nature, to naturalize history and social phenomena: "The (ideological) goal of this technique is to naturalize meaning and thus to give credence to the reality of the story: for (in the West) meaning (system), we are told, is antipathetic to nature and reality. This naturalization is possible only because the significant data released—or summoned—in a homeopathic rhythm, are carried, borne along, by a purportedly 'natural' medium, language; paradoxically language, the integral system of meaning, is employed to systematize the secondary meanings, to naturalize their production and to authenticate the story" (*S/Z*, p. 23/30). We have already seen, above, how the naming system of language functions precisely as just such an illusion that social realities are "natural" ones (proper names being in this respect as natural a taxonomic system as the words for the various species). Where Barthes goes much further in his demystification, furnishing us thereby with an object of study that we have not yet seen in quite this light before, is in his account of the *sentence* itself as the primary vehicle for just such a profoundly ideological process of naturalization: "there is a force in the sentence (linguistic entity) that domesticates the artifice of the narrative, a meaning that denies the meaning. We might call this diacritical element (since it overhangs the articulation of the narrative units): *sentencing*. To put it still another way: the sentence is a *nature* whose function—or scope—is to justify the culture of the narrative. Superimposed on the narrative structure, forming it, guiding it, regulating its rhythm, imposing on it morphemes of a purely grammatical logic, the sentence serves as *evidence* for the narrative. For language (in this case, French), by the way it is learned (by children), by its historical weight, by the apparent universality of its conventions, in short, by its *anteriority*, seems to have every right over a contingent anecdote, one which has begun only some twenty pages back—whereas language has lasted forever" (*S/Z*, pp. 127–28/133–34).

In many ways, however, this mission to track down and to destroy the traces of "naturality" in our culture is very much part of the private thematics of Barthes himself ("the will to burden signification with all the justification of nature itself provokes a kind of nausea," he tells us in *Mythologies*[18]), and it is the other feature of the ideology of representation—the status of the *subject*—that has been perhaps more widely explored in recent French theory. The most graphic dramatization of the intimate relationship between representation and the concept of the subject has indeed been made by Michel Foucault, in the opening chapter of *The Order of Things*, or rather by his object of study in that chapter, Velasquez himself, in his painting *Las Meniñas*. This work, by common agreement one of the summits in the mastery of the techniques of representation, is thus profoundly exemplary of such representational discourse at the very moment when, transcending itself, it begins to offer its own diagnosis: the viewer is indeed astonished to find himself standing in the place of the royal subject—Philip IV and his queen—whose reflections gaze back at us from a mirror on the distant rear wall of the painted room. *Las Meniñas* thus betrays a double and *constitutive* absence: "that of the painter and the spectator when they are looking at or composing the picture. It may be said that in this picture, as in all the representations of which it may be said to reveal the fundamental essence, the profound invisibility of what one sees is inseparable from the invisibility of the person seeing. . . . And indeed, [in *Las Meniñas*] representation undertakes to represent itself in all its elements, with its images, the eyes to which it is offered, the faces it makes visible, the gestures that call it into being. But there, in the midst of this dispersion which it is simultaneously grouping together and spreading out before us, indicated compellingly from every side, is an essential void: the necessary disappearance of that which is its foundation—of the person it resembles and the person in whose eyes it is only a resemblance. This very subject—the two are the same—has been elided. And representation, freed finally from the relation that was impeding it, can offer itself as representation in its pure form."[19]

Such an account, by insisting on the self-consciousness of representation in *Las Meniñas*, would seem in the present context on the point of transforming this "realistic" work into a "modernistic" one. Yet the constitutive link demonstrated here between representation and the repression of the subject will then become the principal feature of poststructuralist diagnosis, and the mediation whereby ideologies (bourgeois versus revolutionary) and artistic discourse (realistic versus modernistic) are linked to psychopathology (neurotic versus psychotic, as in Deleuze and Guattari's *Anti-Oedipus*).

The paradox of this position is that the structuralist critics of representation are led to denounce the active and in-forming presence of the subject precisely in those texts in which it is repressed: on the one hand, they denounce its forgetfulness of itself, and on the other, they call for its suppression. So the following diagnosis of Barthes takes on unexpected overtones in a situation in which, as we shall see, schizophrenia has become a slogan and a whole ethical and political program: "We may say that, in a sense, 'objective' discourse (as in positivist history) [or the realistic novel] resembles schizophrenic discourse; in both cases there is a radical censorship of the utterance, in which negativity cannot be expressed (though it can be felt), and there is a massive reversion of discourse away from any form of sui-reference, or even (in the case of the historian) a reversion towards the level of pure referent—the utterance for which no one is responsible."[20]

As one would be only too inclined to agree that one of the fundamental preconditions of some representational, or "realistic," narrative discourse is to be found in the deliberate effacement of the traces of producer and consumer, and that the viewing eye, faced with representational discourse, has a vested interest in ignoring its own presence; yet in the polemic appropriation of this insight by the realism/modernism debate, a curious reversal takes place in which it is henceforth precisely just such a subversion of the subject that is recommended. Here is Barthes on what is exemplary, in this respect, in Flaubert: "Flaubert, however, . . . working with an irony impregnated with uncertainty, achieves a salutary discomfort in writing: he does not stop the play of codes (or stops it only partially), so that (and this is indubitably the manner of *proof* of his writing) *one never knows if he is responsible for what he writes* (if there is a subject *behind* his language); for the very being of writing (the meaning of the labor that constitutes it) is to keep the question *Who is speaking?* from ever being answered" (*S/Z*, p. 140/46).

Again, the contradictions that arise from the structuralist attack on the subject seem to me resolvable if they are projected onto a more complicated scheme of periodization and articulated in a more properly historical, rather than an ethical, perspective. The trouble is that the attack on the old bourgeois subject can take two forms: that of the attempt to dissolve the subject altogether, and that is, as we shall see in the case of Deleuze, either an anarchist or a countercultural solution, depending on whether "time's livid final flame" is conceived of in terms of a political apocalypse or a private druglike fantasmagoria; or the other quite different solution, which would consist of renewing the primacy of the group and of collective life over the bourgeois optical illusion of individual existence, and returning to a view of the individual subject as a *function* of the collective structure, a condition of which, perhaps, the ethnographic descriptions of tribal existence give us the most adequate glimpse.

The same adjustment must be made in the earlier motif of naturality: what is ahistorical about Barthes's attack on this particular feature of the bourgeois weltanschauung is the implication that the concept of nature is at all times and everywhere in and of itself reactionary. But clearly there have been moments—the preparation of the bourgeois revolution itself and the attack on the "artificiality" of the feudal order—in which the concept of nature has been a profoundly subversive and contestatory weapon; and clearly the only dialectical way of evaluating such a motif is through analysis of its function in a given historical situation. Nothing is, indeed, more idealistic than the notion that a given thought-form (representationality, for instance, or the belief in the subject or in the referent) is always and under all circumstances "bourgeois" and ideological, for such a position—which seems to me that of the *Tel Quel* group, among others—tends precisely to isolate the form of thought (or its equivalent, the form of discourse) from that practical context in which alone its results can be measured. Ideologies can therefore never be evaluated independently of their function in a given historical situation: witness, for a dramatic example of this assertion, Koyre's demonstration of the progressive character of Galileo's Platonism as opposed to the apparently far more realistic and even materialistic Aristotelianism of his contemporaries and immediate predecessors.[21]

A Marxist framework, to be sure, substitutes, for the structuralist opposition between nature and culture, the more dialectical and diachronic one of an opposition between nature and *history:* yet even here the ideological character of "nature" is by no means unequivocal, as may be observed in the works of the very writer from whom Barthes himself first drew his suspicion of naturality, as well as the literary instruments by which to denounce it, namely, Brecht himself. For even in the Brechtian canon, there is a decided alternation between plays like *Mann ist Mann* and *The Good Woman of Sezuan*, which unmask the historical and constructed origins of seemingly natural attributes like aggressivity or acquisitiveness, and *Mother Courage*, which emphasizes the *unnatural* character of the seemingly only-too-natural drive to make a profit (this un-Brechtian reversal would then go a long way toward explaining the peculiar and ambiguous status of the latter play in the writer's work). There is indeed a powerful tradition of what I will call the "naturistic strategy" in Marxism itself, one going back as far as the *Economic and Philosophical Manuscripts of 1844;* with their emphasis on a species being, these works argue, if not for a fixed and immutable human nature in the right-wing sense, then certainly for judgments based on a notion of human potential, of which they demonstrate the contemporary *alienation.* And a communist literature no less powerful than that of Brecht—I'm thinking of the novels of Paul Nizan, particularly *Antoine Bloyé*—draws its force from just such a rhetoric of the natural and the unnatural. Meanwhile, there are signs, particularly in the work of Herbert Marcuse, that in our own peculiarly antinatural society, the concept of nature may once again recover some of its negative and critical virulence as an offensive weapon and a Utopian standard.

Whatever position one takes on these two privileged themes (nature, the centered subject), the "ideology of modernism" can also be seen to confront fundamental problems of historical explanation in its account (when it is willing to offer one) of the *transition* from realism to modernism. The framing and priorities of the commentary form in *S/Z* release this particular Barthes from that historical obligation (which was discharged in a very different way in *Le Degré zero de l'écriture*); but one has the impression that poststructuralist *doxa* includes two relatively distinct alternative ways of telling this particular story.

The first is the apocalyptic or prophetic mode, given paradigmatic voice at the climax of the aforementioned work of Michel Foucault, where the impending dawn of some new "structuralist" age is saluted with what will now look like premature enthusiasm. The passage in question was of course composed before May 1968, a moment that seems on the whole to have spelled an end to such Utopian celebrations, at least by *French* intellectuals, who went on in the next decade with diligence to dissolve and liquidate all remaining traces of the legacy of a political Utopianism (from the Sartrean 1950s) as well as of an aesthetic Utopianism (from the twin currents, in the 1960s, of the *nouveau roman* and of the *nouvelle vague* in film). Still, feeble traces of the old realism/modernism paradigm remained to greet the anachronistic victory of the Left in a 1980s France from which Marxism had been triumphantly delegitimated and virtually expunged. Paradoxically (yet in a peculiar replay of the belated and peculiarly French ideological function of romanticism itself, in the 1820s) it is now the conservatives who are the modernists (a stylistic slogan that reduces itself to a kind of internationalist and pro-American celebration of California-type modernization), while the Socialists are symmetrically positioned within a dreary "realism" to which a whole range of old-fashioned and outmoded attitudes are attributed, which range from traditional French chauvinism and the *esprit de clocher* to traditional French anti-Semitism (since this last is the current code-word for the Soviet Union, it will be clear that such a denunciation of "tradition" also includes traditional, "pro-Soviet," party politics).

The other, alternative version of the contemporary account of the passage from realism to modernism is not specifically French and can be observed at work in the Culler book discussed earlier: the historical paradigm offered here (but it is extremely widespread) is grounded on the hypothesis of the weakening, throughout the nineteenth century, of the "basic enabling convention of the novel as genre," namely a "confidence in the transparency and representative power of language" (p. 80). The possibility that such hypothetical confidence might itself have been a relatively recent historical development, which then demands explanation in its own turn, is not generally taken into account in such narratives of cultural change, which then tend to describe the crisis in question in terms of an intensifying reflexivity, which is most often at one with irony and/or nihilism. When a writer like Baudelaire or Flaubert becomes "self-conscious," that is to say, "aware of his images as interpretations, of his words not as the furniture of the world but as devices that, at least for the moment of this particular perspective, are being used to communicate ends," then the older literary discourse enters a long and terminal crisis, of which canonical modernism can be the only "solution." On this particular road, then, Culler's Flaubert, undermining interpretation in the very moment of soliciting it, comes to be seen as a strategic halfway house.

The conception of a linguistic or a formal "self-consciousness" or "reflexivity" has, however, always been part of the explanatory baggage of the ideology of modernism since its inception; although Hegelian in its first inspiration, it has become the unexamined premise of an enormous variety of pseudo-historical descriptions of modernity and survives anachronistically, under its pseudonym "irony," into the rather different historical narratives of Paul de Man and Hayden White. It does seem to me high time to abandon this particular concept; but as this is not the moment to argue for that more radical act in any great detail, I will limit myself to what seems a more moderate and indeed unassailable suggestion, namely that any such virtually universal presupposition demands systematic reexamination from time to time.

However such literary self-consciousness is to be understood, its functional link with the other specifically modernist conception of "innovation" seems clear enough: an aesthetic reflexivity which, continuing to use older forms, did not, however, in one way or another result in formal change and transformation, would not seem particularly plausible. Leaving aside the analogies between this way of thinking about "high culture" and the rhythms of fashion and commodity production generally (analogies that can only reawaken our suspicions and doubts about these modernist concepts), we may observe that the modernist paradigm is most often staged in terms of the pathos of the museum or the library, the sheer weight of the cultural past, some excess of literature and its dead texts which by way of a kind of fatigued and disabused sophistication ultimately provoke the dialectical reversal of a "coming to awareness" by literature of itself. It is, for example, symptomatic that Culler systematically avoids any perspective that would lead him into a discussion of the relationship between the new raw material of Flaubert's commonplaces and *idées reçues* and the equally new saturation of a commodity society by commercial writing and messages of all kinds. His allegorical reading of the theme of stupidity (which we have already touched on in another context) can now be seen to have the secondary function of excluding a sociological perspective of this kind. Even more symptomatic in his characterization of another theme in the novel—what may be taken as Flaubert's own "sociological" perspective—as "*Madame Bovary*'s greatest flaw. If there is anything that justifies our finding the novel limited and tendentious, it is the seriousness with which Emma's corruption is attributed to novels and romances. If this is an attempt to diagnose Emma's condition, to characterize her alienation, and to explain her fate, it is a singularly feeble one" (p. 146). Culler thereby cuts himself off from what would seem the most promising possibility of linking what the Russian Formalists called the "literary system" proper with those other, distinct, yet still proximate, "systems" of daily life such as those still verbal systems of "popular culture" which are the ancestors of what we would today call the media; but more recent theorizations of what is now called "intertextuality" more successfully manage to incorporate the obvious referencing of other kinds of texts while leaving history and sociology out of it.

Barthes' version of all this, as I have already observed, does not have to theorize "self-consciousness" in any particularly thematized way (pseudo-historical or otherwise), if only because it so elaborately shows interpretive self-consciousness and hyperreflexive reading concretely at work in what must be their strongest forms; yet another twist of the thermostat, and we are across the line into the "scriptible" itself, whether in the sheer act of a Bouvard-and-Pecuchet kind of copying out of lengthy quotations without comment, as in Derrida's "commentary" on Sollers' *Nombres,* or in the writing of new texts—about which, however, since they are "scriptible" rather than "legible," one can no longer, virtually by definition, say anything at all.

This is the moment, then, to propose a more thoroughgoing modification of the dualistic paradigm of realism and modernism, the "legible" and the "scriptible" as it has been found to underpin critical works of this kind. The attempt to unsettle this seemingly ineradicable dualism by adding a prior third term, in the form of some "classical" or precapitalist narrative—the moment of merchant culture and of a Renaissance-style novella that is neither "realistic" nor "modernistic"—proved to have known only partial success, modifying Barthes' working categories, but not his fundamental historical scheme. Let us therefore attempt to displace this last in a different way, by introducing a third term as it were at the other end of its temporal spectrum.

The concept of *postmodernism* in fact incorporates all the features of the Barthesian aesthetic, as it informs *S/Z* (surface, "textualization," intensities of a new affect that surges and fades, decentering of the subject, pulverization of the monumental in favor of fragments and a taste for their momentary configurations, spatialization in place of deep temporality, rewriting rather than interpretation), and presents in addition a threefold explanatory advantage. First, it allows us to situate Barthes' own text—and "theory" or *theoretical discourse* in general—as themselves manifestations of the postmodern, indeed as a new kind of discourse that knows its historical moment of emergence with postmodernism itself. This proposition then restores its historical content to the exercise in metacommentary we have been pursuing here, for it means that the description of Barthes' own discursive structure ceases to be a matter of weighing various critical alternatives against their object of study (Balzac), but has a specific cultural and historical object of study of its own right (the postmodernist "theoretical" text).

Meanwhile, the new distinction clarifies Barthes' otherwise confusing appeals to modernity by separating the classical moment of high modernism—which still retains the centrality of the *auteur* as subject or demiurge, and projects a monumental effort at ultimate reunification in the form of the "book of the world"—from the postmodernist restructuration. As far as I know, Barthes never officially confronted the monumental works of high modernism which he admired (see the reference to *Der Zauberberg* at the conclusion of his "Inaugural Lecture" at the *Collège de France*); the occasional returns to Proust essentially foreground the post modern features of that author, just as Culler does with Flaubert. Yet the critical practice of a related theoretical group—the film theories of the journal *Screen*—suggest that whereas the works of the great modernist *auteurs* (Bergmann, Fellini, Hitchcock, Kurosawa) must be critically devalued owing to the ideology of the modern which informs them (as it equally informs the architecture of Wright or the

International Style, with similar results among the younger postmodernist architects), earlier kinds of representational artifacts—in the area of film, this will mean Hollywood and commercial genre productions—are by no means subject to the same strictures, since in them other (unconscious) forces are at work to subvert the weakly conventional logic of the surface representation. Such possibilities of a radical rewriting of older forms of more conventional storytelling also account for Barthes' own attraction here to Balzac and elsewhere to Jules Verne.

But the concept of the postmodern has a final signal advantage over the various pseudo-historical paradigms we have touched on in the course of this essay, namely to allow a genuinely concrete explanation of such aesthetic and cultural phenomena to emerge as a possibility for the first time. The theory of the postmodern, indeed, is predicated on (or rather indeed, heuristically, confirmed by) a more fundamental periodizing hypothesis about the nature of capitalism itself as a system and a mode of production. According to that economic and social hypothesis, capital has so far historically known three specific mutations, in which a persistence or an identity of the underlying system is maintained throughout moments of expansion (virtual quantum-leaps in the organization of capital), which are also felt as breaks, as the emergence, particularly in culture and the superstructures, of a radically new existential and cultural logic. These three moments can be enumerated as the classical or national market capitalism known to Marx, the moment of monopoly capital or the stage of imperialism (theorized by Lenin), and the permutation, finally, after World War II, into a global form of ''multinational'' capitalism which has as yet received no adequate designation in its own right (but is the object of an ambitious theorization by Ernest Mandel in his pathbreaking book *Late Capitalism*). To each of these systemic moments ''corresponds'' (but this word should be taken to designate, not a theoretical solution, but rather a theoretical and historiographic problem and task) the appropriate cultural moment of realism, modernism and postmodernism respectively. These are less to be grasped as ''styles''—in the older sense of the great period styles like the Baroque—than as so many cultural ''dominants'' that inform a whole range of social and existential phenomena beyond the realm of the aesthetic or of culture, a realm which in any case is modified in each of these moments and knows a dialectically distinct ''space'' within each one.

The development and exploration of this historical hypothesis is, obviously enough, a program that bursts the confines of the present essay. I will conclude it, therefore, with some final remarks on the problem implicitly staged in the two books we have been discussing here, which it seems to me fair to formulate in terms of the relationship between consciousness and form. Indeed, despite the essentially postmodernist content of their aesthetics, both

Barthes and Culler retain one fundamental feature of the ideology of modernism proper, which involves something like a reversal of what above we called the Whorf hypothesis, namely the idea that stylistic or linguistic traits reflect epistemological or ideological ones. For modernism—radical in its rejection of realistic discourse and of the bourgeois world to which the latter corresponds—imagines that if you alter the structure of artistic discourse in a decisive way, the realities to which it corresponds will find themselves thereby similarly modified. Thus, if seeing the world through the old "bourgeois" categories is bad, a change in style will help us to see the world in a new way and thus achieve a kind of cultural or countercultural revolution of its own. And to be sure, if consumer capitalism were a new and qualitatively distinct socioeconomic form in its own right, as many have maintained, something like this would presumably be conceivable, and we would expect the new social form in time to generate its own distinctive kinds of artistic discourse, and to leave the realistic ones behind it like so many dead husks, as antiquated and archaic as the chanson de geste, primitive rituals, or Greek tragedy. But what is peculiar about consumer capitalism is that it is merely a second-degree construction upon classical capitalism itself, the latter continuing in a paradoxical coexistence with it, the fundamental laws of classical capitalism (codified by Marx) operative from a global perspective while seemingly invalidated and outmoded if one looks at them within the limits of the national experience of a single advanced country. So it is that we continue to walk the older world of everyday life of classical capitalism while our heads move about in the apparently quite different hallucinogenic atmosphere of the media and the supermarket/suburb; the first of these realities, not unlike the Lacanian signified, is repressed as far as possible under the second, driven under the crossbar of the semiotic fraction, into something that is not altogether an unconscious. This is why our art, that of modernism, is not a new thing in itself, but rather something like a canceled realism, a realism denied and negated and *aufgehoben* in genuinely Hegelian fashion; and what we do with the works that show the functioning of all those realities of capitalism that have not changed substantially since the time of the great naturalists—wage slavery, money, exploitation, the profit motive—is to decree that since they cannot be said to be untrue, they are boring and old-fashioned. But here boredom is the sign of what is to be repressed, and this automatic and indeed visceral reaction to the older art forms betrays the origin of modernism itself in an aestheticizing reaction against the sordid realities of a business civilization, about which we would prefer not even to have our art remind us. So the death of the referent has been greatly exaggerated; at best, it has only gone underground.

Under these circumstances, there are few enough versions of the modernist apologia consequent enough to stand the test. Let us recall Gombrich's lesson, as a way of radicalizing the literary version of this particular dilemma: in the visual arts, a kind of absolute, or Zenonic, formulation of the problem was reached by asking whether the destruction of perpective by modern painters, and their return to two-dimensionality, could be imagined as affecting in any way the three-dimensional experience of everyday life of their contemporaries. The appeal to lived perspective, like the appeal to the hard sciences, is to be sure an apparently decisive argument, comparable to Dr. Johnson's appeal to the stone; and in literature, the equivalent argument may seem less binding. For the literary equivalent of the phenomenon of perspective—we have implied as much throughout these pages without as yet saying so outright—is surely narrative itself. Gombrich indeed sees an intimate link between the development of naturalistic techniques in painting and the requirements of storytelling; the modernist attack on realism in literature was at one with its repudiation of plot, and Barthes' fluoroscopy of the text has been useful in implying some of the reasons (operation of the proairetic schemata, organization of plot around enigmas and discoveries, naturality of the narrative sentence, dependence of narrative discourse on some type of effacement of the subject) why this should have been so.

A fundamental work of the newer philology, indeed, confirms the analogy between narrative and perspective by suggesting that the very structure of language itself shows a deep functional vocation for storytelling, which must then be seen, not as some secondary pastime, to be pursued around the fireside when praxis is over, but rather as a basic and constitutive element of human life. Harold Weinrich's *Tempus*,[22] following Benveniste, proposes a comprehensive resolution of the vexed problem of verb tenses through which they are systematically sorted out into narrative tenses and what he calls "discussive" (*besprechend*) ones, those of storytelling (where events have become closed off and may be contemplated at a distance, in themselves) and those of an active relationship to the world in which we must ourselves be drawn into the context along with our listeners and our referents. If such a picture of language wins conviction, it can only intensify the peculiarity of a spectable in which modernist writers seek to amputate language of a good half of its essential organs, to suppress one whole dimension of linguistic and literary experience.

Weinrich, like Gombrich, is resolutely anti-Whorfian, and repudiates the idea that a change in language, any more than a change in style, results from—let alone causes—a change in our phenomenological experience of the external world. This skepticism tends to force both of them back into a relatively conservative view of literature, involving the defense of convention (of the schemata, of the structure of narrative tenses) in and for itself, a road down which we will not follow them. We are, however, fortunate in having at our disposition a counterexhibit, a rather astonishing document that pushes to its ultimate limits the modernistic or textual position outlined above. This is the glorification of schizophrenia (and of the schizophrenic as the "true hero of desire") to be found in Deleuze and Guattari's *Anti-Oedipus: Capitalism and Schizophrenia,*[23] where the final step is taken and it is asked of life itself and of lived experience that it conform to the account we have given to the text. For Deleuze and Guattari essentially follow Lacan's description of schizophrenia as a disease of language in which connections have broken down: continuity in speech, for Lacan, is a function of what he calls "the slippage of signifieds" (*le glissement des signifies*), in other words, that relative semantic flux that allows us to disconnect a meaning from one word, or signifier, and attach it to its synonym. For Lacan, indeed, the world of the schizophrenic is quite the opposite of meaningless: if anything, it is too meaningful; each instant, like each signifier, is a closed and full meaning in itself, from which it becomes increasingly difficult to lay a bridge to the subsequent moment of time. So the schizophrenic's reality gradually comes to approximate the Flaubertian text as Culler describes it, a formal or syntactical succession through time that does not correspond to any real progression or perspective at the level of its meanings or signifieds. Here also the ultimate implications of Barthes' critique of the proairetic code are fulfilled: there are no longer any names! and the old conventional words and unities have been swept away in a flux of experience in which everything is by definition always new. And no doubt there is a sense in which it can only be a relief to find one's self liberated from the all-too-familiar continuities of ordinary representational, or "realistic," referential living: the analogous effect of drugs is in no small measure also linked to just this abolition of the logic of time, which releases each instant, and the object in it, to glow and radiate a kind of undifferentiated and autonomous energy. We should also mention the historical context in which Deleuze and Guattari's book became, in France, a kind of manifesto: that widespread disillusionment with the Communist party among students and intellectuals after the failure of May 1968, which predictably drove so many of them across the still-political positions of leftism or anarchism into what in this country we would call a depoliticized counterculture, of which the *Anti-Oedipus* is one of the basic texts. Still, as the Surrealists discovered in a situation that bore some similarities to this one, it is probably easier to praise madness than to practice it; and one does not become a schizophrenic, no matter how heroic an act that would be, simply by the taking of thought.

Deleuze and Guattari's position, indeed, may be seen as the most extreme working out of that Cartesian maxim from which all bourgeois subjectivism may be said to spring: "always to seek to conquer myself rather than fortune, to change my desires rather than the established order, and generally to believe that nothing except our thoughts is wholly under our control."[24] The illusion of freedom and creativity enjoyed by the early modernists was a function of their transitional moment in socioeconomic history, a moment in which features of the new consumer economy, the so-called second industrial revolution, had begun to supersede those of older classical or Balzacian capitalism. Today, however, when modernism no longer represents this conquest of new material but rather has integrated itself into an economy functionally dependent on it for its indispensable fashion changes and for the perpetual resupplying of a media culture, artists and writers who want to change their styles may well once again come to the conclusion that they must first change the world.

Fall 1975—Winter 1976

II

Chapter 3
Imaginary and Symbolic in Lacan

The attempt to coordinate a Marxist and a Freudian criticism confronts—but as it were explicitly, thematically articulated in the form of a problem—a dilemma that is in reality inherent in all psychoanalytic criticism as such: that of the insertion of the subject, or, in a different terminology, the difficulty of providing mediations between social phenomena and what must be called private, rather than even merely individual, facts. But what for Marxist criticism is already overtly social—in such questions as the relationship of the work so its social or historical context, or the status of its ideological content—is often merely implicitly so in that more specialized or conventional psychoanalytic criticism which imagines that it has no interest in extrinsic or social matters.

In "pure" psychoanalytic criticism, indeed, the social phenomenon with which the private materials of case history, of individual fantasy or childhood experience, must initially be confronted is simply language itself. Even prior to the establishment of the literary forms and the literary institution as official social phenomena, language—the very medium of universality and of intersubjectivity—constitutes that primary social instance into which the preverbal, presocial facts of archaic or unconscious experience find themselves somehow inserted.[1] Anyone who has ever tried to recount a dream to someone else is in a position to measure the immense gap, the qualitative incommensurability, between the vivid memory of the dream and the dull, impoverished words that are all we can find to convey it. Yet this incommensurability, between the particular and the universal, between the *vécu* and language itself, is one language itself, is one in which we dwell all our lives, and it is from it that all works of literature and culture necessarily emerge.

What is so often problematical about psychoanalytic criticism is therefore not its insistence on the subterranean relationships between the literary text on the one hand and the "obsessive metaphor" or the distant and inaccessible childhood or unconscious fascination on the other. It is rather the absence of any reflection on the transformational process whereby such private materials become public—a transformation that is often, to be sure, so undramatic and inconspicuous as the very act of speech itself. Yet insofar as speech is preeminently social, in what follows we will do well to keep Durkheim's stern warning constantly before us as a standard against which to assess the various models psychoanalytic criticism has provided: "Whenever a social phenomenon is directly explained by a psychological phenomenon, we may be sure that the explanation is false."[2]

I

In any case, it was Freud himself who, as he did so often, first sensed the methodological problems raised by the application of psychoanalytic techniques to those intersubjective objects which are works of art or literature. It has not sufficiently been observed that his major statement in this area, the essay "Creative Writers and Day-Dreaming" (1907), far from using the identification of literary productivity with private fantasy as a pretext for "reducing" the former to the latter, on the contrary very specifically enumerates the theoretical difficulties such an identification must face. His point is that it is by no means so easy as it might seem to reconcile the collective nature of literary reception with that fundamental tenet of psychoanalysis that sees the logic of the wish-fulfillment (or of its more metaphysical contemporary variant, le désir) as the organizing principle of all human thought and action. Freud tirelessly stresses the infantile egotism of the unconscious, its Schadenfreude and its envious rage at the gratifications of others, to the point where it becomes clear that it is precisely the fantasy or wish-fulfilling component of the literary work that constitutes the most serious barrier to its reception by a public: "You will remember how I have said that the day-dreamer carefully conceals his phantasies from other people because he feels he has reasons for being ashamed of them. I should now add that even if he were to communicate them to us he could give us no pleasure by his disclosures. Such phantasies, when we learn them, repel us or at least leave us cold."[3] Here again the dream provides a useful confirmation, and anyone who has had to listen to the dream narratives of other people can readily weigh that monotony against the inexhaustible fascination of our own dream memories. Thus, in literature, the detectable presence of self-dramatizing, and most often self-pitying, fantasies is enough to cause a withdrawal from the implied contract of reading. The novels of Baron Corvo may serve as illustrations, or most bestsellers; even in Balzac, a good many thinly disguised wish-fulfillments become the object of what is at best amused complicity on the reader's part, but at worst outright embarrassment.[4]

Freud does not conclude, but proposes a twofold hypothesis for exploration as to the nature of the poetic process itself, which he characterizes as "the technique of overcoming the feeling of repulsion in us which is undoubtedly connected with the barriers that rise between each single ego and the others. . . . The writer softens the character of his egoistic day-dreams by altering and disguising it, and he bribes us by the purely formal—that is, aesthetic—yield of pleasure which he offers us in the presentation of his phantasies. We give the name of an *incentive bonus*, or a *fore-pleasure*, to a yield of pleasure such as this, which is offered to us so as to make possible the release of still greater pleasure arising from deeper psychical sources."[5] Repression of the private or individual relevance of the fantasy (in other words, it universalization) on the one hand, and the substitution of a formal play for the immediate gratification of wish-fulfilling content on the other—these two "methods," as Freud calls them, correspond to a dual interpretive system that runs through all his reading of texts, from those of dreams all the way to literary and cultural objects, but is given most striking expression, perhaps, in *Jokes and Their Relation to the Unconscious:* namely, an account of the wish-fulfillment in terms of its content (in other words, the nature of the wish being fulfilled and the symbolic ways in which it may be said to reach fulfillment) side by side with an explanation of the "supplement" of a more purely formal pleasure to be derived from the work's organization itself and the psychic economy the latter realizes. It is thus perhaps not too far-fetched to see at work in this twofold account of the poetic process the subterranean presence of those primordial Freudian powers of Displacement and Condensation; gratification of the wish by its displacement and disguise, and a simultaneous release of psychic energy owing to the formal shortcuts and superpositions of overdetermination. For the moment, however, we must retain, not Freud's solution, but rather his formulation of the problem in terms of a dialectic between individual desire and fantasy and the collective nature of language and reception.

It cannot be said that the literary criticism of orthodox Freudianism—even at its best—has followed the example of Freud himself in these reflections; rather, it has tended to remain locked within the categories of the individual and of individual experience (psychoanalyzing, as Holland puts it, either the character, or the author, or the public) without reaching a point at which those categories themselves become problematical. It is rather in some of the oppositional, or heretical, applications of psychoanalytic method to literature that we will be likely to find suggestive hints toward a further specification of the problem itself.

Thus, for example, Sartre may be said to have pioneered a psychobio-graphical method that cuts across some of the false problems of an orthodox psychoanalytic and a traditional biographical criticism alike. In both Sartre and Erikson, indeed, the conventional opposition between the private and the public, the unconscious and the conscious, the personal or unknowable and the universal and comprehensible, is displaced and reanchored in a new conception of the psychic and historical situation or context. Now the mean-ing of Genêt's style or Luther's theological propositions is no longer a matter for intuition, for the instinctive sensibility of analyst or interpreter in search of a hidden meaning within the outer and external one; rather, these cultural manifestations and individual productions come to be grasped as responses to a determinate situation and have the intelligibility of sheer gesture, provided the context is reconstructed with sufficient complexity. From an effort at em-pathy, therefore, the process of analysis is transformed into one of a hypothetical restoration of the situation itself, whose reconstruction is at one with comprehension (*Verstehen*).[6] Even the problem of evaluation (the "greatness" of Luther's political acts, of Genêt's formal innovations) becomes linked to the way in which each articulates the situation and may thus be seen as an exemplary reaction to it. From this point of view, the response may be said to structure and virtually to bring to being for the first time an objective situation lived in a confused and less awakened fashion by their contemporaries. The concept of the context or situation here is thus not something extrinsic to the verbal or psychic text, but is generated by the lat-ter at the very moment in which it begins to work on and to alter it. It should be added that in both Sartrean and Eriksonian reconstructions, the family proves to be the central mediatory institution between the psychic drama and that social or political realm (papal authority for Luther, nineteenth-century class society for Flaubert) in which the psychic drama is ultimately acted out and "resolved."

At least for Sartre, however, this valorization of the situation goes hand in hand with a radical depersonalization of the subject. Here, despite the Lacanian polemic against the Cartesianism of *Being and Nothingness* and against the alleged ego-psychologizing of the psychobiographies and the evi-dent revisionism of Sartre's early attacks on the Freudian concept of the un-conscious, it must be observed that another Sartre—that of *The Transcendence of the Ego*—was an important predecessor in precisely that struggle against ego psychology that Lacan and his group systematically waged. In that work, as well as in the chapter on the psyche in *L'Etre et le néant* which prolongs it, the ego in the traditional sense—character, personality, identity, sense of self—is shown to be an object for consciousness, part of the latter's "con-tents," rather than a constitutive and structuring element of it. A distance thus emerges within the subject between pure consciousness and its ego or psyche that is comparable to that separating the subject (S) and the ego (a) in

Lacan's L-schema. Sartre's "Cartesianism" is not properly understood unless the attendant stress on the impersonality of consciousness is also grasped, on its utter lack of quality or individuating attributes, its "nature" as a mere speck or point without substance or consistency, in terms of which you, I, Luther, Genêt, Flaubert, are all radically equivalent and indistinguishable. We are thus entitled to speak of an insertion of the subject here, both in the relationship of the historical figure to his situation and in the project of the psychobiography as a reconstruction of it: the opposition of particular to universal has been transformed into the relationship of an impersonal and rigorously interchangeable consciousness to a unique historical configuration. This said, it must also be noted that the psychobiographical form remains shackled to the categories of individual experience, and is thus unable to reach a level of cultural and social generalization without passing through the individual case history (a survival of the classical existential insistence on the primacy of individual experience that continues to govern both the *Critique de la raison dialectique* and the presentation of nineteenth-century objective spirit—there called "objective neurosis"—in volume III of *L'Idiot de la famille*).

In contrast, the synthesis of Marx and Freud projected by the Frankfurt School takes as its province the fate of the subject in general under late capitalism. In retrospect, their Freudo-Marxism has not worn well, often seeming mechanical in those moments in Adorno's literary or musical studies when a Freudian scheme is perfunctorily introduced into a discussion of cultural or formal history.[7] Whenever Adorno or Horkheimer found their historical analyses upon a specific diagnosis, that is, on a local description of a determinate configuration of drive, repressive mechanism, and anxiety, Durkheim's warning about the psychological explanation of social phenomena seems to rematerialize in the middle distance.

What remains powerful in this part of their work, however, is a more global model of repression which, borrowed from psychoanalysis, provides the underpinnings for their sociological vision of the total system, or *verwaltete Welt* (the bureaucratically "administered" world system), of late capitalism. The adaptation of clinical Freudianism proves awkward at best, precisely because the fundamental psychoanalytic inspiration of the Frankfurt School derives, not from diagnostic texts, but rather from *Civilization and Its Discontents*, with its eschatological vision of an irreversible link between development (or Kultur, in the classical German sense of the word as technological and bureaucratic "progress") and ever-increasing instinctual renunciation and misery. Henceforth, for Adorno and Horkheimer, the evocation of renunciation will function less as psychic diagnosis than as cultural criticism; and technical terms like "repression" come to be used less for their own denotative value than as instruments for constructing, negatively, a new Utopian vision of *bonheur* and instinctual gratification. Marcuse's work can then be understood as an adaptation of this Utopian vision to the quite different condition of the *société de consommation,* with its "repressive desublimation," its commercialized permissiveness, so different from the authoritarian character structures and the rigid instinctual taboos of an older European industrial society.

If the Sartrean approach tended to emphasize the individual case history to the point where the very existence of more collective structures becomes problematical, the Frankfurt School's powerful vision of a liberated collective culture tends to leave little space for the unique histories—both psychic and social—of individual subjects. We must not forget, of course, that it was the Frankfurt School which pioneered the study of family structure as the mediation between society and the individual psyche;[8] yet even here the results now seem dated, partly owing to precisely that decay of family structure in modern times that they themselves denounced. Partly, however, this relative obsolescence of their findings results from a methodological shift for which they themselves are responsible, namely the change of emphasis—particularly in their American period—from the family as a social institution to more properly psychological concepts like those of the authoritarian personality or the fascist character structure. Today, however, when it is ever clearer just how banal evil really is, and when we have repeatedly been able to observe the reactionary uses of such psychological interpretations of political positions (for example, the student revolt as an Oedipal manifestation), this will no longer do. Frankfurt School Freudo-Marxism ended up as an analysis of the threats to "democracy" from right-wing extremism, which was easily transferred, in the 1960s, to the Left; but the original Freudo-Marxian synthesis—that of Wilhelm Reich in the 1920s—evolved as an urgent response to what we would today call the problems of cultural revolution, and addressed the sense that political revolution cannot be fulfilled until the very character structures inherited from the older, prerevolutionary society, and reinforced by its instinctual taboos, have been utterly transformed in their turn.

A rather different model of the relationship between individual psychology and social structure from either that of Sartre or of the Frankfurt School may be found in a remarkable and neglected work of Charles Mauron, *Psychocritique du genre comique.* Mauron's work cuts across that static opposition between the individual and the collective whose effects we have observed in the preceding discussion by introducing between them the mediation of a generic structure capable of functioning both on the level of individual gratification and on that of social structuration.

Comedy is in any case a unique and privileged type of cultural and psychic material, as the lasting theoretical suggestiveness of Freud's joke book may testify. Nor is Mauron's Oedipal interpretation of classical comedy as the triumph of the young over the old particularly novel for the Anglo-American reader (a similar analysis of comedy is to be found in Northrop Frye's work).

Even here, however, the psychoanalytic reading raises the fundamental issue of the status of character as such and of the categories that correspond to it: are the characters of classical comedy—hero protagonist, love object, split drives or fragments of libidinal energy, the father as superego or as Oedipal rival—all structurally homogeneous with each other as in other forms of representation, or is there some more basic structural discontinuity at work here that the theatrical framework serves to mask?

It is precisely such a discontinuity that Mauron sees as constituting the originality of the Aristophanic form, in contrast to the classical theater of Molière or of Roman comedy. He shows that the fundamental Oedipal analysis can be made to apply to Old Comedy only if the framework of representation and the primacy of the category of character be broken: the place of the love object of Oedipal rivalry is then seen to be taken, not by another individual character, as in the heroines of Molière or of Plautus, but rather by the *polis* itself, that is, by an entity that dialectically transcends any individual existence. Aristophanic comedy thus reflects a moment of social and psychic development that precedes the constitution of the family as a homogeneous unit, a moment in which libidinal impulses still valorize the larger collective structures of the city or the tribe as a whole; and Mauron's analysis may be profitably juxtaposed with the results of the investigation by Marie-Cécile and Edmond Ortigues of the functioning of the Oedipus complex in traditional African society: "The question of the Oedipus complex cannot be assimilated to a characterology, or to a genetic psychology, or to a social psychology, or to a psychiatric semiology, but circumscribes the fundamental structures according to which, for society as well as for the individual, the problem of evil and suffering, the dialectic of desire and demand, are articulated. . . . The Oedipus complex cannot be reduced to a description of the child's attitudes toward his or her father and mother. . . . The father is not only a second mother, a masculine educator; rather, the difference between the father and the mother, insofar as it projects that of man and woman in society as a whole, is part of the logic of a structure that manifests itself at several levels, both sociological and psychological. . . . The principal distinction [between the manifestation of the Oedipal problem in Senegalese society and that of Europe] lies in the form taken by guilt. Guilt does not appear as such; in other words, as the absence of depression and of any delirium of self-denunciation testifies, it does not appear as a splitting of the ego, but rather under the form of an anxiety at being abandoned by the group, of a loss of object."[9] The source of these modifications is then seen by the Ortigues to be the ancestor cult, into which much of the authority function of the Western father figure is absorbed: "It is the collectivity that [in Senegalese society] takes the death of the father upon itself. From the outset traditional Senegalese society announces that the place of each individual in the community is marked by reference to an ancestor, the father of the lineage. . . . Society, by presenting the law of the fathers, thus in a sense neutralizes the diachronic series of generations. In effect the death fantasies of the young Oedipal subject are deflected onto his collaterals, his brothers or his contemporaries. Instead of developing vertically or diachronically in a conflict between generations, aggressivity tends to be restricted to a horizontal expression within the limits of a single generation, in the framework of a solidarity and rivalry between collaterals.''[10]

The methodological recourse to formally different textual structures, as in Mauron, or sociologically different contexts, as in *Oedipe africain*, thus has the merit of freeing the psychoanalytic model from its dependency on the classical Western family, with its ideology of individualism and its categories of the subject and (in matters of literary representation) of the character. It suggests in turn the need for a model that is not locked into the classical opposition between the individual and the collective, but rather is able to think these discontinuities in a radically different way. Such is indeed the promise of Lacan's conception of the three orders (the Imaginary, the Symbolic, and the Real), of which it now remains for us to determine whether the hypothesis of a dialectically distinct status for each of these registers, or sectors of experience, can be maintained within the unity of a single system.

II

For the difficulties involved in an exposition of the three orders spring at least in part from their inseparability. According to Lacanian epistemology, indeed, acts of consciousness, experiences of the mature subject, necessarily imply a structural coordination between the Imaginary, the Symbolic, and the Real. "The experience of the Real presupposes the simultaneous exercise of two correlative functions, the imaginary function and the symbolic function.''[11] If the notion of the Real is the most problematical of the three—since it can never be experienced immediately, but only by way of the mediation of the other two—it is also the easiest to bracket for the purposes of this presentation. We will return to the function of this concept—neither an order nor a register, exactly—in our conclusion; suffice it to underscore here the profound heterogeneity of the Real with respect to the other two functions, between which we would then expect to discover a similar disproportion.

Yet to speak of the Imaginary independently of the Symbolic is to perpetuate the illusion that we could have a relatively pure experience of either. If, for instance, we overhastily identify the Symbolic with the dimension of language and the function of speech in general, it becomes obvious that we can hardly convey any experience of the Imaginary without presupposing the former. Meanwhile, insofar as the Imaginary is understood as the place of the insertion of my unique individuality as *Dasein* and as *corps propre*, it will become increasingly difficult to form a notion of the Symbolic Order as some pure syntactic web, which entertains no relationship to individual subjects at all.

In reality, however, the methodological danger is the obverse of this one, namely, the temptation to transform the notion of the two orders into a binary opposition, and to define each relationally in terms of the other—something it is even easier to find oneself doing when one has begun by suspending the Real itself and leaving it out of consideration. We will, however, come to learn that this process of definition by binary opposition is itself profoundly characteristic of the Imaginary, so that to allow our exposition to be influenced by it is already to slant our presentation in terms of one of its two objects of study.

Fortunately, the genetic preoccupations of psychoanalysis provide a solution to this dilemma; for Freud founded his diagnosis of psychic disorders, not only on the latter's own aetiology, but on a larger view of the process of formation of the psyche itself as a whole, and on a conception of the stages of infantile development. And we will see shortly that Lacan follows him in this, rewriting the Freudian history of the psyche in a new and unexpected way. But this means that even if they are inextricable in mature psychic life, we ought to be able to distinguish Imaginary from Symbolic at the moment of emergence of each; in addition, we ought to be able to form a more reliable assessment of the role of each in the economy of the psyche by examining those moments in which their mature relationship to each other has broken down, moments that present a serious imbalance in favor of one or the other registers. Most frequently, this imbalance would seem to take the form of a degradation of the Symbolic to an Imaginary level: "The problem of the neurotic consists in a loss of the symbolic reference of the signifiers that make up the central points of the structure of his complex. Thus the neurotic may repress the signified of his symptom. This loss of the reference value of the symbol causes it to regress to the level of the imaginary, in the absence of any mediation between self and idea."[12] On the other hand, when it is appreciated to what degree, for Lacan, the apprenticeship of language is an alienation for the psyche, it will become clear that there can also be a hypertrophy of the Symbolic at the Imaginary's expense that is no less pathological; the recent emphasis on the critique of science and of its alienated *sujet supposé savoir* is indeed predicated on this overdevelopment of the Symbolic function: "The symbol is an imaginary figure in which man's truth is alienated. The intellectual elaboration of the symbol cannot disalienate it. Only the analysis of its imaginary elements, taken individually, reveals the meaning and the desire that the subject had hidden within it."[13]

Even before undertaking a genetic exposition of the two registers, however, we must observe that the very terms themselves present a preliminary difficulty, which is none other than their respective previous histories: thus Imaginary surely derives from the experience of the image—and of the imago—and we are meant to retain its spatial and visual connotations. Yet as Lacan uses the word, it has a relatively narrow and technical sense, and should not be extended in any immediate way to the traditional conception of the imagination in philosophical aesthetics (nor to the Sartrean doctrine of the *imaginaire*, although the latter's material of study is doubtless Imaginary in Lacan's sense of the term).

The word "Symbolic" is even more troublesome, since much of what Lacan will designate as Imaginary is traditionally designated by expressions like symbol and symbolism. We will want to wrench the Lacanian term loose from its rich history as the opposite number to allegory, particularly in Romantic thought; nor can it maintain any of its wider suggestion to the figural as opposed to the literal meaning (symbolism versus discursive thought, Mauss' symbolic exchange as opposed to the market system, and so forth). Indeed, we would be tempted to suggest that the Lacanian Symbolic Order has nothing whatsoever to do with symbols or with symbolism in the conventional sense, were it not for the obvious problem of what then to do with the whole classical Freudian apparatus of dream symbolism proper.

The originality of Lacan's rewriting of Freud may be judged by his radical reorganization of this material, which had hitherto—houses, towers, cigars, and all—been taken to constitute some storehouse of universal symbols. Most of the latter will now be understood rather as "part-objects" in Melanie Klein's sense of organs and parts of the body that are libidinally valorized; these part-objects then, as we will see shortly, belong to the realm of the Imaginary rather than to that of the Symbolic. The one exception—the notorious "phallic" symbol dear to vulgar Freudian literary criticism—is the very instrument for the Lacanian reinterpretation of Freud in linguistic terms. For the phallus—not, in contradistinction to the penis, an organ of the body—now comes to be considered neither image nor symbol, but rather a signifier, indeed the fundamental signifier of mature psychic life, and thus one of the basic organizational categories of the Symbolic Order itself.[14]

In any case, whatever the nature of the Lacanian Symbolic, it is clear that the Imaginary—a kind of preverbal register whose logic is essentially visual—precedes it as a stage in the development of the psyche. Its moment of formation—and that existential situation in which its specificity is most strikingly dramatized—has been named the "mirror stage" by Lacan, who thereby designates that moment between six and eighteen months in which the child first demonstrably "recognizes" his or her own image in the mirror, thus tangibly making the connection between inner motricity and the specular movements stirring before him. It is important not to deduce too hastily from this very early experience some ultimate ontological possibility of an ego or an identity in the psychological sense, or even in the sense of some Hegelian self-conscious reflexivity. Whatever else the mirror stage is, indeed, for Lacan it marks a fundamental gap between the subject and its own self or imago that can never be bridged: "The important point is that this form [of the subject in the mirror stage] fixed the instance of the ego, well before any social determination, in a line of fiction that is forever irreducible for the individual himself—or rather that will rejoin the subject's evolution in asymptotic fashion only, whatever the favorable outcome of those dialectical syntheses by which as an ego he must resolve his discordance with his own reality."[15] In our present context, we will want to retain the words "dans une ligne de fiction," which underscore the psychic function of narrative and fantasy in the attempts of the subject to reintegrate his or her alienated image.

The mirror stage, which is the precondition for primary narcissism, is also, owing to the equally irreducible gap it opens between the infant and its fellows, the very source of human aggressivity; and indeed, one of the original features of Lacan's early teaching is its insistence on the inextricable association of these two drives.[16] How could it indeed be otherwise, at a moment when, the child's investment in images of the body having been achieved, there does not yet exist the ego formation that would permit him to distinguish his own form from that of others? The result is a world of bodies and organs that in some fashion lacks a phenomenological center and a privileged point of view: "Throughout this period the emotional reactions and verbal indications of normal transitivism [Charlotte Bühler's term for the indifferentiation of subject and object] will be observed. The child who hits says he has been hit, the child who sees another child fall begins to cry. Similarly, it is by way of an identification with the other that the infant lives the entire spectrum of reactions from ostentation to generosity, whose structural ambiguity his conduct so undisguisedly reveals, slave identified with despot, actor with spectator, victim with seducer."[17] This "structural crossroads" (Lacan) corresponds to that preindividualistic, premimetic, pre-point-of-view stage in aesthetic organization that is generally designated as "play,"[18] whose essence lies in the frequent shifts of the subject from one fixed position to another, in a kind of optional multiplicity of insertions of the subject into a relatively fixed Symbolic Order. In the realm of linguistics and psychopathology, the fundamental document on the effects of "transitivism" remains Freud's "A Child Is Being Beaten," which has had considerable emblematic significance for recent theory.[19]

A description of the Imaginary will therefore on the one hand require us to come to terms with a uniquely determinate configuration of space—one that is not yet organized around the individuation of my own personal body, or differentiated hierarchically according to the perspectives of my own central point of view, but that nonetheless swarms with bodies and forms intuited in a different way, whose fundamental property is, it would seem, to be visible without their visibility being the result of the act of any particular observer, to be, as it were, always-already seen, to carry their specularity upon themselves like a color they wear or the texture of their surface. In this—the indifferentiation of their *esse* from a *percipi* that does not know a *percipiens*—these bodies of the Imaginary exemplify the very logic of mirror images; yet the existence of the normal object world of adult everyday life presupposes this prior, imaginary, experience of space: "It is normally by the possibilities of a game of imaginary transposition that the progressive valorization of objects is achieved, on what is customarily known as the affective level, by a proliferation, a fanlike disposition of all the imagination equations that allow the human being, alone in the animal realm, to have an almost infinite number of objects at his disposition, objects isolated in their form."[20]

The affective valorization of these objects ultimately derives from the primacy of the human imago in the mirror stage; and it is clear that the very investment of an object world will depend in one way or another on the possibility of symbolic association or identification of an inanimate thing with the libidinal priority of the human body. Here, then, we come upon what Melanie Klein termed "part-objects"—organs, like the breast, or objects associated with the body, like feces, whose psychic investment is then transferred to a host of other, more indifferent contents of the external world (which are then, as we will see below, valorized as good or as evil). "A trait common to such objects, Lacan insists, is that they have no specular image, which is to say that they know no alterity. 'They are the very lining, the stuff or imaginary filling of the subject itself, which identifies itself with these objects.' "[21] It is from Melanie Klein's pioneering psychoanalysis of children that the basic features of the Lacanian Imaginary are drawn: there is, as we might expect for an experience of spatiality phenomenologically so different from our own, a logic specific to Imaginary space, whose dominant category proves to be the opposition of container and contained, the fundamental relationship of inside to outside, which clearly enough originates in the infant's fantasies about the maternal body as the receptacle of part-objects (confusion between childbirth and evacuation, and so forth).[22]

This spatial syntax of the Imaginary order may then be said to be intersected by a different type of axis, whose conjunction completes it as an experience: this is the type of relationship that Lacan designates as aggressivity, and that we have seen to result from that indistinct rivalry between self and other in a period that precedes the very elaboration of a self or the construction of an ego. As with the axis of Imaginary space, we must again try to imagine something deeply sedimented in our own experience, but buried under the adult rationality of everyday life (and under the exercise of the Symbolic): a kind of situational experience of otherness as pure relationship, as struggle, violence, and antagonism, in which the child can occupy either term indifferently, or indeed, as in transitivism, both at one. A remarkable sentence of St. Augustine is inscribed as a motto to the primordiality of this rivalry with the imagoes of other infants: "I have myself seen jealousy in a baby and know what it means. He was not old enough to speak, but, whenever his foster-brother was at the breast, would glare at him pale with envy [et intuebatur pallidus amaro aspectu conlactaneum suum]."[23]

Provided it is understood that this moment is quite distinct from that later intervention of the Other (Lacan's capital A—for *Autre*—the parents, or language itself) that ratifies the assumption of the subject into the realm of language or the Symbolic Order, it will be appropriate to designate this primordial rivalry of the mirror stage as a relationship of otherness. Nowhere better can we observe the violent situational content of those judgments of good and evil that will later cool off and sediment into the various systems of ethics. Both Nietzsche and Sartre have exhaustively explored the genealogy of ethics as the latter emerges from just such an archaic valorization of space, where what is "good" is what is associated with "my" position, and the "bad" simply characterizes the affairs of my mirror rival.[24] We may further document the archaic or atavistic tendencies of ethical or moralizing thought by observing that it has no place in the Symbolic Order, or in the structure of language itself, whose shifters are positional and structurally incapable of supporting this kind of situational complicity with the subject momentarily occupying them.

The Imaginary may thus be described as a peculiar spatial configuration, whose bodies primarily entertain relationships of inside/outside with one another, which is then traversed and reorganized by that primordial rivalry and transitivistic substitution of imagoes, that indistinction of primary narcissism and aggressivity, from which our later conceptions of good and evil derive. This stage is already an alienation—the subject having been captivated by his or her specular image—but in Hegelian fashion it is the kind of alienation from which a more positive evolution is indistinguishable and without which the latter is inconceivable. The same must be said for the next stage of psychic development, in which the Imaginary itself is assumed into the Symbolic Order by way of its alienation by language itself. The Hegelian model of dialectical history—as Jean Hyppolite's interventions in Lacan's first Seminar make clear—remains the fundamental one here: "This development [of the human anatomy and in particular the cortex] is lived as a temporal dialectic that decisively projects the formation of the individual as history: the *mirror stage* is a drama whose internal dynamic shifts from insufficiency to anticipation—a drama that, for its subject, caught in the mirage of spatial identification, vehiculates a whole series of fantasies which range from a fragmented image of the body to what we will term an orthopedic form of its unity, and to that ultimate assumption of the armature of an alienating identity, whose rigid structure will mark the subject's entire mental development. Thus the rupture of the circle in which *Innenwelt* and *Umwelt* are united generates that inexhaustible attempt to square it in which we reap the ego."[25]

The approach to the Symbolic is the moment to suggest the originality of Lacan's conception of the function of language in psychoanalysis. For neo-Freudianism, it would seem that the role of language in the analytical situation, or the "talking cure," is understood in terms of what we may call an aesthetic of expression and expressiveness: the patient unburdens himself or herself; his "relief" comes from his having verbalized (or even, according to a more recent ideology, from having "communicated"). For Lacan, on the contrary, this later exercise of speech in the analytical situation draws its therapeutic force from being as it were a completion and fulfillment of the first, imperfectly realized, accession to language and to the Symbolic in early childhood.

For the emphasis of Lacan on the linguistic development of the child—an area in which his work necessarily draws much from Piaget—has mistakenly been criticized as a "revision" of Freud in terms of more traditional psychology, a substitution of the psychological data of the mirror stage and of language acquisition for the more properly psychoanalytic phenomena of infantile sexuality and the Oedipus complex. Obviously Lacan's work must be read as presupposing the entire content of classical Freudianism, otherwise it would be simply another philosophy or intellectual system. The linguistic materials are not intended, it seems to me, to be substituted for the sexual ones; rather we must understand the Lacanian notion of the Symbolic Order as an attempt to create mediations between libidinal analysis and the linguistic categories, to provide, in other words, a transcoding scheme that allows us to speak of both within a common conceptual framework. Thus, the very cornerstone of Freud's conception of the psyche, the Oedipus complex, is transliterated by Lacan into a linguistic phenomenon, which he designates as the discovery by the subject of the Name-of-the-Father, and which consists in the transformation of an Imaginary relationship with that particular imago which is the physical parent into the new and menacing abstraction of the paternal role as the possessor of the mother and the place of the Law. (Meanwhile, we have already seen above how this conception allows the Ortigues to posit a continuing validity for the Freudian notion of the Oedipus complex in a social and familial situation in which many of the more parochial and purely European features of this relationship no longer obtain.)

The Symbolic Order is thus, as we have already suggested, a further alienation of the subject; and this repeated emphasis further serves to distinguish Lacan's position (what we have called his Hegelianism) from many of the more facile celebrations of the primacy of language by structuralist ideologues. Perhaps the link with Lévi-Strauss' primitivism may be made across Rousseau, for whom the social order in all its repressiveness is intimately linked with the emergence of language itself. In Lacan, however, an analogous sense of the alienating function of language is arrested in Utopian mid-course by the palpable impossibility of returning to an archaic, preverbal stage of the psyche itself (although the Deleuze–Guattari celebration of schizophrenia would appear to attempt precisely that). Far more adequately than the schizophrenic or natural man, the tragic symbol of the unavoidable alienation by language would seem to have been provided by Truffaut's film, *L'Enfant sauvage* (The Wild Child), in which language learning comes before us as a racking torture, a palpably physical kind of suffering upon which the feral child is only imperfectly willing to enter.

The clinical equivalent of this agonizing transition from the Imaginary to the Symbolic is then furnished by an analysis, by Melanie Klein, of an autistic child, which makes it clear that the "cure," the accession of the child to speech and to the Symbolic, is accompanied by an increase, rather than a lessening, of anxiety. This case history (published in 1930 under the title "The Importance of Symbol-Formation in the Development of the Ego") may also serve to correct the imbalance of our own presentation, and of the very notion of a "transition" from Imaginary to Symbolic, by demonstrating that the acquisition of the Symbolic is rather the precondition for a full mastery of the Imaginary as well. In this case, the autistic child, Dick, is not only unable to speak but unable to play as well—unable, that is, to act out fantasies and to create "symbols," a term that in this context means object substitutes. The few meager objects handled by Dick all represent in a kind of undifferentiated state "the phantasied contents [of the mother's body]. The sadistic phantasies directed against the inside of her body constitute the first and basic relation to the outside world and to reality."[26] Psychic investment in the external world—or in other words, the development of the Imaginary itself—has been arrested at its most rudimentary form, with those little trains that function as representations of Dick and of his father, and the dark space or station that represents the mother. The fear of anxiety prevents the child from developing further symbolic substitutes and expanding the narrow limits of his object world.

Melanie Klein's therapy then consists in introducing the Symbolic Order, and language, into this impoverished realm; and that, as Lacan observes, without any particular subtlety or precautions ("Elle lui fout le symbolisme avec la denière brutalité, Melanie Klein, au petit Dick! Elle commence tout de suite par lui flanquer les interprétations majeures. Elle le flanque dans une verbalisation brutale du mythe oedipien, presque aussi révoltante pour nous que pour n'importe quel lecteur"[27]). Verbalization itself heavy-handedly superposes a Symbolic relationship upon the Imaginary fantasy of the train rolling up to the station: "The station is mummy; Dick is going into mummy."[28]

It is enough: from this point on, miraculously, the child begins to develop relationships to others, jealousies, games, and much richer forms of substitution and of the exercise of language. The Symbolic now releases Imaginary investments of ever new kinds of objects, which had hitherto been blocked, and permits the development of what Melanie Klein in her paper calls "symbol formation.'' Such symbol or substitute formation is a fundamental precondition of psychic evolution, since it can alone lead the subject to love objects that are equivalents for the original, now forbidden or taboo, maternal presence: Lacan will then assimilate this process to the operation of the trope of metonymy in the linguistic realm,[29] and the profound effects of this new and complex ''rhetorical'' mechanism—unavailable in the preverbal realm of the Imaginary, where, as we have seen, only the rudimentary oppositions of inside/outside and good/bad are operative—may serve to underscore and to dramatize the extent of the transformation language brings to what without it could not yet have been called desire.

We may now attempt to give a more complete picture of Lacan's conception of language, or at least of those features of articulate speech that are the most essential in the structuration of the psyche, and which may thus be said to constitute the Symbolic Order. It will be convenient to consider these features in three groups, even though they are obviously all very closely interrelated.

The first of these groups—we have already seen it at work in the Oedipal phenomenon of the Name-of-the-Father—may be generalized as the naming function of language, something that has the most momentous consequences for the subject. For the acquisition of a name results in a thoroughgoing transformation of the position of the subject in its object world: ''That a name, no matter how confused, designates a particular person—this is precisely what the passage to the human state consists in. If we must define that moment in which man [sic] becomes human, we would say that it is at that instant when, as minimally as you like, he enters into a symbolic relationship.''[30] It would seem fair to observe that Lacan's attention to the components of language has centered on those kinds of words, primarily names and pronouns, on those slots that, like the shifters generally, anchor a free-floating syntax to a particular subject, those verbal joints, therefore, at which the insertion of the subject into the Symbolic is particularly detectable.

Even here, however, we must distinguish among the various possible effects of these types of words: nouns, in particular the Name-of-the-Father itself, awaken the subject to the sense of a function that is somehow objective and independent of the existence of the biological father. Such names thus provide a liberation from the here-and-now of the Imaginary; for the separation, through language, of the paternal function from the biological father is precisely what permits the child to take the father's place in his turn. The order of abstraction—the Law, as Lacan calls it—is thus also what releases the subject from the constraints of the immediate family situation and from the ''bad immediacy'' of the pre-Symbolic period.

Pronouns, meanwhile, are the locus for a related, yet distinct, development, which is none other than the emergence of the unconscious itself. Such is indeed for Lacan the significance of the bar that divides signifier from signified in the semiotic fraction: the pronoun, the first person, the signifier, results in division of the subject, or *Spaltung*, which drives the "real subject" as it were underground, and leaves a "representative"—the ego—in its place: "The subject is figured in symbolism by a stand-in or substitute [un tenant-lieu], whether we have to do with the personal pronoun 'I,' with the name that is given him, or with the denomination 'son of.' This stand-in is of the order of the symbol or the signifier, an order that is only perpetuated laterally, through the relationships entertained by that signifier with other signifiers. The subject mediated by language is irremediably divided because it has been excluded from the symbolic chain [the lateral relations of signifiers among themselves] at the very moment at which it became 'represented' in it."[31] Thus, the discontinuity insisted on by linguists between the *énoncé* and the subject of the enunciation (or, by Humboldt's even broader distinction between language as *ergon*, or produced object, and language as *energeia*, or force of linguistic production) corresponds to the coming into being of the unconscious itself, as that reality of the subject that has been alienated and repressed through the very process by which, in receiving a name, it is transformed into a representation of itself.

This production of the unconscious by way of a primary repression— which is none other than the acquisition of language—is then reinterpreted in terms of the communicational situation as a whole; and Lacan's redefinition of the signifier, "the signifier is what represents the subject for another signifier,"[32] now illuminates what it may be artificial to call a different form of linguistic alienation than either of the above features, but what is certainly a distinct dimension of that alienation, namely, the coming into view of the inescapable mediation of other people, and more particularly of the Other with a capital O, or A, or, in other words, the parents. Yet here the Law represented by the parents, and in particular by the father, passes over into the very nature of language itself, which the child receives from the outside and which speaks him or her just as surely as he or she learns to speak it. At this third moment of the subject's alienation by language we therefore confront a more complex version of that strategy which we have elsewhere described as the fundamental enabling device of structuralism in general, namely, the possibility—provided by the ambiguous nature of language itself—of imperceptibly shifting back and forth between a conception of speech as a linguistic structure, whose components can then be tabulated, and a conception of speech as communication, which permits a virtual dramatization of the linguistic process (sender/receiver, *destinaire/destinateur*, etc.).[33] Lacan's "Other" (capital A) is the locus of this superposition, constituting at one and the same time the dramatis personae of the Oedipal situation (but most particularly the father or his substitutes) and the very structure of articulate language itself.

So it is that this third aspect of Symbolic alienation, the alienation by the Other, passes over into the more familiar terms of the accounts of the *chaîne du signifiant* given in Lacan's mature doctrine,[34] which, embattled in a struggle against ego psychology, and emerging from a long polemic with the neo-Freudian emphasis on the analysis of resistances and the strengthening of the subject's ego, has found its fundamental principle and organizing theme in "a conception of the function of the signifier able to demonstrate the place at which the subject is subordinated to it to the point of being virtually subverted [*suborné*]."[35] The result is a determination of the subject by language—not to say a linguistic determinism—which results in a rewriting of the classical Freudian unconscious in terms of language: "the Unconscious," to quote what must be Lacan's best-known sentence, "is the discourse of the Other."[36] For those of us still accustomed to the classical image of the Freudian unconscious as a seething cauldron of archaic instincts (and inclined, also, to associate language with thinking and consciousness rather than the opposite of those things), the Lacanian redefinition must inevitably scandalize. As far as language is concerned, the references to Hegel have a strategic role to play in confronting this scandal with the philosophically more respectable idea of alienation in general, and alienation to other people in particular (the master/slave chapter is of course the basic text here). Thus, if we can bring ourselves to think of language itself as an alienating structure, particularly in those features enumerated above, we are halfway toward an appreciation of this concept.

The other half of the way, however, presents the more serious obstacle of our preconceptions, not about language, but rather about the unconscious itself. To be sure, the relationship between the unconscious and the instincts will seem less problematical when we recall the enigma posed by Freud's notion of the *Vorstellungsrepräsentanz* ("ideational representative"),[37] one of those rare moments when, as with his hypothesis of the death wish, Freud himself seems terminologically and theoretically inarticulate. Yet the function of the concept seems clear: Freud wants to avoid giving the impression that instincts or drives (*Triebe*) are conceivable in a pure state, even for the purposes of building a model of the psyche; and his tautological term is meant to underscore the indissociable link, no matter how far back we go in the history of the psyche, between the instincts to be found there and the fantasies or objects to which they are bound and through which alone they must express themselves. What is this to say but that the instincts, indeed, the libido itself, no matter how energetically boiling, cannot be conceived independently of their representations—in short, that, in Lacanian terms, no matter how archaic they may be, the instincts are already of the order of the signifier? So it is that the place *A* of the Lacanian topology indifferently designates the Other (the parents), language, or the unconscious, now termed the "treasurehouse of the signifier," in other words, the lumber-room in which the subject's most ancient fantasies or fragments of fantasy are still stored. Two well-known, if less well understood, graphs illustrate this topology, in dynamic as well as in static forms. The static version is, of course, the so-called L-schema,[38] in which the subject's conscious desire, which she understands as a relationship between the desired object (*a*) and her ego or self *(á)*, is mediated by the more fundamental relationship between the real subject *(S)* and the capital *A* of the Other, language, or the unconscious. In the dynamic version of this topology (the so-called *graphe du désir*),[39] this structure of the subject is as it were put in motion by the movement of desire, considered as a *parole*, or act of enunciation: the inexhaustible fascination of this graph comes from the difficulty of thinking its intersections, in which the speech act of the subject, on its way from sender to receiver, is traversed by the retroactive effect of the "chain of the signifier" traveling, *nachträglich*, in the opposite direction, in such a way that the capital *A* constitutes the source of the fulfillment of both trajectories.

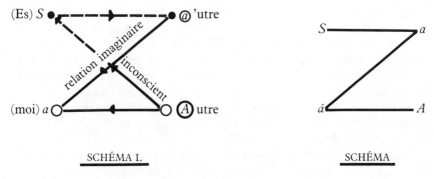

SCHÉMA L   SCHÉMA

Two versions of Lacan's L-schema. By way of wordplay on the German, *S* is the unconscious (or place of the subject of desire); capital *A* is the Other, the adult, or language itself; and lowercase *a* and *á* are the ego and the object of desire, respectively (note their interesting exchange of positions in Lacan's two versions). *Autre* must obviously be rendered in English with "*O*," which does not simplify matters. The schema is so-called on account of the *z*-related shape of the *L* in French penmanship, which has the advantage of inscribing the initial of its author. (Jacques Lacan, *Ecrits*, Paris, 1966, p. 53 and p. 548.)

Still, it will be observed that even if language can be invested to this degree with the content of the subject's alienations, it remains to square the Lacanian linguistic bias with the predominantly sexual emphasis of psychoanalysis' inaugural period. Even if, in other words, one were willing to grant the phallus provisional status as a signifier, the relationship between language and sexuality remains to be defined, the suspicion lingering that a system that permits you to talk about language instead of sexuality must betray a revisionist, if not a downright idealistic, impulse. The connection is made by way of the distinction between need ("pure" biological phenomenon) and demand (a purely interpersonal one, conceivable only after the emergence of language). Sexual desire is then that qualitatively new and more complex realm opened up by the lateness of human maturation in comparison with the other animal species, in which a previously biological instinct must undergo an alienation to a fundamentally communicational or linguistic relationship— that of the demand for recognition by the Other—in order to find satisfaction. Sexuality thus charts a middle course between physical need and interpersonal demand, satisfying neither and maintained at distance from each by the gravitational pull of both "forces." This alienation also explains why, for Lacan, sexual desire is structurally incapable of ultimate satisfaction: *plaisir*—as the momentary reduction of a purely physical tension—not being the same as *jouissance*, which involves that demand for recognition by the Other which in the very nature of things (in the very nature of language?) can never be fulfilled. This structural distance between the subject and his or her own desire will then serve as the enabling mechanism for the Lacanian typology of the neuroses and the perversions; and nowhere is Lacan more eloquent than in his defense of the ontological dignity of these primordial malfunctionings of the human psyche: "Hieroglyphics of hysteria, blazons of phobia, labyrinths of the *Zwangsneurose*—charms of impotence, enigmas of inhibition, oracles of anxiety—armorial bearings of character, seals of self-punishment, disguises of perversion—these are the hermetic elements that our exegesis resolves, the equivocations that our invocation dissolves, the artifices that our dialectic absolves, in a deliverance of the imprisoned sense, which moves from the revelation of the palimpsest to the pass-word of the mystery and the pardon of speech."[40]

Meanwhile, this conception of desire as a protolinguistic demand, and of the unconscious as a language, or "chain of signifiers," then permits something like a rhetorical analysis of psychic processes to come into being. As is well known, not only is desire a function of metonymy for Lacan, but the symptom is a product of metaphor, and the entire machinery of the psychic life of the mature subject—which consists, as we have seen above, in the indefinite production of substitutes, or, in other words, in Melanie Klein's "symbol-formation"—may be said to be figural in its very essence, figuration being that property of language that allows the same word to be used in several senses. The correlative of the chain of signifiers is thus the conception of a *glissement du signifié*, or "slippage of signifieds," which allows the psychic signifier to be displaced from one object to another. Here once again, the material of the Imaginary serves as a useful contrast by which to define the Symbolic: for not only does the latter, with its slippage of signifieds, know a structural malfunction in the language of the schizophrenic (whose syntagmatic experience of the signifying chain has broken down, on account of a radical *forclusion*, or expulsion of the Other), but it may also be said to have something like a zero degree in the so-called animal languages, which constitute the very prototype of the code proper to the Imaginary, involving no demands on the Other, but simply a fixed one-to-one relationship between signifier and signified, between signal and place, from which the more properly human phenomenon of figuration is absent.[41]

Displacement of the subject and redefinition of the unconscious as a language, topology and typology of desire and of its avatars—this brief sketch of "Lacanianism" would not be complete without a mention of that third overriding preoccupation of Lacan's life work, the one that it is most tempting and convenient for lay readers to overlook, namely, the strategy of the analytic situation itself, and in particular the role to be played in it by the analyst's interventions and the nature of transference. It is clear that in the Lacanian scheme of things, the uniqueness of the analytic situation—its emblematic as well as therapeutic value—derives from the fact that it is the one communicational situation in which the Other is addressed without being functionally involved: the analyst's silence thus causes the structural dependency of the subject on the capital A of the Other's language to become visible as it never could in any concrete interpersonal situation. So the subject's gradual experience of his or her own subordination to an alienating signifier is at one with the theorist's denunciation of philosophies of the subject and his Copernican attempt to assign to the subject an ec-centric position with respect to language as a whole.

We may now ask what, apart from the incidental mention of phenomena like that of animal language, above, can be said to be the place of the Imaginary in Lacan's later teaching; we will have occasion to see that its gradual eclipse in the later work is not foreign to a certain overestimation of the Symbolic that may be said to be properly ideological. For the moment, we may suggest that Imaginary thought patterns persist into mature psychic life in the form of what are generally thought of as ethical judgments—those implicit or explicit valorizations or repudiations in which "good" and "bad" are simply positional descriptions of the geographical relationship of the phenomenon in question to my own Imaginary conception of centrality. It is a comedy we may observe, not only in the world of action, but also in that of thought, where, in that immense proliferation of private languages which characterizes the intellectual life of consumer capitalism, the private religions that emerge around thinkers like the one presently under consideration are matched only by their anathematization by the champions of rival "codes." The Imaginary sources of passions like ethics may always be identified by the operation of the dual in them and the organization of their themes around binary oppositions; the ideological quality of such thinking must, however, be accounted for, not so much by the metaphysical nature of its categories of centrality, as Derrida and Lyotard have argued, as rather by its substitution of the categories of individual relationships for those—collective—of history and of historical, transindividual phenomena.

This view of ethics would seem to find confirmation in Lacan's essay

"Kant avec Sade," in which the very prototype of an attempt to construct a rationally coherent (in other words, Symbolic) system of ethics by Kant is thoroughly discredited by a structural analogy with the delirious rationality of Sade. By attempting to universalize ethics and to establish the criteria for universally binding ethical laws that are not dependent on the logic of the individual situation, Kant merely succeeds in stripping the subject of his object (*a*) in an effort to separate pleasurability from the notion of the Good, thereby leaving the subject alone with the Law (*A*): "Cannot moral law be said to represent desire in that situation in which it is not the subject, but rather the object, that is missing?"[42] Yet this structural result turns out to be homologous with perversion, defined by Lacan as the fascination with the pleasure of the Other at the expense of the subject's own, and illustrated monotonously by the voluminous pages of Sade.

Whatever the philosophical value of this analysis, in the present context it has the merit of allowing us to conceive the possibility of transforming the topological distinction between Imaginary and Symbolic into a genuine methodology. "Kant avec Sade" would seem indeed to be the equivalent in the realm of moral philosophy of those logical paradoxes and mathematical exercises that have so disoriented the readers of Lacan in other areas. Thus, for example, we find a properly psychoanalytic reflection on the timing of the analytical situation unexpectedly punctuated by a meditation on a logical puzzle or metalogical paradox (see "Le Temps logique"), whose upshot is to force us to reintroduce the time of the individual subject back into what was supposed to be a universal or impersonal mental operation. Elsewhere the experiment is reversed, and the laws of probability are invoked to demonstrate the Symbolic regularity (in Freudian terms, the repetitive structure) of what otherwise strikes the subject as sheer individual chance. Lacan has, however, explained himself about these excursions, designed, he says, to lead "those who follow us into places where logic itself is staggered by the glaring incommensurability between Imaginary and Symbolic; and this, not out of complacency with the resultant paradoxes, nor with any so-called intellectual crisis, but rather on the contrary to restore its illicit glitter to the structural gap [*béance*] thereby revealed, a gap perpetually instructive for us, and above all to try to forge the method of a kind of calculus able to dislodge its secret by its very inappropriateness."[43]

In the same way, "Kant avec Sade" transforms the very project of a moral philosophy into an insoluble intellectual paradox by rotating it in such a way that the implicit gap in it between subject and law catches the light. It is time to ask whether a similar use of the distinction between Imaginary and Symbolic may not be possible in the realm of aesthetic theory and literary criticism, offering psychoanalytic method a more fruitful vocation than it was able to exercise in the older literary psychoanalyses.

III

We cannot do so, however, before first asking whether, alongside that Freudian criticism, of which everyone—for good or ill—has a fairly vivid idea what it ends up looking like, a properly Lacanian criticism is also conceivable. Yet it is here that the ambiguity of Lacan's relations to his original—is he rewriting him or merely restoring him?—becomes problematic. For at the point of interpretation, either the attempt at a Lacanian reading simply again generates the classic themes of all psychoanalytic literary criticism since Freud—the Oedipus complex, the double, splitting, the phallus, the lost object, and so forth—or else, trying to keep faith with the linguistic inspiration of "L'Instance de la lettre," it exercises the distinction between metaphor and metonymy to the point where the orthodox psychoanalytic preoccupations seem to have been forgotten without a trace.[44] In part, of course, this methodological fluctuation can be accounted for by what we have suggested above: namely, that on the level of interpretive codes Lacan's position is not one of substituting linguistic for classical psychoanalytic concepts, but rather of mediating between them, and this is clearly a matter of some tact that cannot be successfully realized on the occasion of every text.

But there is another, more structural, side to this problem, which raises the question of the syntagmatic organization of the work of art, rather than the issue—a more properly paradigmatic one—of the interpretive schemes into which it is to be "transcoded" or interpreted. Freud's own two greatest narrative readings, that of Jensen's *Gradiva* and that of Hoffmann's *Sandmann*, turn on delusions that either come to appeasement or culminate in the destruction of the subject. They thus recapitulate the trajectory of the cure, or of the illness, or—ultimately, and behind both—of the evolution and maturation of the psyche itself. We have here, therefore, narratives that formally require the final term of a norm (maturity, psychic health, the cure) toward which to steer their itineraries, whether catastrophic or providential; or that ultimate norm itself, however, the narrative can have nothing to say, as it is not a realm, but rather only an organizational device or term limit.

It would not be difficult to imagine a Lacanian criticism—although I do not know that there has been one[45]—in which the transition from the Imaginary to the Symbolic described above played an analogous role in organizing the syntagmatic movement of the narrative from disorder to the term limit of the Symbolic Order itself. The risk of an operation like this lies clearly in the assimilation of what is original in Lacan to the more widespread and now conventionalized structuralist paradigm of the passage from nature to culture; and this is surely the moment to ask ourselves whether the Lacanian emphasis on the Law and on the necessity of the castration anxiety in the evolution of the subject—so different in spirit from the instinctual and revolutionary Utopias of Brown's polymorphous perversity, Reich's genital sexuality, and Marcuse's maternal super-id—shares the implicit conservatism of the classical structuralist paradigm. Insofar as the Lacanian version generates a rhetoric of its own that celebrates submission to the Law, and indeed, the subordination of the subject to the Symbolic Order, conservative overtones and indeed the possibility of a conservative misappropriation of this clearly anti-Utopian scheme are unavoidable. On the other hand, if we recall that for Lacan "submission to the Law" designates, not repression, but rather something quite different, namely alienation—in the ambiguous sense in which Hegel, as opposed to Marx, conceives of this phenomenon—then the more tragic character of Lacan's thought, and the dialectical possibilities inherent in it, become evident.

Indeed, the one sustained literary exegesis that Lacan has published, the seminar on Poe's "Purloined Letter,"[46] suggests that for Lacan, in contradistinction to Freud himself, the norm *can* be the locus of a properly narrative exploration, albeit one of a uniquely didactic or "illustrative" type.[47] Poe's story is for Lacan the occasion of a magisterial demonstration of the way "a formal language determines the subject."[48] Three distinct positions are structurally available in relationship to the Letter itself, or the signifier: that of the king, that of the queen, and that of the Minister. When in the sequel to the narrative the places change, Dupin taking the place of the Minister, who then moves to that previously held by the queen, it is the positions themselves that exercise a structurating power over the subjects who momentarily occupy them. So the signifying chain becomes a vicious circle, and the story of the norm itself, of the Symbolic Order, is not that of a "happy end," but rather of a perpetual alienation. Obviously, Lacan's interpretation of the narrative is an allegorical one, in which the signified of the narrative proves to be simply language itself. Once again, the relative richness of the reading derives from the dramatic structure of the communicational process and the multiplicity of different positions available in it; but while more lively because of the musical chairs being played in it, Lacan's exegesis in this respect rejoins that now conventional structuralist conception of the autoreferentiality of the text that we have shown at work in *Tel Quel* and Derrida, as well as in Todorov's interpretations.[49] Read in this way—but as I will suggest later, it is not the only way one can read Lacan's essay—the "Seminar on 'The Purloined Letter,' " by its programmatic demonstration of the primacy of the signifier, furnishes powerful ammunition for what must properly be called, in distinction to its other achievements, the ideology of structuralism. (It may rapidly be defined here as the systematic substitution of "referent" for "signified," which allows one to pass logically from the properly linguistic assertion that the signified is an effect of the organization of signifiers to the quite different conclusion that therefore the "referent"—in other words, History—does not exist). Yet the present context suggests an explanation for this excess charge of ideology, this ideological effect, vehiculated or produced by Lacan's exposé. Indeed, its opening page, with its polemic repudiation of those "imaginary incidences [which], far from representing the essence of our experience, reveal only what remains inconsistent in it,"[50] makes a diagnosis of an overestimation of the Symbolic at the expense of the Imaginary in its presentation well-nigh inescapable.

Strengthened by this detour through Lacan's own literary criticism, we have thus returned to our hypothesis that whatever else it is, the distinction between the Imaginary and the Symbolic, and the requirement that a given analysis be able to do justice to the qualitative gap between them, may prove to be an invaluable instrument for measuring the range or the limits of a particular way of thinking. If it is always unsatisfying to speculate on what a Lacanian literary criticism ought to be in the future, if it is clear that the "Seminar on 'The Purloined Letter' " cannot possibly constitute a model for such criticism—since on the contrary the literary work is in it a mere pretext for a dazzling illustration of a nonliterary thesis—then at least we may be able to use the concept of the two orders, or registers, as a means for demonstrating the imbalance of other critical methods, and of suggesting ways in which they may be coordinated and an eclectic pluralism overcome. So, for instance, it seems abundantly clear that the whole area of image study and image hunting takes on a new appearance when we grasp the image content of a given text, not as so many clues to its ideational content (or "meaning"), but rather as the sedimentation of the imaginary material on which the text must work, as the raw materials it must transform. The relationship of the literary text to its image content is thus—in spite of the historic preponderance of the sensory in modern literature since Romanticism—not that of the production of imagery, but rather of its mastery and control in ways that range from outright repression (and the transformation of the sensory image into some more comfortable conceptual symbol) to the more complex modes of assimilation of surrealism and, more recently, of schizophrenic literature.[51] Only by grasping images—and also the surviving fragments of authentic myth and delusion—in this way, as that trace of the Imaginary, of sheer private or physiological experience, which has undergone the sea change of the Symbolic, can criticism of this kind recover a vital and hermeneutic relationship to the literary text.

Yet image criticism raises a problem that we have postponed until this time, namely, as a matter of critical practice now rather than abstract theory, how to identify Imaginary materials as such, particularly insofar as the same contents can at different times or in different contexts have been part of an imaginary experience as well as of a symbolic system? Leclaire's useful example of the bronze ashtray[52] enumerates this gradual shifting of registers, as the initial perception of the shape and the blackened metal surface of the object, of its density in the hand and its slickness for the eye, then is slowly by means of names ranged in the various symbolic systems in which it seems to find a momentary home—first as a functional object ("ashtray"), then as an antique, further as the specimen of a particular style of rural furnishing, and so forth. This distinction between the experience of immediate sense perception and the various systems of abstraction into which the name of an object allows it to be inserted, has already become familiar to us.

It should, however, be possible to formulate more specific rules for the determination of the respective Imaginary or Symbolic function of a given object, such as the following one: "The same term may be considered imaginary if taken absolutely and symbolic if taken as a differential value correlative of other terms that limit it reciprocally."[53] This excellent formula, which we owe to Edmond Ortigues, should probably not be generalized into the kind of ahistorical system he goes on to offer us, in which the Imaginary becomes the regime of the eye, the Symbolic that of the ear and of language; in which the "material imagination," with its fascination with a single sense plenum, is opposed to all those differential systems that are essentially linguistic and social in character. Such an opposition is unfortunately, as we have come to learn, a properly Imaginary one. Yet the formula usefully insists on the tendency of the Imaginary object to absolutize itself, to exclude relationship and to overshadow the perceptual apparatus in a freestanding and isolated way, in contrast to the ways in which elements of Symbolic systems are always implicitly or explicitly embedded in a complex of binary oppositions and subjected to the whole range of what Greimas calls the "play of semiotic constraints."

The problem with such a definition is that when we reintroduce the subject into such relationships, the proportions change, and what it was useful to designate in terms of the isolation of the single Imaginary object, now becomes a two-term relationship, while the binary systems of the Symbolic must now be understood as introducing a third term into the hitherto duplex logic of the Imaginary:

> This is the sense of J. Lacan's definition of the essence of the Imaginary as a "dual relationship," an ambiguous redoubling, a "mirror" reflection, an immediate relationship between the subject and its other in which each term passes immediately into the other and is lost in a never-ending play of reflections. Imagination and desire are the realities of a finite being that can emerge from the contradiction between self and other only by the genesis of a third term, a mediatory "concept" which, by determining each term, orders them into reversible and progressive relations that can be developed in language. The whole problem of symbolization lies here, in this passage from a dual opposition to a ternary relation, a passage from desire to the concept.[54]

On the other hand, as we have suggested above, to stage the relationship in terms of so radical an opposition is somehow covertly to reintroduce Imaginary thinking itself into a thought that was apparently attempting to overcome it; nor is it really a question of repudiating the Imaginary and substituting the Symbolic for it—as though the one were "bad" and the other "good"—but rather of elaborating a method that can articulate both while preserving their radical discontinuity with each other.

In this perspective, returning now to our critique of current literary methods, it becomes clear that above and beyond image criticism, it is phenomenology itself that must become the object of critical reconsideration, insofar as its fundamental materials of analysis—the lived experience of time and space, of the elements, of the very texture of subjectivity—are drawn almost exclusively from the Imaginary realm. Phenomenological criticism, whose program was heralded by Husserl's well-known slogan of a "return to things," clearly had a role to play as a kind of therapeutic corrective to overly intellectualized conceptions of the work of art, as an attempt to restore the authenticity of lived experience and sensory plenitude to the aesthetic text.

In retrospect, however, the aesthetic developed by the phenomenologists, and in particular by Merleau-Ponty, with its notion of the primacy of perception in the elaboration of the languages of art, would seem to be the very prototype of a theory of the Symbolic conceived almost exclusively from the perspective of the Imaginary. On the other hand, it cannot be said that in its most rigorous form, phenomenological criticism as such has been widely applied in the United States; what has tended to replace it, but sometimes to claim its authority, is the far more obviously ideological interpretation of works in terms of the "self" and its various identity crises. On readings of this kind—which have obviously become the dominant academic interpretive ideology, along with so-called pluralism—readings whose interminable oscillation between the subject, the ego, and the Other reflects the optical illusions of the Imaginary register itself, the full force of the Lacanian denunciation of ego psychology may be allowed to fall.[55]

We must, however, specify an important variant of this approach, which, framed in protosocial terms, has genuinely political consequences. This approach—the reading of cultural phenomena in terms of otherness—derives from the dialectic of the relationship to the Other in Sartre's *Being and Nothingness*, and beyond that, from the Hegelian account of the master and the slave in the *Phenomenology*. It is a dialectic that, particularly as developed in *Saint Genêt*, seemed to lay the basis for an aggressive critique of the relations of domination—hence, in particular, its extension by Frantz Fanon to the whole realm of Third World theory and of the psychopathology of the colonized and the colonial Other. And something like just such a theory of otherness must surely always be implicit in a politics that for whatever reason substitutes categories of race for those of class, and the struggle for colonial independence for that of the class struggle proper.

Meanwhile, the work of Michel Foucault testifies to the growing influence of a similar theory of otherness in the analysis of culture and history, where it has taken on the more structural form of a theory of exclusion. So, following Sartre's analysis of criminality in *Saint Genêt*, Foucault showed how a society developing a conception of Reason found it necessary to devise one of insanity and abnormality as well, and to generate marginal realities against which to define itself; and his more recent work on imprisonment and incarceration proper rejoins what has become one of the most significant currents of American political reality since Attica, namely, the movement within the prisons themselves.

On the other hand, it cannot be denied that *"Saint Genêt* is the epic of the 'stade du miroir' ";[56] and political reality, as well as the theoretical framework offered here, suggests that the Lumpenpolitics, the politics of marginality or "molecular politics" (Deleuze), of which such theories are the ideology and which is in some ways the successor to the student movements of the 1960s both here and in France, is essentially an ethical—when not an overtly anarchist—politics dominated by the categories of the Imaginary. Yet, in the long run, as we will see in our concluding section, an ethical politics is a contradiction in terms, however admirable may be its passions and the quality of its indignation.

Such are, then, some of the forms taken in recent criticism by what we may diagnose as an overestimation of the Imaginary at the expense of the Symbolic. That it is not simply a question of method or theory but has implications for aesthetic production may be suggested by the example of Brecht, whose conception of an anti-Aristotelian theater, an aesthetic that refuses spectator empathy and "identification," has raised problems that are clarified by our present context. We would suggest, indeed, that the Brechtean attack on "culinary" theater—as well as the apparent paradoxes to which the ideal of "epic theater" gives rise—can best be understood as an attempt to block Imaginary investment and thereby to dramatize the problematical relationship between the observing subject and the Symbolic Order or history.

As for the complementary extreme, the overestimation of the Symbolic itself, it is easier to say what this particular "heresy" or "illusion" looks like since the development of semiotics, whose fundamental program may in this respect be described as a veritable mapping of the Symbolic Order. Its blind spots may therefore be expected to be particularly instructive as to the problems of the insertion of the Imaginary into the model of a Symbolic system. I will here point to only one of them, but it is surely the most important one in the context of literary criticism, namely, the problem of the category of the "character" in a structural analysis of narrative.[57]

For, as the ideologies of "identification" and "point of view" make plain, "character" is that point in the narrative text at which the problem of the insertion of the subject into the Symbolic most acutely arises. It can surely not be solved by compromises like those of Propp and Greimas—whatever their undoubted practical value—in which the anthropomorphic remnant of a "subject" of the action persists beneath the guise of the "function" or the *actant*. What is wanted is not only an instrument of analysis that will maintain the incommensurability of the subject with its narrative representations—or, in other words, the incommensurability between the Imaginary and the Symbolic in general—but also one that will articulate the discontinuities within the subject's various "representatives" themselves, not only those that Benveniste has taught us to observe between the first and second pronouns on the one hand and the third on the other, but also, and above all, that discontinuity, stressed by Lacan, between the nominative and the accusative forms of the first person itself. To a certain degree, the theoretical problem of the status of the subject in narrative analysis is itself a reflection of the historical attempt of modernistic practice to eliminate the old-fashioned subject from the literary text. My own feeling is that you cannot deny the possibility of an adequate representation of the subject in narrative on the one hand, and then continue the search for a more satisfactory category for such representation on the other. If this is so, the notion of some relationship—still to be defined—between the subject and this or that individual character or "point of view" should be replaced by the study of those character systems into which the subject is fitfully inserted.[58]

In a more general way, however, this dilemma suggests that the most crucial need of literary theory today is for the development of conceptual instruments capable of doing justice to a postindividualistic experience of the subject in contemporary life itself, as well as in the texts. Such a need is underscored by the persistent contemporary rhetoric of a fragmentation of the subject (most notably, perhaps, in the *Anti-Oedipe* of Deleuze and Guattari, with their celebration of the schizophrenic as the "true hero of desire"); but it is not satisfied any more adequately by the (still very abstract) Marxist conviction that the theory as well as the experience of the decentering of consciousness must serve "to liquidate the last vestiges of bourgeois individualism itself and to prepare the basis for some new postindividualistic thought mode to come."[59] At the least, however, and whatever their practical value as analytic machinery turns out to be, the Lacanian graphs of a properly structural "subversion of the subject" allow us in retrospect to measure the anticipatory value, but also the Hegelianizing limits, of such conceptual precursors as the dialectics of *Saint Genêt* and of René Girard's *Deceit, Desire and the Novel*, as well as of Sartre's later concept of "seriality" in the *Critique*, while suggesting future areas for exploration in Bakhtin's prestructural notion of a properly dialogical speech and the preindividualistic forms of social experience from which it springs.[60] It is therefore tempting to reverse Lacan's polemics (in the "Seminar on 'The Purloined Letter'" and elsewhere) and to suggest that at a time when the primacy of language and the Symbolic Order is widely understood—or at least widely asserted—it is rather in the underestimation of the Imaginary and the problem of the insertion of the subject that the "un-hiddenness of truth" (Heidegger) may now be sought.

IV

For Derrida's accusation is undoubtedly true, and what is at stake, in Lacan as well as in psychoanalysis in general, is truth; even worse, a conception of truth peculiarly affiliated to the classical existential one (that of Heidegger as a veiling/unveiling, that of Sartre as a fitful reclamation from *mauvaise foi*).[61] For that very reason, it seems arbitrary to class as logocentric and phonocentric a thought that—insofar as it is structural—proposes a decentering of the subject, and—insofar as it is "existential"—is guided by a concept of truth, not as adequation with reality (as Derrida suggests), but rather as a relationship, at best an asymptotic approach, to the Real.

This is not the place to deal with Lacan's epistemology, but it is certainly the moment to return to this term, the third of the canonical Lacanian triad, of which it must be admitted that it is at the very least astonishing that we have been able to avoid mentioning it for so long. Just as the Symbolic Order (or language itself) restructures the Imaginary by introducing a third term into the hitherto infinite regression of the duality of the latter's mirror images, so we may hope and expect that the tardy introduction of this third term, the Real, may put an end to the Imaginary opposition into which our previous discussion of Lacan's two orders has risked falling again and again. We must not, however, expect much help from Lacan himself in giving an account of a realm of which he in one place observes that it—"the Real, or what is perceived as such,—is what resists symbolization absolutely."[62]

Nonetheless, it is not terribly difficult to say what is meant by the Real in Lacan. It is simply History itself; and if for psychoanalysis the history in question here is obviously enough the history of the subject, the resonance of the word suggests that a confrontation between this particular materialism and the historical materialism of Marx can no longer be postponed. It is a confrontation whose first example has been set by Lacan himself, with his suggestion that the notion of the Symbolic as he uses it is compatible with Marxism (whose theory of language, as most Marxists would be willing to agree, remains to be worked out).[63] Meanwhile, it is certain that his entire work is permeated by dialectical tendencies, the more Hegelian ones having already been indicated above, and beyond this that the fascination of that work lies precisely in its ambiguous hesitation between dialectical formulations and those, more static, more properly structural and spatializing, of his various topologies. In Lacan, however, unlike the other varieties of structural mapping, there is always the proximity of the analytic situation to ensure the transformation of such structures back into "moments" of a more process-oriented type. Thus, in the "Seminar on 'The Purloined Letter,' " which we have hitherto taken at face value as a "structuralist" manifesto against the optical illusions of the signified, other passages on the contrary suggest that the circular trajectory of the signifier may be a little more closely related to the emergence of a dialectical self-consciousness than one might have thought, and project a second, more dialectical reading superimposed upon the structural one already outlined. In particular, the dilemma of Poe's Minister implies that it is in awareness of the Symbolic that liberation from the optical illusions of the Imaginary is to be sought:

> For if it is, now as before, a question of protecting the letter from
> inquisitive eyes, he can do nothing but employ the same technique
> he himself has already foiled: leave it in the open. And we may prop-
> erly doubt that he knows what he is thus doing, when we see him
> immediately captivated by a dual relationship in which we find all
> the traits of a mimetic or of an animal feigning death, and, trapped
> in the typically imaginary situation of seeing that he is not seen,
> misconstrue the real situation in which he is seen not seeing.[64]

Even if the structural self-consciousness diagnostically implied by such a passage is a properly dialectical one, it would not necessarily follow that the dialectic is a Marxist one, even though psychoanalysis is unquestionably a materialism. Meanwhile the experience of a whole series of abortive Freudo-Marxisms, as well as the methodological standard of the type of radical discontinuity proposed by the model outlined in the present essay, suggests that no good purpose is to be served by attempting too hastily to combine them into some unified anthropology. To say that both psychoanalysis and Marxism are materialisms is simply to assert that each reveals an area in which human consciousness is not "master in its own house": only the areas decentered by each are the quite different ones of sexuality and of the class dynamics of social history. That these areas know local interrelationships—as when Reich shows how sexual repression is something like the cement that holds the authority fabric of society together—is undeniable; but none of these instinctual or ideological ion-exchanges, in which a molecular element of one system is temporarily lent to the other for purposes of stabilization, can properly furnish a model of the relationship of sexuality to class con-sciousness as a whole. Materialistic thinking, however, ought to have had enough practice of heterogeneity and discontinuity to entertain the possibility that human reality is fundamentally alienated in more than one way, and in ways that have little enough to do with each other.

What one can do, however, more modestly but with better hope of suc-cess, is to show what these two systems—each one essentially a hermeneutic—

have to teach each other in the way of method. Marxism and psychoanalysis indeed present a number of striking analogies of structure with each other, as a checklist of their major themes can testify: the relation of theory and practice; the resistance of false consciousness and the problem as to its opposite (is it knowledge or truth? science or individual certainty?); the role and risks of the concept of a "midwife" of truth, whether analyst or vanguard party; the reappropriation of an alienated history and the function of narrative; the question of desire and value and of the nature of "false desire"; the paradox of the end of the revolutionary process, which, like analysis, must surely be considered "interminable" rather than "terminable"; and so forth. It is therefore not surprising that these two nineteenth-century "philosophies" should be the objects, at the present time and in the present intellectual atmosphere, of similar attacks, which focus on their "naive semanticism."

It is at least clear that the nineteenth century is to be blamed for the absence until very recently, in both Marxism and psychoanalysis, of a concept of language that would permit the proper answer to this objection. Lacan is therefore in this perspective an exemplary figure, provided we understand his life's work, not as the transformation of Freud into linguistics, but as the disengagement of a linguistic theory that was implicit in Freud's practice but for which he did not yet have the appropriate conceptual instruments; and clearly enough, it is Lacan's third term, his addition of the Real to a relatively harmless conceptual opposition between Imaginary and Symbolic, that sticks in the craw and causes all the trouble. For what is scandalous for contemporary philosophy in both of these "materialisms"—to emphasize the fundamental distance between each of these "unities-of-theory-and-practice" and conventional philosophy as such—is the subborn retention by both of something the sophisticated philosopher was long since supposed to have put between parentheses, namely a conception of the referent. For model-building and language-oriented philosophies, indeed (and in our time they span an immense range of tendencies and styles from Nietzsche to common language philosophy and from pragmatism to existentialism and structuralism)—for an intellectual climate dominated, in other words, by the conviction that the realities we confront or experience come before us preformed and preordered, not so much by the human "mind" (that is the older form of classical idealism), as rather by the various modes in which human language can work—it is clear that there must be something unacceptable about this affirmation of the persistence, behind our representations, of that indestructible nucleus of what Lacan calls the Real, of which we have already said above that it was simply History itself. If we can have an idea of it, it is objected, then it has already become part of our representations; if not, it is just another Kantian *Ding-an-sich* (a formulation that will probably no longer satisfy anyone). Yet the objection presupposes an epistemology for which

knowledge is in one way or another an identity with the things, a presupposition peculiarly without force over the Lacanian conception of the decentered
subject, which can know union neither with language nor with the Real and
which is structurally at a distance from both in its very being. The Lacanian
notion of an "asymptotic" approach to the Real, moreover, maps a situation
in which the action of this "absent cause" can be understood as a term limit,
both indistinguishable from the Symbolic (or the Imaginary) and also independent of it.

The other version of this objection—that history is a text, and that in that
case, as one text is worth another, it can no longer be appealed to as the
"ground" of truth—raises the issue of narrative fundamental both for
psychoanalysis and for historical materialism, and requires us to lay at least
the groundwork for a materialist philosophy of language. For both psychoanalysis and Marxism depend very fundamentally on history in its other
sense, as story and storytelling: if the Marxian narrative of the irreversible
dynamism of human society as it develops into capitalism be disallowed, little
or nothing remains of Marxism as a system and the meaning of the acts of all
those who have associated their praxis with it bleeds away. Meanwhile, it is
clear that the analytic situation is nothing if not a systematic reconstruction or
rewriting of the subject's past,[65] as indeed the very status of the Freudian
corpus as an immense body of narrative analyses testifies. We cannot here
fully argue the distinction between this narrative orientation of both Marxism
and Freudianism and the nonreferential philosophies alluded to above. Suffice it to observe this: that history is not so much a text, as rather a text-to-
be-(re-)constructed. Better still, it is an obligation to do so, whose means and
techniques are themselves historically irreversible, so that we are not at liber-
ty to construct any historical narrative at all (we are not free, for instance, to
return to theodicies or providential narratives, or even to the older na-
tionalistic ones), and the refusal of the Marxist paradigm can generally be
demonstrated to be at one with the refusal of historical narration itself, or at
least, with its systematic strategic delimitation.

In terms of language, we must distinguish between our own narrative of
history—whether psychoanalytic or political—and the Real itself, which our
narratives can only approximate in asymptotic fashion and which "resists
symbolization absolutely." Nor can the historical paradigm furnished us by
psychoanalysis or by Marxism—that of the Oedipus complex or of the class
struggle—be considered as anything more Real than a master text, an abstract
one, hardly even a protonarrative, in terms of which we construct the text of
our own lives with our own concrete praxis. This is the point at which the intervention of Lacan's fundamental distinction between truth and knowledge
(or science) must be decisive: the abstract schemata of psychoanalysis or of
the Marxian philosophy of history constitute a body of knowledge, indeed, of
what many of us would be willing to call scientific knowledge, but they do

not embody the "truth" of the subject, nor are the texts in which they are elaborated to be thought of as a *parole pleine*. A materialistic philosophy of language reserves a status for scientific language of this kind, which designates the Real without claiming to coincide with it, which offers the very theory of its own incapacity to signify fully as its credentials for transcending both Imaginary and Symbolic alike. "Il y a des formules qu'on n'imagine pas," Lacan observes of Newton's laws: "Au moins pour un temps, elles font assemblée avec le réel."[66]

The chief defect of all hitherto existing materialism is that it has been conceived as a series of propositions about matter—and in particular the relationship of matter to consciousness, which is to say of the natural sciences to the so-called human sciences[67]—rather than as a set of propositions about language. A materialistic philosophy of language is not a semanticism, naive or otherwise, because its fundamental tenet is a rigorous distinction between the signified—the realm of semantics proper, of interpretation, of the study of the text's ostensible meaning—and the referent. The study of the referent, however, is the study, not of the meaning of the text, but of the limits of its meanings and of their historical preconditions, and of what is and must remain incommensurable with individual expression. In our present terms, this means that a relationship to objective knowledge (in other words, to what is of such a different order of magnitude and organization from the individual subject that it can never be adequately "represented" within the latter's lived experience save as a term limit) is conceivable only for a thought able to do justice to radical discontinuities, not only between the Lacanian "orders," but within language itself, between its various types of propositions as they entertain wholly different structural relations with the subject.

The Lacanian conception of science as a historically original form of the decentering of the subject[68]—rather than as a place of "truth"—has much that is suggestive for a Marxism still locked in the outmoded antinomy of that opposition between ideology and science whose bewildering changes are rung in the various and contradictory models of that relationship proposed by Althusser at various stages of his work. And in view of the use to which we will elsewhere see Althusser put the Lacanian notion of the orders, it is all the more surprising that he should not have profited from a scheme in which knowledge and science, the subject and his or her individual truth, the place of the Master, the ec-centric relationship both to the Symbolic and to the Real, are all relationally mapped.

For clearly, in Marxism as well as in psychoanalysis, there is a problem—even a crisis—of the subject: suffice it to evoke on the level of praxis the intolerable alternative between a self-sacrificing and repressing Stalinism and an anarchistic celebration of the subject's immediate here-and-now. In the area of theory, the crisis in the Marxian conception of the subject finds its most dramatic expression in the contrast between what we may call the German and the French traditions—the Hegelianizing and dialectical current that, emerging from Lukács' *History and Class Consciousness*, found its embodiment in the work of the Frankfurt School, and the structural and science-oriented reading of Marx that, combining the heritage of Saussure with the lessons of Mao Tse-tung's *On Contradiction* (and also with Lacanian psychoanalysis), informs the theoretical practice of Althusser and his group.

The theme of the subject, indeed, clarifies many of the ambiguities of Althusser's positions. His polemic against that particular ideology of the subject called humanism was to be sure a relatively local one, directed not only against currents in the non- and even anti-Communist Left in France, but also against some elements of the French Communist party; whereas his polemic against Hegel is clearly intended to forestall the use of the early, Hegelianizing Marx, the Marx of the theory of alienation, against the later Marx of *Capital*.[69] Neither of these polemics is particularly relevant to the fortunes of Marxism in the Anglo-American world, where Hegel has never been a name to conjure with in the first place, and where the dominant individualism has never flirted very extensively with the rhetoric of humanism. Our present context, however, makes it easier to see the markings of the Imaginary and its distortion in that "idealism" with which Althusser reproaches Hegel, whose conceptual instruments—totality, negativity, alienation, *Aufhebung*, and even "contradiction" when understood in a fundamentally idealist sense—he takes such pains to distinguish from his own discontinuous and structural ones.[70] To rewrite Althusser's critique in these terms is to escape the antithesis between that affirmation of a "materialist kernel" in Hegel to which he rightly objects, and his own blanket repudiation, and to evolve a more productive way of handling the content of "idealistic" philosophies. Some such approach, indeed, seems implicit in Althusser's later conception of history as a "process without a subject"[71] (a polemic aimed at the Hegelianism of Lukács, whose characterization of the proletariat as the "subject of history" is here alluded to). Yet it must not be thought that this difference has to do with the content of a Marxian vision of history shared by Lukács and Althusser alike; rather, it would seem a question for Althusser of rejecting the use of categories of the subject in the discussion of a collective process structurally incommensurable with them, and with individual or existential experience.[72] Indeed, the Althusserian emphasis on science is in this respect such an extreme overreaction as to leave no place for that very rich field of study that emerged from Lukács' tradition and that is customarily designated as the phenomenology of everyday life.

The lasting achievement of the Frankfurt School, meanwhile, lies precisely in this area, and in particular, in its vivid demonstration of the reification of the subject under late capitalism—a demonstration that ranges from Adorno's diagnoses of the fetishization of aesthetic perception (and of artistic form) all the way to Marcuse's anatomy of the language and thought patterns of *One-Dimensional Man*. What we must now observe is that the demonstration depends for its force on the hypothesis of some previous historical stage in which the subject is still relatively whole and autonomous. Yet the very ideal of psychological autonomy and individualism, in the name of which their diagnosis of the atomized subject of late capitalism is made, precludes any imaginative appeal back beyond bourgeois civil society to some preindividualistic and precapitalist social form, since the latter would necessarily precede the constitution of the bourgeois subject itself. Inevitably, then, the Frankfurt School drew its norm of the autonomous subject from that period in which the bourgeoisie was itself a rising and progressive class, its psychological formation conditioned by the then still vital structure of the nuclear family; and this is the sense in which their thought has with some justification been taxed as potentially regressive and nostalgic.

Whereas in France in the 1960s and 1970s, the left-wing celebration of the "end of man" (Foucault) has generated a rhetoric in which it is precisely the so-called autonomous subject (in other words, the ego, the illusion of autonomy) that is denounced as an ideological and a bourgeois phenomenon, and the various signs of its decay—what the Frankfurt School took to be symptoms—are welcomed as the harbingers of some new postindividualistic state of things. The historical reasons for this theoretical divergence—the Frankfurt School's experience of the quality of consciousness among the subjects of Nazism, the absence from the France of the *société de consommation* of anything like a countercultural "revolution" in daily life of the American type—do not suffice to solve the theoretical problem of the status the subject ought to have for Marxism today.

The solution can only lie, it seems to me, in the renewal of Utopian thinking, of creative speculation as to the place of the subject at the other end of historical time, in a social order that has put behind it class organization, commodity production and the market, alienated labor, and the implacable determinism of a historical logic beyond the control of humanity. Only thus can a third term be imagined beyond either the "autonomous individualism" of the bourgeoisie in its heyday or the schizoid part-objects in which the fetishization of the subject under late capitalism has left its trace; a term in the light of which both these forms of consciousness can be placed in their proper historical perspective.

To do so, however, would require the elaboration of a properly Marxist "ideology," something that will be more fully explored in the following two chapters.

It seems appropriate, however, to conclude this "Lacanian" evaluation of different discourses with a return to Lacan himself, who proposed another kind of typology in his 1969–1970 seminar. As this is very specifically a structural typology—organized around the logical permutations that obtain in relationships to the signifier—the Imaginary no longer plays any role in it (but reappears in the very different dialectical scheme of the "knots" that link the three orders, at the end of Lacan's career). The system of the "four discourses," however, is organized around the idea that a distinct discursive structure will appear as each of the four fundamental elements in that relationship is foregrounded and "overemphasized" (it being understood that no real harmony between them is possible that would allow the proper "ratio" and that could therefore be understood as a "solution" to the problem of overemphasis or, in other words, as a kind of norm; whereas, on the other hand, it is not possible to avoid foregrounding and privileging one of these elements over the others in any given situation). The four terms of this discursive system (along with their specific Lacanian notations) are as follows:

> the signifier as such (S_1),
> the signifying chain (S_2),
> the subject in its division ($\mathcal{S}$),
> the object of desire (a).

Each unit is defined by its relations to two others:

I will gloss these terms very impressionistically as follows: the "signifier" is the source of meaning; it is what, inside us, seems to be the absent center of reference—the basic private experience, the most charged private word or thing. Yet the signifier is not a reified object that one contemplates for its own sake; its power derives from its capacity and function to organize syntax, the signifying chain, signification for us (this is the sense in which Lacan describes the phallus as the "signifier of desire"). The signifier is thus rarely in that sense identified with a person, whether our self or another; yet, when that does happen, the person in question becomes, as we will see shortly, invested with a strange prestige, that evoked by the word "master" (taken in both its Hegelian and its pedagogical senses).

The "signifying chain," then, is that specific set of private or public meanings, that pattern or cluster of more provisional and interrelated signifiers, in which our desire is invested and which organizes the content of our psychic life in shifting and provisional (but sometimes long-term) constellations. This is, if you like, a "text," provided that the term is given the proper metaphorical extensions to such things as my daily routine (familiar and organized to the point of compulsiveness), my habitual emotional reactions (for example, immediate resignation that is then punctuated by fits of revolt or rage), or my "ideology" (now grasped as a relatively routinized system of protonarrative evaluations, as when a reaction to a particularly charged topic—taxes, say, or "big government"—then triggers a familiar mental journey across all my inner obsessions and subjects of complaint).

What is here designated as the "subject in its division" can just as well be described in the more imperfect but more familiar existential terminology of the "subject of desire," the repressed subject, the authentic source of desire that still from time to time makes its presence felt, penetrating consciousness in the form of a throb or impulse of a nature unmistakably different from our customary velleities. The term "division," however, is meant to remind us that this deep, unconscious, authentic "subject" exists only in repressed form and is the structural consequence of primal repression (speech, consciousness), without which it would cease to offer the mirage of some "true" desire or true being; this is to say, of course, that it can never be recovered as such and is a most unreliable space for nostalgia or instinctual Utopianism.

As for the final term, the "object of desire" itself (or lower case *a*), it can of course not be specified, since it is in perpetual modification and substitution for all of us at all times. This is perhaps the moment to say something, however, about the practical wisdom of Lacanianism—whose dead letter, like all forms of practical wisdom, may seem relatively banal—and also about the relationship of Lacanian ethics to the more familiar Socratic kind. Neurotics, Lacan has often said, are people who imagine that happiness exists (but that only other people have it). The formula obviously dramatizes what we have called the tragic character of Lacan's thought, which, closely related to Freudian stoicism, sees the "problem" of desire as being structurally unresolvable, as being forever a problem and an "existential" dilemma in its very nature. There is therefore in such a scheme of things nothing like a "cure" in its pop-psychological sense. What replaces it is a specifically Lacanian version of the "know thyself" that turns precisely on the matter of lower case *a*, or the object of desire, and that is often conventionally expressed by the Lacanians in the form of a question to which there is no correct answer, namely, *Où en es-tu par rapport à ton désir?* (Where do you stand with respect to your desire?) The momentary self-consciousness or "authentic" consciousness such a question seeks to probe or therapeutically awaken demands the coordination between two kinds of "self-knowledge": what my desire—my "object" *a*—is right now; and how—also right now—I mean to handle it, what I am in the process of doing with it, what position on it I can see myself adopting (resignation, active appropriation, contemplation, repression, and so forth). Even the first of these forms of self-knowledge makes the greatest demands on most of us, who most of the time are never really clear what our desire does happen to be; and we recall, in this context, Lacan's interpretation of the origins of psychoanalysis as a historical confrontation with hysteria as such, which he describes as a "desire to desire," a state in which desire—and desiring—has itself become a problem and is no longer "natural." As for the second kind of self-consciousness measured by the Lacanian question, it should be understood that it does not call for action, but it seeks to reveal or deconceal the practical distance that we already entertain to our object of desire, which is somehow already implicit in the desire itself. Indeed, no "practical" recommendations at all are implied by this ethics, which is an "existential" one in the sense that it deliberately abandons the subject before the void of the choice itself. Nonetheless, these remarks about the status of the object of desire in Lacan will help us evaluate his conception of the four discourses, whose able résumé by Mitchell and Rose follows:

> What matters is the primacy or subordination given by each form of discourse to the subject in its relation to desire. Permutation of the four basic units produces four discourses as follows:

1/ the discourse of the master:

$$\frac{S_1}{\$} \rightarrow \frac{S_2}{a}$$

tyranny of the all-knowing and exclusion of fantasy; primacy to the signifier (S_1), retreat of subjectivity beneath its bar $(\$)$, producing its knowledge as object (S_2), which stands over and against the lost object of desire (a).

2/ discourse of the university:

$$\frac{S_2}{S_1} \rightarrow \frac{a}{\$}$$

knowledge in the place of the master; primacy to discourse itself constituted as knowledge (S_2), over the signifier as such (S_1), producing knowledge as the ultimate object of desire (a), over and against any question of the subject $(\$)$.

3/ discourse of the hysteric:

$$\frac{\$}{a} \rightarrow \frac{S_1}{S_2}$$

the question of subjectivity; primacy to the division of the subject $(\$)$, over his or her fantasy (a), producing the symptom in the place of knowledge (S_1), related to but divided from the signifying chain which supports it (S_2).

4/ discourse of the analyst:

$$\frac{a}{S_2} \rightarrow \frac{\$}{S_1}$$

the question of desire; primacy to the object of desire (a), over and against knowledge as such (S_2), producing the subject in its division

(S) ($a \longrightarrow S$ as the very structure of fantasy), over the signifier through which it is constituted and from which it is divided (S_1).[73]

These positions seem to me to have interesting equivalents in that other "unity-of-theory-and-practice" which is Marxism. The recognition involved in the "discourse of the master" is there, of course, that of charismatic authority, and of the historical originality and foundational innovations of key individuals, from Marx himself and Lenin, to Mao Tse-tung and Fidel Castro. Lacan's scheme makes it clear that this veneration of a freshness of conceptuality and of the authority of the word, or even of prophecy, is to be sharply distinguished from the "discourse of the university"—or, in other words, the authority of the letter, texts, doctrine; the scholastic weighing and comparing of juridical formulas; the concern with coherency and system; and the punctilious textual distinction between what is orthodox and what is not.

Still, these are familiar distinctions. What is more interesting is the second set of positions, in which rather different relationships to desire become identified. The "discourse of the hysteric," for example, as it is described here, seems to me to correspond to a commitment to existential authenticity, to the obedience of Hegel's "law of the heart," and to a repudiation of the letter for the "spirit" when the latter can be identified within us as true meaning and as what we instinctively "know" and recognize. In politics, this stance often

THE WORD
prophecy
speaking
annunciation

THE TEXT
the letter
writing
knowledge

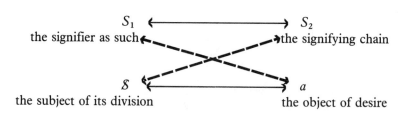

S_1 ←→ S_2
the signifier as such   the signifying chain

S ←→ a
the subject of its division   the object of desire

MEANING
desire,
the spirit,
"lived experience,"
    the existential
    reading/understanding

ANALYSIS
listening

corresponds to essentially anarchist positions and to what Lenin uncharitably called "infantile leftism," a revolutionary but also existential purism, in which political acts must also—im-mediately—constitute political expressions, the expressions of the passions of indignation and justice, which can only be sullied and obscured, and rendered inauthentic and reified, by translation into the instrumental thinking of strategies and tactics.

The "discourse of the analyst," finally, is the subject position that our current political languages seem least qualified to articulate. Like the "discourse of the hysteric," this position also involves an absolute commitment to desire as such at the same time that it opens a certain listening distance from it and suspends the latter's existential urgencies—the illusions of conscious experience—in a fashion more dialectical than ironic. The "discourse of the analyst," then, which seeks to distinguish the nature of the object of desire itself from the passions and immediacies of the experience of desire's subject, suggests a demanding and self-effacing political equivalent in which the structure of Utopian desire itself is attended to through the chaotic rhythms of collective discourse and fantasy of all kinds (including those that pass through our own heads). This is not, unlike the discourse of the master, a position of authority (although those dutifully enumerated as masters above have always possessed extraordinary "analytic" sensitivity to the deepest currents of collective desire, which it was also their task to un-bind, to articulate, and to demystify); rather, it is a position of articulated receptivity, of deep listening (L'écoute), of some attention beyond the self or the ego, but one that may need to use those bracketed personal functions as instruments for hearing the Other's desire. The active and theoretical passivity, the rigorous and committed self-denial, of this final subject position, which acknowledges collective desire at the same moment that it tracks its spoors and traces, may well have lessons for cultural intellectuals as well as politicians and psychoanalysts.

1978

Chapter 4
Criticism in History

If Marxism is a system among others, if Marxist literary criticism is a literary *method* among others, then it ought to be possible to spell it out in a relatively straightforward way, or so the objection runs, without that complicated dialectical apparatus, derived as much from Hegel as from Marx, that seems to make such presentations into tortuous affairs of reflexivity and auto-reference at every step of the way. Can we not simply talk about class and history, about ideology, and about the function of a given literary work in a given situation, with a polemic honesty that dispenses with the philosophical refinements? What about Brecht's and Benjamin's defense of *plumpes Denken*—crude thinking? Surely, as all real Marxists know, there is something intolerable about the use of the accusation of "vulgar Marxism" to frighten us away from the real issues and to encourage a kind of intellectual discourse more respectable and more acceptable in the university.

I think that the problem lies in this, that we are always *in situation* with respect to class and ideology and cultural history, that we are never able to be mere blank slates, and that truth can never exist as a static system, but always has to be part of a more general process of *demystification*. This, in its simplest form, is the justification and the essence of the dialectical method; and the proof is that even *plumpes Denken* takes its value from the intellectual positions that it corrects—the overcomplicated Hegelianism or philosophic Marxism for which it substitutes some hard truths and plain language. So *plumpes Denken* is not a position in its own right either, but the demystification of some prior position from which it derives its acquired momentum and of which it comes as a genuinely Hegelian *Aufhebung,* or cancellation/transcendence.

This is why it seems to me at least as important to come to terms with the various critical methods practiced today as to outline the method of the future. Not only is there the evident fact that most of us have been formed in one or the other of those older "methods"; there is the far more basic presupposition that the Marxist point of view is secretly present in all those methods—if only as the reality that is repressed, or covertly opposed, the consciousness that is threatening and that the *mauvaise foi* of critical formalism then projects out of itself as its converse or its nightmare. So we do not have to be defensive about a Marxist literary criticism; that is more properly the stance of those who want to flee history. Nor do we need to suggest that Marxism is an *alternative* to those methods; rather, it is to be seen as their completion, and as the only method that can really finish what it is they all in their various ways set out to do.

Our hypothesis is, then, that all apparently formal statements about a work bear within them a concealed historical dimension of which the critic is not often aware; and it follows from this that we ought to be able to transform those statements about form and aesthetic properties and the like into genuinely historical ones, if we could only find the right vantage point for doing so. The picture is then not one of turning away from the formalizing kinds of criticism to something else, but rather of going all the way through them so completely that we come out the other side; and that other side, for Marxists, is what is loosely known as history. Only to put it that way is to suggest all the wrong things too, and to convey the idea that it is simply a question of substituting one specialized discipline—that of the historian—for another—that of the literary critic. What I have in mind, however, is the point at which a specialized discipline is transcended toward reality itself, the point at which—and this under its own momentum, under its own inner logic—literary criticism abolishes itself as such and yields a glimpse of consciousness momentarily at one with its social ground, of what Hegel calls the "concrete."

In what follows, I would like to give a sense of this momentary contact with the real, at least insofar as it takes place in the realm of literary studies, and in so doing, to touch on some of the critical methods that have seemed the most rewarding or at least the most prevalent in recent years, and also the most self-contained and mutually exclusive. I would propose in particular to say something about stylistic analysis, about ethical criticism and myth criticism, about Freudian approaches, and about structuralism. No doubt what follows will be by way of a critique of these various methods; yet it is a critique that does not seek to dissolve their relative autonomy, or to abolish any of them as semi-independent methodologies. What I want to show is that none of these modes of interpretation are complete in themselves, and that their appearance of autonomy results from limits and boundaries arbitrarily fixed on the interpretative process. I would like to show that if you prolong any one of these methods even on its own terms, you always reemerge into the historical dimension itself, which thus comes as an implicit or explicit completion of all literary analysis or interpretation. I think in this connection of Serge Doubrovsky's striking description of the Marxist critical process, where he says, "you reach the heart of a text at the very moment you pass beyond it to its social context."[1] Such a formulation has the advantage of reminding us that the historical dimension does not come as a merely formal or academic type of completion—it reemerges with a kind of shock for the mind, as a kind of twist or a sudden propulsion of our being onto a different plane of reality. It involves what is properly a transformational process, conversion techniques, a shift in mental perspective that suddenly and powerfully enlarges our field of vision, releasing us from the limits of the various, purely literary methods, and permitting us to experience the profound historicity of their application, as indeed of all mental operations in general.

I

To begin with stylistics, it would seem that as generally practiced today, it tends to fall into two rather distinct and mutually exclusive types of investigation. In what we might call the classical or philological stylistics—that of Spitzer and Auerbach, or Jean-Pierre Richard—the various aspects of a syntax or of a style are understood as so many manifestations or externalizations of a more fundamental and indeed fictive entity—the style of Rabelais or Faulkner, the spirit of the Baroque or of European realism, the genius of place, or whatever. The other stylistics—I take David Lodge's *Language of Fiction* as a convenient example, Riffaterre would be another—deliberately limits itself to the intrinsic effects of the individual work, enumerating the linguistic traits or features characteristic of that work—the vocabulary field, the predilection for certain types of sentence structure and for certain types of verbal patterns over others—and attempts to show how each of these features, or the totality of them, contributes to the construction of the unique effect on the reader that is the aesthetic end or aim of the individual work in question. The distinction between these two antagonistic methods may become clearer if we characterize the second one as essentially a rhetorical analysis—dealing not with a corpus or a period but rather with the properties of discourse in general and of a single verbal object in particular—whereas the first is more properly *stylistic* in its emphasis on the uniquely personal, in the etymological sense of the *stilus*, the inimitable and well-nigh physiological specificity of my own handwriting. How to choose between these two methods, the one idealistic and speculative, the other empirical and analytic?

I would prefer to suggest that each in its own way corresponds to a different view of language and thereby to a distinct historical mode of the latter's development. Rhetoric is an older and essentially precapitalist mode of linguistic organization; it is a collective or class phenomenon in that it serves as a means of assimilating the speech of individuals to some suprapersonal oratorical paradigm, to some non- or preindividualistic standard of *beau parler*, of high style and fine writing. A profound social value is here invested in spoken language, one that may be gauged by the primacy of such aristocratic forms as the sermon and the verse tragedy, the salon witticism and the poetic epistle.

Style, on the other hand is a middle-class phenomenon and reflects the increasing atomization of middle-class life and the sapping of the collective vitality of language itself, as the older collective and precapitalist social groupings are gradually undermined and dissolved. Style thus emerges, not from the social life of the group, but from the silence of the isolated individual: hence its rigorously personal, quasi-physical or physiological content, the very materiality of its verbal components.

We may put all this the other way around by reformulating it in terms of the literary public. Rhetoric would then reflect the existence of that relatively homogeneous public or class to which the speaker addresses himself/herself and may be detected by the predilection for standardized formulas and fixed forms and by the continuing influence of the oratorical tradition as codified in classical antiquity. Style is, on the contrary, always an individual and problematical solution to the dilemma of the absence of a public and emerges against the background of that host of private languages into which the substance of the modern work has been shattered.

Such a distinction now permits us a more genuinely historical evaluation of the results achieved by both of the two stylistic or rhetorical methods I have been describing. It also permits us to understand such things as the relative disparity between the English and the French traditions of the novel (and incidentally between the types of literary criticism to which each has given rise). For if the English novel is modernized at a far later date than the French—around 1900, say—this is surely to be accounted for by the vitality of the rhetorical strain in it. The English novel, all the way to Conrad and Ford and beyond, is irrepressibly spoken—elegant or chatty, Ciceronian or intimate—in a way that has no equivalent in the French tradition after the great letter novels, or at least after the death of Balzac. Such narratives (I mean the English) have their readership vividly built into them, and one cannot read them without at once visualizing the drawing rooms and Victorian furniture in which they find their natural setting. The great English novels of the eighteenth and nineteenth centuries are thus forms of direct and quasi-immediate social communication and embody an aesthetic essentially oral in character: hence the linguistic priorities in them, which are those of the spoken rather than written composition, and whose sentences are not conceived as precious objects to be fashioned one by one, but rather emerge and disappear with all the permanent provisionality of spoken communication—telling, digressing, repeating, exclaiming, rambling, and apostrophizing. This is to say that in the English tradition the individual prose sentence and the individual prose paragraph have not yet become dominant literary and stylistic categories in their own right: the spoken period, albeit on a familiar and intimate level, here clearly outweighs the later structures of a more modernistic aesthetic of the art sentence and of the visual text. The rhetorical dimension of the English novel thus only too clearly reflects the British class compromise, in which the older feudal aristocracy is able to maintain its control of the apparatus of the state to the very middle of the First World War by granting privileges to the bourgeoisie at the same time that it appropriates for itself the techniques of the latter's commercial and productive activity.

In France, however, rhetoric in the novel is at one stroke abolished in 1857 with the publication of *Madame Bovary.* Henceforth the novel is no longer the written prospectus of some essentially natural and quasi-oral storytelling, but rather the pretext for the forging of individual sentences, for the practice of style as such. And what was hitherto a cultural institution—the storytelling situation itself, with its narrator and class public—now fades into the silence and the solitude of the individual writer, confronted with the absence of a reading public as with some form of the absence of God. For in the development of France, which has so often seemed paradigmatic of modern political and class history in general, the July revolution of 1830 signals the definitive retirement of the aristocracy from the realm of governmental control, whereas the June massacre of 1848 confirms henceforth permanent antagonism between bourgeoisie and proletariat. After 1848 in France, therefore, the primacy of the middle classes announces the beginning of that process of social atomization and monadization of which the modern literary language—stylistic rather than rhetorical, profoundly subjectivistic rather than collective—is one ideological reflex among others. Under such circumstances, clearly enough, there can be no stylistic analysis that is not ultimately political or historical in character.

II

If we turn now to what may be called ethical or moral criticism, the Marxist position may well seem paradoxical, if not scandalous, to those trained in some Arnoldian tradition and for whom it goes without saying that literature is always an ethical force and always takes as its subject, or has as its content, ethical choices. And, of course, if everything is a matter of ethics, then clearly enough so is literature. But the proposition that in our time politics and political questions have superseded ethical or moral ones implies a complete transformation of the status of the individual in society: it suggests that we would do better to limit the notion of ethical choices and ethical acts to those situations alone in which individuals face each other as conscious and responsible moral or rational agents, or in which such an autonomous individual or subject confronts his or her own self or personal development. To put it this way is to realize that in the modern world, and therefore in modern literature as well, there are many experiences and situations that are far more complex than this, where an individual or a character is faced not with an interpersonal relationship, with an ethical choice, but rather with a relationship to some determining force vaster than the self or any individual, that is, with society itself, or with politics and the movement of history; and there are other situations in which that individual confronts the influence of forces and instincts within the former "self" that cannot be assimilated to consciousness in the older sense of autonomous reason. In both these cases, we have left ethical content and ethical criticism behind for a literature and a criticism of a more political or psychological cast, and it follows that a literature for which ethics or moral choices are the principal subject matter will require a fairly stable class context for its development—you cannot explore sophisticated questions of interpersonal relationships in the midst of social upheaval or extreme psychic disintegration.

Thus the very project of an ethical literature is itself socially and historically symptomatic. To take an illustrious example of what no one doubts to be a work with ethical content, George Eliot's *Middlemarch*, we may briefly summarize that content under the form of a double lesson. *Middlemarch* teaches us, on the one hand, that as isolated as our individual lives are from each other, they nonetheless continue to exert a mysterious subterranean influence on each other of which we ourselves are scarcely aware. The network of such influences—George Eliot calls it a "stealthy convergence of human lots"—constitutes the very body and reality of the social fabric, hidden except in moments of unusual vision from our everyday awareness.

> Dorothea's full nature, like that river of which Cyrus broke the strength, spent itself in channels which had no great name on the earth. But the effect of her being on those around her was incalculably diffusive: for the growing good of the world is partly dependent on unhistoric acts; and that things are not so ill with you and me as they might have been, is half owing to the number who lived faithfully a hidden life, and rest in unvisited tombs.[2]

The other lesson of *Middlemarch* has to do with the reliability of consciousness itself and with the profound difference there is between ideas, concepts, and values that we understand in a purely intellectualized way and those somehow concretely realized for us in our life experience. Only think, in this connection, of the comical disparity between Mr. Casaubon's universal key to mythology, with its hypothesis of an unbroken tradition from the earliest generations to our own time, and his shattering discovery of the imminence of his own death; think of Dorothea's initial vapid pietism and of her later, painfully won understanding of the realities to which those doctrines correspond. Here the novel triumphantly reassumes its function as a demystification of consciousness and as the guardian and the purifier of genuine ethical content.

From a historical point of view, however, such content is to be received with a certain methodological suspicion; or rather, like the interpretation of statutes and ordinances in the legal superstructure, it is first and foremost to be understood negatively. Just as you do not legislate against things nobody does, just as the existence of a given taboo at a certain period in history tends to suggest the prevalence of the crimes against which it is directed, so also no one needs to teach what everybody knows; and ethical doctrines are in this sense to be understood as symptoms of a social situation that calls out for the supplement or the corrective of the doctrine in question. So George Eliot's novelistic construction of a community or a *Gemeinschaft,* her doctrine of the secret interweaving of human existences, stands itself as a symptom of the increasing disintegration of community, of the increasing difficulty her contemporaries have in feeling and experiencing their society as an organic totality. This—rather than the overt political, or I should say antipolitical, attitudes expressed in the book—is the most basic way in which it reflects the realities of its social context.

As for the second major theme of the work, or what we might call the existential dimension of George Eliot, it expresses that distrust of the abstract to be found everywhere in modern middle-class culture, growing more and more pronounced in the present century, and of which existentialism is itself one of the more striking manifestations. Such distrust—a kind of philosophical anti-intellectualism, a growing conviction of the gap between words and real meaning or real experience—arises from the increasing autonomy of culture in the middle-class world. It reflects the disintegration of the older codified social wisdom; a proliferation of private languages and private philosophies that is itself but the reflection of the increasing automization of private existence; the alienation of language by commercial uses and the commercial media; in short, the division of labor and the structural mystification of the middle classes about their own social reality, a mystification more complex and of a far greater intensity than that obtaining in any previous kind of society. George Eliot's novel, as language, is obliged to work its way back up the current of a debased speech in order to find some original and unsullied content; yet, not that content, but rather the process of linguistic reinvention itself yields the surest clue to the concrete historical reality in question. So we cannot even understand *Middlemarch* in the fullest way without replacing its ethical concerns in their historical situation, without seeing them as a response to an essentially social dilemma, without indeed translating them into political terms of which George Eliot was not always herself aware; and the ethical categories—which are semiautonomous to the degree to which George Eliot herself considered them ultimates or absolutes, a semiautonomy of moral philosophy and religious problematics that has its source in the English situation, and of which a sociological analysis could be made in its own right—are least of all the final terms of our literary comprehension.

III

With myth criticism it is much the same, except that the myth critic is the prisoner, not of some concrete historical class or in-group situation, as rather of a Utopian vision of his own devising. For myth is the imaginative consciousness of primitive social life, of the archaic or neolithic *Gemeinschaft;* it is a preindividualistic storytelling that seals the unity of the tribe, confirms their common past through the celebration of the heroic founders of culture itself, and unites their individual minds through a shared symbolism and a shared ritual (Durkheim's description of religion). If, therefore, in the modern world we find or seem to find mythic patterns in our literature, this is surely not because the novelist in question has been able once again to tap archaic sources of the imagination or of the collective unconscious, but only because he has experienced the nostalgia for such sources and such origins. Northrop Frye knows this very well, as his insistence on the translation or degradation of myth into literature shows:

> The structural principles of a mythology, built up from analogy and identity, become in due course the structural principles of literature. The absorption of the natural cycle into mythology provides myth with two of these structures; the rising movement that we find in myths of spring or the dawn, of birth, marriage and resurrection, and the falling movement in myths of death, metamorphosis, or sacrifice. These movements reappear as the structural principles of comedy and tragedy in literature.[3]

Or again:

> Total literary history moves from the primitive to the sophisticated, and here we glimpse the possibility of seeing literature as a complication of a relatively restricted and simple group of formulas that can be studied in primitive culture. If so, then the search for archetypes is a kind of literary anthropology, concerned with the way that literature is informed by pre-literary categories such as ritual, myth and folk tale.[4]

What we do not find in Frye, however, any more than we find it in Lévi-Strauss, is some genuinely historical account of how history itself began, how the cold societies were transformed into hot societies, how the mythic storytelling of neolithic life gave way to the literature of the more complex social forms. (As for Frye's own recent statements about art and society, I would have to characterize them as making room for the *social* function of literature at the expense of its *historical* function. In Ricoeur's terminology, Frye offers us a positive hermeneutic not unlike that of Ernst Bloch, one that stresses the origins of art in the deepest and most primal longings of the collectivity. He does not betray, however, the slightest awareness that hermeneutic can serve another, equally vital but negative, purpose, namely that of demystification–what Ricoeur calls the hermeneutic of suspicion, that of the critique of ideology and of false consciousness. Yet it is precisely that negative hermeneutic that takes as its object historical individuals, and that is alone capable of dealing with and correcting the distortions of the Utopian wish as the latter emerges into the repressive structure of a given concrete situation in history itself.)

Still, I do not mean by this to recommend that we jettison myth criticism, only that we invert its priorities. After all, in such works as those of Bakhtin[5] we find something like a myth criticism whose sound has been turned back on, a myth criticism willing to account historically and socially for its own content and to defend the position that the forms that come out of the older collectivities, the literature of festival and of the saturnalian celebration of a whole community, have precisely the value *for us today* of standing in accusation of our own social life, of constituting a condemnation of the market system as such from which, henceforth, all genuine popular elements have disappeared. So where Frye tries to mystify us and, implying mythic elements still at work in our own society, uses his doctrine of the literary archetypes to reinforce our sense of the Identity between the literary present and this distant mythical past, and to inspire some sense of the continuity between our psyches and those of tribal peoples, it seems to me equally feasible, and more realistic, to do the reverse, and to use the raw material shared by both myth and literature to stimulate our sense of historical Difference and to help us to an increasingly vivid apprehension of what happens when plot falls into history, so to speak, and enters the force field of modern societies. So what myth criticism ought to be telling us is not that modern writers recreate myths, but rather that they wish they could; and it ought to be explaining the origins of such a compensatory wish in the very structure of modern social life itself.

IV

We must, however, sharply distinguish this kind of archetypal or Jungian or religious myth criticism from the Freudian variety, which has a very different intent and very different implications. Genuine Freudianism is, like Marxism, a materialism, which is to say that it cannot really be assimilated to the ideal coherence and consistency of a purely philosophical system. It stresses, on the contrary, the contingency and lack of autonomy of consciousness, the scandalous and irrevocable dependency of the mind on something that is irreconcilable with the latter's sense of order and meaning—in the occurrence, on human sexuality itself. It would no doubt be a mistake to speak of a Freudian criticism, as though there were only one, or worse yet, as though there existed a single authentic or fully accredited, orthodox variety. Just as Freud himself throughout his career evolved a series of distinct models or hypotheses about the psyche, models not always reintegrated into some definitive synthesis, so a literary criticism inspired by Freud's discoveries finds itself confronted with a very rich series of themes, around any one of which a distinctive interpretative practice might be organized. What I would like to suggest is that most of the methods thus inspired tend to result in literary interpretations that are essentially allegorical, the most representative being no doubt one that sees the various elements of the work as figures for the parts of the psyche—for the id, the ego, and the superego. To say so, however, may appear at first glance to damn Freudian interpretation by association and to burden it with the ignominy that has for so long clung to allegorical interpretation in general, as a kind of artificial refraction of the organic unity of a work into lifeless parts and mechanical personifications.

If, however, you regard allegory in general, and Freudian allegory in particular, as a cultural and historical symptom rather than as one intellectual option among others, this is perhaps no longer quite the case. We may recall, in this context, Adorno's recommendation that we understand the Freudian psychic model as a new *event* rather than a new *theory;* that we understand the Freudian system as a sign of profound new changes and restructurations taking place in Western consciousness in general. So, no doubt, for Freud himself, the Oedipus complex is a constant throughout history, along with the superego and the id, along with repression and sublimation; but in the present context it seems more useful, or at least more interesting, to understand the Freudian vision of the psyche as being itself a reflection of the historic moment when the older autonomous rational consciousness begins to disintegrate, when the subject can no longer be felt as an autonomous and intelligible whole in its own right, can no longer be seen as the responsible agent posited by ethical criticism, but rather begins to project an Other out of itself, and to feel itself surrounded by the dark and inaccessible, yet ultimately determinate, realm of the unconscious. The Freudian psychic model is thus a kind of allegory of the mind, in which consciousness suddenly understands itself in relationship to other hidden absent zones of energy. Such a discovery is tantamount to the realization by consciousness that it is not a complete thing in itself, not really autonomous, not wholly in control or wholly intelligible in its own terms; but this discovery is just as surely a social event as it is a scientific hypothesis.

Seen in this light, the works that call out for Freudian interpretation reflect through their allegorical structure some fundamental dispersal of the lived experience of consciousness, some fundamental disintegration of the psyche. Such works foretell the end of the age of individualism, and nothing is quite so comparable to the medieval practice of allegory in, say, *Le Roman de la rose*, as the great surrealist film of Buñuel and Dali, *An Andalusian Dog*, with its multiple levels, its looping temporal sequences and its use of doubles of the hero to represent the superego and the id. *Un chien andalou* shares with the poem of Guillaume de Lorris the conviction that to give a complete picture of the story of love—the central theme of both works—requires us to transcend the subjective point of view of the individual lover, and indeed point of view in general as a literary category, and to present materials—in the one case cultural, in the other psychic—that are largely inaccessible to the lover's own limited consciousness. Yet in spite of the peculiar stylization of such works, in spite of their depersonalized and well-nigh inhuman surface, they represent an attempt to construct a new and intelligible totality upon the ruins of the older individualistic one; they reflect psychic disintegration, to be sure, but at the same time they mark an effort at overcoming that state by the very fact of making it present to us as a complete process.

Freudian interpretation thus designates a fragmentation, but also a reunification of existence. In a situation in which consciousness is now but a minimal zone of our being, and a doubtful one, whose introspection and whose self-knowledge is no longer trustworthy, the Freudian schemes come as larger coordinates within which we may relocate the data of consciousness and correct their distortions. Allegorical criticism of this kind thus corresponds to the structure of a postindividualistic world, one in which neither the older unity of the *Gemeinschaft* nor the newer unity of the autonomous and individualistic bourgeois subject is available.

At the same time such allegory has a political dimension of a far more specific import than the symptomatic character of its form. If indeed we remember the frequency with which, in Freud, the psyche is compared to a city or to a government, it will not be terribly surprising to find that all Freudian interpretation is in its very structure susceptible to expression in political terms, amounting, thus, to a political, as well as a psychic, allegory. Thus Buñuel's "passionate appeal to murder" is also an explosive document of modern anarchism and finds its explicit political expression in his next movie, *L'Age d'or*. Or, to take another familiar illustration, Thomas Mann's *Death in Venice* is the story of the return of the repressed, the destruction of the psyche by its own rigid mechanisms of censorship, but it is also a prophetic allegory of the internal collapse of the authoritarian Prussian state, in that respect far closer to *Der Untertan* or *The Blue Angel* than, say, to Kafka or Hofmannsthal. So it is that the allegories revealed by the Freudian method prove to harbor a very explicit political content in their structures themselves at the same time that by their existence as forms they stand as signs of the crippling effects of monopoly capitalism on the consciousness of modern man.

V

When we turn, finally to structuralism, we may find it equally difficult to isolate some official structural literary method. In actual practice, the literary criticism to which structuralism has given rise tends to fall into two relatively distinct groups. On the one hand, there is what we might call the apolitical branch, or right wing, of the structuralist movement, which through complicated descriptive analyses of individual forms aims at the construction of a grammar and a taxonomy of narrative or plot structures using surface oppositions or deeper quasi-syntactic structures to establish the essential movement of the narrative from contract broken to contract reestablished, from object lost to object restored, from contradiction through mediation to final synthesis.

On the other side of the political spectrum, we find a whole body of work—particularly centering around the literary review *Tel Quel*—that aims at making explicitly political correlations between the forms of discourse—the internal mechanisms of a text, the relative dosage of written and spoken, the reification or process-oriented character of a given style and attitude toward language—the forms of bourgeois or revolutionary consciousness.

Yet it should be understood that in reality both these kinds of research are post-Marxist and that even the relatively formalistic kinds of structuralism tend to imply correlations between literary and extraliterary structures. Our task here is thus a little more complicated than it was with respect to the other methods we have touched on; for it is here a question, not so much of revealing some historical dimension implicit or concealed in the method, as rather of passing judgment on sociological conclusions already suggested by the critics themselves.

The vices of structural method, however, are not terribly difficult to localize: they arise almost exclusively from strategic and self-imposed methodological limits on the type of statements to be made, from a purely empirical attitude toward the individual text under study, and from a refusal, after the completion of the analytical procedure, to turn the attention back upon the structural method and categories themselves as part of the larger object of study. So what is at issue is not the technique of structural analysis as such: such techniques have permitted us to isolate the finest mechanisms of plot and narrative with something of that same microscopic precision that the

New Criticism taught us to bring to bear on the verbal texture of poetry. What is at issue is rather the nature of the conclusions to be drawn from such research.

To illustrate this with a well-known and widely reprinted essay by Jacques Ehrmann, "The Structures of Exchange in Corneille's *Cinna*,"[6] no one can fail to be both impressed and convinced, I think, by the patterns there shown to be present in the very language of tragedy—patterns of giving and taking, receiving, buying and selling, pillage, heaping high with gifts or, on the contrary, the struggle to obtain a just recompense—such are some of the ways in which Corneille and his characters see the consequences of an act. It is clear that for them acts take place within a complex exchange system in which every move commits your interlocutor to some reciprocal—immediate or mediated—obligation in return. With such an analysis, Ehrmann is of course in the very mainstream of the structuralist tradition, for his model derives from Marcel Mauss' *Essay on the Gift,* an essay whose seminal insights were adapted by Lévi-Strauss to the marriage rules that govern the exchange of women in primitive societies in his study *The Elementary Structures of Kinship,* which may be said to amount to the first great monument of structuralism as an intellectual and philosophical movement.

What conclusions does Ehrmann go on to draw from the existence of these exchange patterns in the work of Corneille? It is only fair to observe that he refuses to be drawn beyond the limits of a purely literary study of a single isolated text. "A critic who enlarged his investigation to include all the works, or the major works, of an era," he tells us, "would see his goal metamorphosed. At that point, with the goal changed, the nature of his study would change. Instead of being literary, it would be either sociological or anthropological. The question is then raised of knowing at what moment the analysis of literary structures ceases to isolate the esthetic or literary aspects of an object and moves on to isolate its anthropological and sociological aspects."[7]

Unfortunately it is not quite so simple as all that, and the anthropological and sociological dimensions of which Ehrmann speaks are already included in his analysis in potential form in the very concept of exchange itself. A category like exchange comes to literary and structural analysis from the fields of anthropology, sociology, and economics and is thus already profoundly comparative in nature. So at that point it does not really matter very much whether the analyst himself refuses, as does Ehrmann here, to take the final step and to assimilate the verbal structures of *Cinna* to those deeper socioeconomic ones—Mauss' potlatch, or the mechanisms of feudal hierarchy, or the market system of nascent capitalism—that are already latent in the concept of exchange itself. Such assimilation is already implicit in the analysis, and this seems to me indeed the fundamental contradiction of the structural method as such: the comparative nature of its conceptual instruments forces the reader to draw generalizing conclusions that can never be corroborated by the isolated object of a purely empirical type of study.

Even those conclusions, however, are historical in appearance only, for structural theory goes on to assimilate all these varied social forms—potlatch, feudal hierarchy, market system—to some more abstract linguistic or communicational relationship. And with this further development, we find ourselves in a wholly ahistorical realm for which categories such as exchange are seen as a priori and universal categories of the human mind and of human society in general.

Still, it is only fair to point out that particularly in the most theoretically sophisticated specimens of structural plot analysis, those of Lévi-Strauss himself, we are offered a somewhat different model of the relationship of literary to extraliterary structures. For Lévi-Strauss, not content to isolate and describe the structures of a narrative, goes on to ask the *function* of such a narrative in the life of the tribe. It then emerges that primitive narrative or myth is yet another form of primitive thinking—*pensée sauvage*, or preconscious reasoning; the narrative is an attempt to reconcile irreconcilable contraries, to solve, through a kind of picture language, like a rebus or a dream, the conceptual antinomies or concrete contradictions that haunt the social life of the primitive commune.[8] Thus narrative becomes once again an act—an act through which tribal people attempt, in the imaginary, to come to grips with their social context and to resolve its most crucial problems. So at length we glimpse a kind of literary analysis that, without even abandoning the purely formal specificity of the work of art itself, may immediately be reformulated in terms of an event in history; a kind of analysis for which the intrinsic and purely formal structures of the work are at one and the same time invested with all the value of a protopolitical act.

VI

Such are then some of the ways in which literary analysis touches the ultimate ground of history itself. And perhaps it will have come to seem that in all this I have been systematically delivering literary criticism over into the hands of the historians and subsuming literary study a little too hastily beneath the more all-embracing discipline of history itself. Yet the history I have in mind is not at all to be confused with the common garden-variety empirical history. To use an offensive but convenient phrase, it is indeed not "bourgeois historiography" at all, for the latter is not a genuine philosophy of history and does not posit a unified overall meaning to the stages of social development. It will be objected, no doubt, that the very notion of a philosophy of history has been discredited and that the concept of a meaning in history as a whole has been shown to be the solution to a false problem. "Nietzsche" is the signature for this new and widespread philosophical position, which may also be taken as an existential symptom of the extinction of historicity, and of a lived sense of the past and tradition, peculiar to our own social formation. The Marxist "philosophy of history," however, needs to be sharply distinguished from its traditional predecessors at least to the degree that it stresses breaks and radical discontinuities in history, what I have called historical Difference, fully as much as the continuities and Identities of the older "master narratives." Just as Marxism is both the end and the fulfillment of philosophy in general, so in much the same way it may be said to be both the end and the fulfillment of philosophies of history, and to demonstrate how the scattered and disparate events of history share common themes and common dilemmas, which link the toil and misery of Neolithic peoples to the most dramatic, as well as the most obscure, struggles of our own age.

A few years ago, it might have been necessary at this point to defend the Marxist vision of history, if not, indeed, to remind people what it was in the first place. Today I doubt if that is any longer really the case. In the past few years, we have witnessed the intellectual and political collapse of that liberal world view that for so long served as an explanation as well as a justification of our economic development and of the aims of our foreign policy. I doubt if there are very many people left today who still believe either in the promise of the older American liberalism or in the theoretical accounts it used to give of the organization of American life. Now that we have come to understand counterinsurgency warfare and neocolonialism, not as freely chosen options of good or evil political leaders, but rather as deeper and more ominous structural necessities of the American system; now that we have been able to observe what is left of the American way of life bombarded and pulverized by the twin corrosive forces of racism and commercialism and indeed to witness the beginnings of the deterioration of the American economic system as a whole; now that we have learned the facts about American responsibility for the beginnings of the Cold War, let alone more recent conflicts—Marxism has once again seemed to many to provide the only intellectually coherent and fully satisfying historical and economic explanation for the things that have been happening to us. It is a totalizing explanation, and this is its formal superiority over all the other partial kinds of accounts—the culture critiques and existential diagnoses, the psychological analyses and the liberal and reformist appeals to the ethics—which use the amount of validity they do contain to obscure the sources of all those cultural sicknesses in the very economic structure of capitalism itself.

Still, to commit ourselves to a Marxist theory of history is not necessarily to identify the historical themes in terms of which our ultimate interpretation will be made. You will have observed, in particular, the use in the present essay of an interpretative code based on Tönnies' classic concept of the difference between *Gemeinschaft* and *Gesellschaft*, between the older organic societies and those fragmented and atomistic social agglomerations with which we are familiar in the modern world, with their profound subjectivization and their monadization of individual experience. Such an opposition is already implicit in Hegel and is quite consistent with socialist thought, but unfortunately it is just as consistent with conservative or fascist thought as well, which brandishes a return to the older national or racial *Gemeinschaft*. The trouble with this particular theme as an ultimate description of social reality is that it amounts to a description of that reality from the point of view of the bourgeoisie alone, since it is in the forms of bourgeois life that such social disintegration is taking place. Yet the opposition between *Gemeinschaft* and *Gesellschaft*—one after all between two types of *society*—sometimes strikes me as being far more adequate and far less misleading than some of the psychological and existential concepts, such as that of alienation, which have come increasingly to be thought of as the principal Marxist contributions to modern sociological theory.

As far as alienation is concerned, it has always seemed to me ironic, if not downright comic, that a concept intended by the Marx of the *Economic and Philosophical Manuscripts* to apply to the way in which the labor power of working people was appropriated from them, along with their work satisfaction and the very products of their labor, should have been so enthusiastically adopted by the middle classes of the affluent society as a glamorous and pathetic way of characterizing their own subjective malaise and psychological complications.

The basic terms of any genuinely Marxist interpretation must surely remain those older and more familiar ones of commodity production and of class struggle; and if they tend to summon up specters of the worst excesses of vulgar Marxism or of Soviet dogmatism, I can only point to that brilliant series of works in which only yesterday Adorno showed the commodity form to be at the very heart of twentieth-century modernism.[9] As for the class struggle itself, its all-informing presence in our private lives as well as in the daily life of our society is the very first lesson that the Marxist textbook has to teach us, and in the absence of such an experience and such a concept there can be no Marxist theory worthy of the name.

Even granting these fundamental themes of Marxism, however, there remains the problem of the proper way of relating a literary analysis to them; and to characterize this very briefly in closing I would like to return for a moment to the essay of Jacques Ehrmann from which I quoted a moment ago. "I have said," he goes on to tell us there, "that I was not interested in looking upon literature as a form of economics. But that doesn't necessarily mean that the phenomenon of literature should be seen as unlike the phenomenon of economics. Using this perspective, it would be as much a question, with the one, of understanding the system established for the exchange of services, merchandise, and women which form the network of communications in ancient and modern collectivities, as it would be, for the other, a question of understanding the system of word and image exchange in literary and artistic communication. The latter system of exchange is, in effect, readily comparable to the former."[10]

In short, we find evoked here what Lucien Goldmann called homologies, or isomorphisms, or structural parallelisms between various types of social realities. This is indeed the principal sociological method of structuralism and the form that most structuralist versions of Marxism tend to take, involving analogies between the purely literary and verbal structures of the work and the various spheres of the legal system, the political ideology, and the organization of the market obtaining in the period in question.

To return to *Cinna* in this light, we find that for Ehrmann the various events of the tragedy—the gradual elaboration of the conspiracy against the Emperor, the doubts of Cinna himself, torn between his admiration for Augustus and his love for a woman who is the latter's mortal enemy, the Emperor's ultimate gesture of clemency with which the conspiracy is unraveled and the play concluded—all amount to so many stages along a "circuit of gift-giving" that can be buckled and fulfilled only by the supreme magnanimity of Augustus' pardon itself as a kind of absolute gift, self-founding and self-motivated. The play thus constitutes for Ehrmann a kind of narrative dramatization of the structural permutations inherent in the exchange mechanism current at the time of Corneille.

That there can be another and far less static way of relating a literary form to its underlying social reality I would like to demonstrate by reference to the literary sociology of Paul Bénichou in his pathbreaking book *Les Morales du grand siècle*.[11] For Bénichou the plays of Corneille are the literary and ideological expression of the rebellious feudal nobility of the Fronde—a declining class, suffering increasingly from the centralizing absolutism, first of Richelieu and Mazarin, and then of Louis XIV, and increasingly edged out of positions of power by the parliamentary nobility (drawn from the upper bourgeoisie) as well as by the rising middle class itself. The politics of these great nobles is profoundly contradictory, for their revolt against the crown is born of a deep longing to return to the feudal license of an earlier era, but at the same time, insofar as the king is a *primus inter pares*, they cannot strike at his power without dealing a blow to their own pretensions as well and sapping the ideological bases of the feudal system as a whole. (And when, a century and a half later, the French Revolution itself began in precisely this way, as a revolt of the nobles against the king, the consequences for those who set it in motion were appropriately disastrous.) In such a situation, therefore, where no real solution is available, an imaginary one is born, a kind of ideological or political wish fulfillment, of which *Cinna* is one of the most striking manifestations. For the dilemma of the nobility could be resolved only if the monarch, maintaining his own legal authority, nonetheless in all his feudal generosity freely turned back to the nobles themselves all those privileges for which they had rebelled against him. Thus the theatrical gesture of Augustus is something more than a mere static reflection of the thought patterns of the baroque weltanschauung; it is an act charged with significance, which seems to suspend and appease for an instant all the deepest contradictions of the age. For such a point of view, Corneille's tragedy is not some mere document in the correlation between works and social classes, between forms of thought and forms of social life; it is first and foremost an event, one that can be shown to have a precise ideological function at a unique moment in history.

For me, therefore, the method of homologies, while not necessarily false in its results, is static and documentary, and derives ultimately from the history of ideas on the one hand, and from a non-Marxist sociology of literature on the other. I would call instead for a *situational* model of the relationship between a work and its social context, one capable of articulating the central paradox of a Marxist aesthetics: namely, that the force of a work of art is directly proportional to its historicity, that there is indeed no contradiction between our present-day appreciation of a work and its concrete historical content, that the greatness of Corneille is not atemporal, but springs immediately from the force with which his plays reflect the struggles of an event like the Fronde—itself apparently a mere historical curiosity for us today, the convulsion of an extinct class whose values mean nothing to us. Indeed, it will be recalled that it was precisely the Fronde that Lévi-Strauss chose as his example when, at the close of *The Savage Mind,* he undertook to discredit history itself as a mode of knowledge. He there implied that history was a matter of taking sides, and that if such a relationship, which requires a delicate assessment of progressive and reactionary positions within a given historical situation, still makes sense for events of a middle-class era in which we are still ourselves implicated, it becomes senseless when we return to an earlier period whose struggles no longer concern us. And of course the ideals of the Fronde are both progressive and reactionary: reactionary in that they serve the ideological function of enlisting the people of Paris in support of an archaic feudal aristocracy, progressive insofar as they nonetheless foreshadow a revolt against the centralization of the feudal power itself. Yet the example of Corneille shows that such contradictions have a very special way of coexisting in the literary work, and that as a desperate and vital episode in the long class struggle of human history, it is precisely not in the history books that the Fronde lives on, but rather in the very bones and marrow of literary form itself. With such a vision of the work of art, the techniques of literary criticism find their ultimate ground in historical reality, and literature may be said once again to recover for us its value as a social act.

1976

Chapter 5
Symbolic Inference; or, Kenneth Burke and Ideological Analysis

What has today for better or for worse come to be known as literary theory may be distinguished from an older, "philosophical" criticism by its emphasis on the primacy of language; and it has come to be widely, if loosely, felt that it is the discovery of the Symbolic in the most general sense that marks the great divide between thinkers and writers who belong to our world and those who speak a historical language we have first to learn. In what follows I will have much to say, at least implicitly, about this proposition, but it is certain that the older, philosophical criticism was content simply to "apply" various philosophical systems to literature in an occasional way, so that we had the curiosities of an existential or a phenomenological criticism, or a Hegelian or a gestalt or indeed a Freudian criticism available on specialized shelves for the philosophically venturesome.

It is clear, however, that in an atmosphere in which technical philosophy—no less than literature itself—is felt to be the emanation of specific powers of language; in an atmosphere in which "literary form," to gloss a famous title of Kenneth Burke's, is felt to be a philosophy in its own right, and in which language is itself theory in action; in such an atmosphere the older, philosophical criticisms are as outmoded as the older, philosophical aesthetics or "systems of the fine arts." Not only does Burke's pioneering work on the tropes mark him as the precursor of literary theory in this new, linguistics-oriented sense, his Freudo-Marxism itself is the sign of a different structural relationship to the abstractions of technical philosophy than that of many of his contemporaries; and it is a modification then supremely visible in the *Grammar* and *Rhetoric of Motives*, where the older, philosophical systems are piled in one after the other to be melted down and lose their separate identities, much as the old bourgeois selves and individualisms were boiled down and transmuted by Ibsen's Button Moulder.

Paradoxically, however, this displacement of traditional criticism and traditional philosophy by what has come to be known as theory turns out to allow the critic a wider latitude for the exercise of personal themes and the free play of private idiosyncrasies. The transcendence of the older academic specializations and the heightened appreciation of the inner logic and autonomy of language itself thus make for a situation in which the temperament of the individual critic—if the latter is not too self-indulgently aware of that fact—can serve as a revealing medium for the textual and formal phenomena to be examined. So it is that when we think of the greatest of contemporary critics and virtuoso readers—besides Burke himself the list would probably include Empson and Frye, Roland Barthes, Walter Benjamin, Viktor Shklovsky—we thereby instinctively designate bodies of criticism in which the practice of idiosyncratic and sometimes eccentric textual interpretations is at one with the projection of a powerful, nonsystematized theoretical resonance, and this even where the critic himself—Frye and Burke are the obvious examples, but also the Empson of *The Structure of Complex Words* or the Barthes of *Système de la mode*—misguidedly but compulsively submits his materials to a rage for patterns and symmetries and the mirage of the metasystem.

Yet it is not enough to say that Burke's notion of the symbolic act is an anticipation, indeed a privileged expression, of current notions of the primacy of language; seen from a different angle, it allows us to probe the insufficiencies of the latter, which is in so much of today's critical practice little more than a received idea or unexamined presupposition. Indeed, Burke's conception of the symbolic as act or praxis may equally well be said to constitute a critique of the more mindless forms of the fetishism of language, and this to the point where one of the most interesting historical issues raised by his work finds its implicit resolution: I mean the question as to why this immense critical corpus, to which lip service is customarily extended in passing, has had shamefully limited influence in literary studies (the social scientists seem to have been more alert to its implications) and is customarily saluted as a monument of personal inventiveness and ingenuity (in the sense in which I have just spoken of the idiosyncrasies of the great critics) rather than as an interpretative model to be studied and a method to be emulated.

A really full and concrete solution to this particular enigma would of course involve us in a reconsideration and a virtual rewriting of the whole history of our recent intellectual past; in particular it commits us to rectify that falsification of the literary and critical history of the 1930s and 1940s which, an ongoing legacy of McCarthyism, has in our own field never been systematically challenged, even where its sterility is widely recognized. It is to be hoped that a generation of students and scholars no longer hysterical about Stalinism will undertake the task of this fundamental historical revision, which is under way in all of the social sciences but has not even been breathed as a distant and unconfirmed rumor in the human sciences, and most particularly in literature or philosophy.

A very different Burke emerges, indeed, when we have understood that in the period in which his most important work was being elaborated, his stress on language, far from reinforcing as it does today the ideologies of the intrinsic and of the antireferential text, had on the contrary the function of restoring to the literary text its value as activity and its meaning as a gesture and a response to a determinate situation. Thus conceived, literary and cultural criticism takes its place among the social sciences, and the study of language and of aesthetic objects in general recovers something of the dignity it had for the founders of philology when their program foresaw the analysis of literary texts and monuments as a unique means of access to the understanding of social relations. It is from this perspective that I here want to reevaluate Burke's contribution.[1] More specifically, I want to determine whether his work can be reread or rewritten as a model for contemporary ideological analysis, or what in my own terminology I prefer to call the study of the ideology of form—the analysis, in other words, of the linguistic, narrative, or purely formal ways in which ideology expresses itself through and inscribes itself in the literary text.

But this displacement of the terminology of the symbolic by that of ideology will seem arbitrary unless I add a word or two about the concept of ideology it presupposes, and which is clearly construed in a much wider sense than that of sheer opinion, of those extraneous and annoying authorial interventions with which a Balzac or a Faulkner suspend their narratives and indulge some heart-felt prejudice. The view of ideology endorsed here is one that springs from and indeed completes the whole rich development of narrative analysis today. And to put it this way is already to measure something of the distance across which we mean to interrogate Burke's achievement, for it is evident that to reexamine his descriptions of symbolic action in terms of narrative analysis is fundamentally to change the terms and the givens, the coordinates, of the problem and to cut across it in a new way. The older debates, indeed, raised the issue of the status of the aesthetic within the framework of an opposition between truth and poetry, an opposition that tended to box the latter, and literary discourse in general, into categories of fiction or the fictive, the imitated, the unreal, the merely imaginary. But to defend the aesthetic on the terrain of an opposition of this kind was clearly to have surrendered everything in advance and to have resigned one's self to a sandbox conception of literature and culture and their respective efficacy.

When now we substitute the term "narrative" for "fiction," this epistemological false problem disappears, or at least goes out of focus; for it becomes clear, not only that narrative is a specific mode of conceptualizing the world, which has its own logic and which is irreducible to other types of cognition, but also that much of what passes for conceptual or scientific writing is itself secretly narrative in character. If, therefore, narrative is one of the basic categorical forms through which we apprehend realities in time and under which synchronic and analytic thinking is itself subsumed and put in perspective, we no longer have to be defensive about the role of culture and the importance of its study and analysis. From this point of view, then, Burke's apologia for literature as gesture and ritual—once an uncompromising statement of the active power and social function of the aesthetic—may no longer strike us as being uncompromising enough.

As far as the relationship of ideology and narrative is concerned, however, it may be most useful first to grasp the function of the words "ideology" and "ideological" as the bearers and the signals of a kind of Brechtian estrangement effect to be applied to the operation of literary and cultural analysis itself. To pronounce these words on the occasion of a literary interpretation or a literary or artistic form itself—as when, for instance, John Berger speaks of the "ideology of light" in certain Renaissance paintings, or when the Althusserians denounce the conception for which ideology is mere false consciousness as being itself "ideological"[2]—to use these terms in such a way is less to pass judgments than to reproblematize the entire artistic discourse or formal analysis thereby so designated. The term "ideology" stands as the sign for a problem yet to be solved, a mental operation that remains to be executed. It does not presuppose cut-and-dried sociological stereotypes like the notion of the "bourgeois" or the "petty bourgeois" but is rather a mediatory concept: that is, it is an imperative to reinvent a relationship between the linguistic or aesthetic or conceptual fact in question and its social ground. Yet this relationship is not programmed in advance, and indeed there are many strategically different ways in which such a relationship can be projected or formulated, just as, correlatively, there are many distinct ways in which the literary fact itself or, on the other hand, what I have very loosely called its "social ground" can be described and thematized. This is obviously not the place to make an inventory of such possibilities, whose range is great but which have little more in common than the repudiation of the ideology of the "intrinsic" and of the "autonomy" of the verbal artifact. It will have already become clear, however, that the usefulness of the term "ideology" lies—whatever the terms of the solution ultimately decided on—in its exacerbation of the problem, in its capacity to make the reinvention of such a relationship as unavoidable as it is philosophically demanding.

It has therefore seemed to me preferable to describe ideological analysis phenomenologically, in terms of the mental and textual operations it involves, rather than in the framework of any of the specific historical conceptions of ideology available to us. Ideological analysis may therefore be described as the rewriting of a particular narrative trait, or seme, as a function of its social, historical, or political context. Still, in the present atmosphere of theoretical sophistication, it is probably futile, if not regressive, to argue for an ideological analysis of literature in ontological terms by asserting the priority of historical or social or political reality over the literary artifacts produced within it or, in other words, by affirming the ontological priority of the context over the text itself. While such assertions still seem to me to be true and obvious, it is equally certain that we need today to respond to the widespread realization that what used to be called a context is itself little more than a text as well, one you find in history manuals or secondary sources, if not in that unexamined pop history or unconscious collective representation by which groups or classes or nations tend to organize their vision and their reading of individual events. But this does not mean that history is itself a text, only that it is inaccessible to us except in textual form, or, in other words, that we approach it only by way of its prior textualization.

This is why it has seemed more satisfactory to me to describe ideological analysis as the rewriting of the literary text in such a way that it may itself be grasped as the rewriting or restructuration of a prior ideological or historical subtext, provided it is understood that the latter—what we used to call the "context"—must always be (re)constructed after the fact, for the purposes of the analysis. The literary or aesthetic gesture thus always stands in some active relationship with the real, even where its activity has been deliberately restricted to the rather sophisticated operation of "reflecting" it. Yet in order to act on the real, the text cannot simply allow reality to persevere in its being outside of itself, inertly, at a distance; it must draw the real into its own texture. And the ultimate paradoxes and false problems of linguistics, and in particular of semantics, are to be situated here, in the way in which language and the texts of language carry the real within themselves as their own "intrinsic" subtexts. Insofar, in other words, as symbolic action—Burke will map it out as "dream," "prayer," or "chart"[3]—is a way of doing something to the world, to that degree what we are calling "world" must inhere within it, as the content it has to take up into itself in order to give it form. The symbolic act therefore begins by producing its own context in the same moment of emergence in which it steps back over against it, measuring it with an eye to its own active project. The whole paradox of what we are calling the subtext can be measured by this, that the literary work or cultural object itself, as though for the first time, brings into being that situation to which it is also at one and the same time a reaction. It articulates its own situation and textualizes it, encouraging the illusion that the very situation itself did not exist before it, that there is nothing but a text, that there never was any extra- or con-textual reality before the text itself generated it. Meanwhile, this simultaneous production and articulation of "reality" by the text is reduplicated by an active, well-nigh instrumental, stance of the text toward the new reality, the new situation, thus produced; and the latter is accompanied immediately by gestures of praxis—whether measurements, cries of rage, magical incantations, caresses, or avoidance behavior. Now to insist on either of these two dimensions of symbolic action without the other—to overemphasize the way in which the text organizes its subtext (in order, presumably, to reach the triumphant conclusion that the "referent" does not exist) or on the other hand to stress the instrumental nature of the symbolic act to the point where reality, understood no longer as a subtext but rather as some mere inert given, is once again delivered over into the hands of that untrustworthy auxiliary, Common Sense—to stress either of these functions of symbolic action at the expense of the other is surely to produce sheer ideology, whether it be, in the first alternative, the ideology of structuralism or, in the second, that of vulgar materialism.

This said, we must add that the refusal of literary semantics, of the categories of the context or the referent, and the various assertions of the autonomy of the literary text, or the timeless universality of its themes and forms, is not mere opinion either, but is itself a historical phenomenon that reflects the historic process by which in recent times literature and culture have acquired at least a *relative* autonomony. Such aesthetics of the intrinsic thus reflect the realities of artistic production under the market system itself and give expression to the free-floating portability of artistic texts in search of an impossible public, texts released from the social functionality that once controlled their meanings and uses in precapitalist social formations which have now broken down or been dissolved.

From this initial fall, however, from the unavoidable historical reality of a breach between text and context, there can only spring mechanical efforts to reconnect what is no longer an organic whole. So the forced linkages of yesterday's "interdisciplinary" experiments, in which one whole field of study—in our case, the formal or literary—is somehow wired up to other disciplines, gives way to no less unsatisfactory models, which can be best exemplified by Lucien Goldmann's "homologies," in which the structure of the literary text is somehow supposed to be "the same," at some level of abstraction, as the other related structures of economic exchange, conceptual epistēmē, class psychology, or whatever. Yet the conception of "levels," whether within the work or between the work and the extratextual systems that surround it, is unsatisfactory not merely because it projects the model of a merely additive or quantitative juxtaposition, but above all because it does not allow for an active or functional relationship between the text itself and its various conceivable subtexts; rather, its "expressive causality" folds each of these separate levels back into the other in a kind of global identity.

This is then the context, if I may put it that way, in which the power of Burke's conception of symbolic action can best be appreciated. The notion of language, of the linguistic artifact, as a verbal act is a strategy for going around behind the dilemma we have been describing, and for setting forth at a point before the fall, and positing a place of emergence that precedes the breach which so many mechanical models have proved unable to heal. *Im Anfang war die Tat:* this place of emergence is that of praxis, or, in other words, of a unity in which subject and object, thing and language, context and projected action, are still at one in the wholeness of a unique gesture. In the act—and this is as true of Sartrean praxis philosophy as of Burke's dramatism, and explains the affinities of both for a certain Marxism—not only is human intention still inseparable from its scene or situation, but language and the mental or structural categories that govern it are still at one with the raw material, the facticity, the data it is in the process of organizing. Hereby, or so it would seem, the false antitheses of an intrinsic and an extrinsic criticism are dispelled, and a new and more adequate conception of the function of literature and its criticism and history can begin to be developed; unfortunately, it is a conception not without some serious new ambiguities in its own right.

This is therefore the moment to evaluate Kenneth Burke's theory of verbal praxis and to reach some judgment as to his contribution to a theory of ideological analysis proper. The lesson I want us to learn and then to unlearn from Burke comes in two stages: the first of these is associated with the word that he, more than anyone else, added to our critical vocabulary, namely, the notion of literary "strategy"; the second inevitably centers on his fundamental theory of dramatism and of the organization of all symbolic action according to the five basic coordinates of Act, Scene, Agent, Agency, and Purpose.

In one sense, of course, the term "strategy" is itself merely shorthand for that complex of symbolic determinants in their totality; it is the term that governs their relations to each other, that names the provisional hierarchy established between them on the occasion of a given act—the dominance of Agency over Scene, or alternatively of Scene over Agent and Act, that confers to any given act, or analysis of action, its structure and its specific flavor. On the other hand, strategy precedes accomplishment and indeed action or realization itself; thus, since what we have to do with here is a theory of *symbolic* action, there is a sense in which none of the symbolic acts in question can be said to have come to its execution, in which all will have remained forever at the stage of project or sheer intention—a kind of permanently provisional hesitation on the threshold of being that the term "strategy" strategically perpetuates. One of the fundamental ambiguities of the concept of symbolic action is indeed precisely this shifting distance from nonsymbolic or practical or instrumental action itself, which sometimes it seems to want to absorb into itself on the grounds that all action is symbolic, all production is really communication, and from which at other times it seems to ebb and retreat, leaving behind it some inhospitably arid and stony ledge to which all mere practical activity in the world is summarily assigned.

I suppose that it is only since we have witnessed the immense and paradoxical good fortunes of this term "strategy" in all kinds of formalizing critical
discourse that we have thus come to sense its own inner ambiguity, to suspect
it of harboring some secret strategy in its own right. The problem is that this
concept, which so boldly proclaims itself a praxis-word, tends, by focusing
our attention on the inner mechanisms of the symbolic act in question, to end
up bracketing the act itself and to suspend any interrogation of what constitutes it as an act in the first place, namely, its social and ideological purpose. Thus Burke's great essay on the "Ode on a Grecian Urn" maps more
triumphantly than any textbook illustration of structural or semiotic analysis
the transformation systems whereby Keats' poem prepares a "transcendent
scene ... [in] which the earthly laws of contradiction no longer prevail":[4]

> the poem begins with an ambiguous fever which in the course of the
> further development is "separated out," splitting into a bodily fever
> and a spiritual counterpart. The bodily passion is the malign aspect
> of the fever, the mental action its benign aspect. In the course of the
> development, the malign passion is transcended and the benign ac-
> tive partner, the intellectual exhilaration, takes over.[5]

Such a description luminously articulates the strategy of Keats' "alchemy of
the word" and isolates its exchange mechanisms and the key moments of its
transfer of energies; yet what it takes for granted, what it "brackets" and
therefore represses from its critical discourse, is what such an operation could
possibly be symbolic of, in the largest sense what it means, the concrete situation or context in which the ultimate identification of truth with beauty and
beauty with truth can be seen itself to be the symbolic resolution of some
more fundamental social contradiction or ideological antinomy. The concept
of "strategy" in Burke's critical practice thus seems to rule out of bounds the
very perspective it began by promising us, namely, the vaster social or
historical or political horizon in which alone the symbolic function of those
symbolic acts that are the verbal and literary artifacts can become visible to us.

Let me now quickly generalize this critique and apply it to the larger
dimensions of the overall theory of dramatism itself. I believe that the
Achilles heel of this system is to be located in the shrunken function left over
for Purpose in its grandiose mapping scheme (Purpose being, in the *Grammar
of Motives*, amalgamated with Agency, and rather summarily dispatched as a
kind of providential survival, a mystical or metaphysical "telos"). Here are
Burke's own reflections on this development:

> All told, of the five terms, Purpose has become the one most suscep-
> tible of dissolution. At least, so far as its formal recognition is con-
> cerned. But once we know the logic of its transformations, we can
> discern its implicit survival; for the demands of dramatism being the
> demands of human nature itself, it is hard for man, by merely taking

thought, to subtract the dramatist cubits from his stature. Implicit in the concepts of act and agent there is the concept of purpose. It is likewise implicit in agency, since tools and methods are for a purpose.[6]

To which one might add that it is evidently implicit in the category of Scene also, inasmuch as Marxism and historical materialism are not very satisfactorily assigned to that particular rubric of the system. The overall problem would appear to be that of the metacategory or metalanguage: insofar as the five "ratios" are inclusive, they must also include their own fundamental principle as well, which thus proves to govern a set of which it is itself a member.

The consequence of this for practical criticism is that in its application to the texts the category of Purpose turns out to designate two very different things at once. On the one hand, it names the inner logic of the symbolic act itself, its immediate aims and official objectives—in other words, the terms in which it explains its own activity to itself. On the level of kinesics, then, this category would designate the strategic organization of the gesture, the immediate end toward which this particular muscular effort is mobilized; in the case of Keats' *Ode*, Purpose construed according to this first limited or restricted sense would have to be reconstructed from its *terminus ad quem*, as the intent to overcome the opposition felt to obtain between beauty and truth.

Such an account of the restricted sense of Purpose in the analysis of a gesture or a symbolic act makes it clear that there is also room for a generalized use of the same term that would govern, not the immediate end and inner organization of a given gesture, but rather its place among all the other possible gestures I might have made at that particular moment, and its more general relationship to the other gestures and symbolic acts in course and under way in the historical network of intersubjectivity of which I am myself a part. The restricted concept of Purpose thus stands to this generalized one as an immanent interpretation to a transcendent one, or, to use another opposition that has been central in recent debates on hermeneutics, as the study of the *Sinn*, or "sense," of a given text, its inner structure and syntax, as opposed to that of its *Bedeutung*, or "meaning," its "historically operative" significance or function. Only the first operation can be carried out without attention to the situation of the work; I would argue that the second, interpretation proper, is impossible without some preliminary (re)construction of what I have called its subtext.

This is the point at which to admit that such reconstruction, the beginnings of a (re)writing of the subtext of Keats' *Ode*, is in fact also present in Burke's essay; and it may be worth taking a moment to watch this process at work:

"Truth" being the essential word of knowledge (science) and "beauty" being the essential word of art or poetry, we might substitute accordingly. The oracle would then assert, "Poetry is science, science poetry." It would be particularly exhilarating to proclaim them one if there were a strong suspicion that they were at odds. . . . It was the dialectical opposition between the "aesthetic" and the "practical," with "poetry" on the one side and utility (business and applied science) on the other that was being ecstatically denied. The *relief* in this denial was grounded in the romantic philosophy itself, a philosophy which gave strong recognition to precisely the *contrast* between "beauty" and "truth.". . .
      An abolishing of romanticism through romanticism![7]

The central interpretative operation in this passage is clearly enough what Burke himself designates as the substitution—or, in our own terms, the rewriting—of "truth" and "beauty" as *science* and *poetry*. This rewriting then furnishes a subtext such that Keats' *Ode* can be seen as its symbolic resolution—what Burke describes with sensory vividness as the "relief" of the concluding affirmation of the poem. What has to be resolved is evidently contradictory—Burke speaks of a "dialectical opposition" between poetry and science, and begins to rewrite the latter even more fundamentally as the "practical," as "applied science" or "utility," "business," and implicitly, although he does not use the word, as capitalism. Still, we must observe that the operation by which this subtext has been constructed remains essentially incomplete. We may indeed formulate a further principle of ideological analysis as follows: the subtext must be so constructed or reconstructed as to constitute not merely a scene or background, not an inert context alone, but rather a structured and determinate situation, such that the text can be grasped as an active response to it (of whatever type). The text's meaning then, in the larger sense of *Bedeutung,* will be the meaningfulness of a gesture that we read back from the situation to which it is precisely a response. The "dialectical opposition" Burke posits here between poetry and science is not yet a situation of that kind. If it is easy enough to see how this opposition might take on the form of a contradiction or an antinomy, a dilemma or a double-bind, a crisis that required some immediate resolution, we must nonetheless conclude that the critic has not been willing to go that far (although, given the urgency of the opposition between science and poetry during the heroic age of the New Criticism, it may be supposed that he felt this opposition to be too familiar to his readers to need any further development).
      Indeed, in place of the construction of a subtext in the form of a situation, we find something significantly different, which we can only call a strategy of containment, a substitution designed to arrest the movement of ideological analysis before it can begin to draw in the social, historical, and political

parameters that are the ultimate horizon of every cultural artifact. What shuts off the process of mediation and transcoding is the appeal to an entity Burke calls "romanticism," which effectively enough fixes his "ultimately determining instance," or ultimate explanatory code, in the area of the history of ideas, if not in the even more ahistorical area of the psychology of the great world views. Here, too, an examination of the subtext of Burke's own work would reveal "romanticism" as a particularly charged term, a complex of moral, political, and poetic dilemmas whose formulation can be traced back to the attack on Rousseau by which Irving Babbitt dramatized his influential counterrevolutionary position. Yet this specification of the ideological context in which Burke is here working only allows us to admire more intelligently the prestidigitation, the intellectual acrobatics, by which he manages to square this particular circle. The problem posed would then be that of saving the arch-romantic Keats from the inevitable contamination of the romanticism that for the generation of the New Critics vitiated poets like Shelley or Swinburne: the trick is turned by having Keats' romanticism criticize itself, and under its own momentum resolve the very contradictions for which it was itself responsible—"an abolishing of romanticism through romanticism!" Keats can remain a great poet, not merely in spite of, but even because of that romanticism directly responsible for the "dissociation of sensibility" of the bad romantics of his period. In the meantime, from the point of view of ideological analysis, it may be observed that this way of construing romanticism, by projecting a situation that is its own response, seals us off from any further need to consult the historical circumstances of romanticism itself and makes this particular superstructural subtext a kind of autoreferential *causa sui*. We must therefore take the passage just quoted as evidence for a discouraging reversal in Burke's critical strategy: his conception of literature as a symbolic act, which began as a powerful incitement to the study of a text's mode of activity in the general cultural and social world beyond it, now proves to have slipped back over the line and (passing from the generalized sense of the word "Purpose" to its immanent and strategic, restricted sense) now furnishes aid and comfort to those who want to limit our work to texts whose autonomy has been carefully secured in advance, all the blackout curtains drawn before the lights are turned back on.

Still, it is a measure of the ambiguous power of Burke's dramatism that we can use it to study its own strategies of containment and to flush out those concepts external to his own system to which he tends to have recourse when it is necessary to arrest the evolution of his concept of symbolic action in the direction of a full-fledged analysis of the ideological function of literary and cultural texts. In what follows I want briefly to mention three of these borrowed interpretative devices, three of these local strategies of containment that can be observed at work in Burke's criticism: they are the notion of art as ritual, the appeal to the bodily dimension of the verbal act, and the concept of the self or of identity as the basic theme or preoccupation of literature in general.

The insistence on the bodily elements, as it were the physiological infrastructure, of the literary work or verbal act—and some such physiological interpretation served as the strategy of containment for the other end of the Keats essay from which I just quoted—needs little comment. Here Burke is the precursor of a kind of analysis that, from phenomenology to structuralism, has become associated with the name Bachelard, and about which it is perhaps enough to distinguish Bachelard's own rather static interpretation, in terms of physical elements or humors, from that more dynamic language of gesture and bodily alchemy that we find in Burke. The rhetoric of the body, however, remains ambiguous: it can inaugurate the celebration of a kind of private materialism, from Bataille and "desire" all the way to certain readings of Bakhtin; or it can lead us dialectically beyond these individualizing and organic limits into some more properly collective apprehension of space and spatiality itself.

The question of ritual, indeed, demands greater attention, insofar as ritual has become, along with myth, one of the great fetishes of present-day American literary criticism and a strategy of containment scarcely restricted to Burke alone. Still, a closer look at the idea of ritual shows that it is scarcely less ambiguous, in its uses and consequences, than that of the symbolic itself. The Cambridge School, and their earliest followers among the literary critics, were indeed concerned to reground tragic and comic drama in the social life of the primitive collectivity. In that context, the interpretation of the work of art in ritual terms dictated its rewriting as a trace or survival of ways in which the primitive collectivity came to the consciousness of itself and celebrated its own social unity. Now the problem arises—and this concept begins to release its dangerous ambiguity—when we seek to transfer this model of the ritual function of primitive art to the culture and the literature of modern societies. The idea of ritual indeed entails as one of its basic preconditions the essential stability of a given social formation, its functional capacity to reproduce itself over time. Ritual as an institution can therefore not be understood except as a function of a society of this kind, as one of the fundamental mechanisms for ensuring the latter's collective coherence and historical perpetuation. It is precisely this precondition, however, that no longer holds for modern society, that is, for capitalism itself; and it would seem to me misguided, not to say historically naive, to attribute a Parsonian stability and functionality of the former primitive or tribal type to a social formation whose inner logic is the restless and corrosive dissolution of traditional social relations into the atomized and quantified aggregates of the market system. Far from assuming a ritual function, far from ensuring the lawful reproduction of our own social formation over geological ages of time, the greatest aesthetic productions of capitalism prove on the contrary to be the cries of pain of isolated individuals against the operation of transindividual laws, the invention of so many private languages and subcodes in the midst of a reified speech, the symptomatic expressions, finally, of a damaged subject and the marks of his or her vain efforts to subvert and to negate an intolerable social order.

To appropriate the rhetoric and conceptuality of primitive ritual to describe these broken fragments of the artistic discourse of capitalism is therefore a sheerly ideological enterprise. Enough has been said about the concept of ideology, however, to make it clear that such a characterization is not gratuitous invective, but rather designates our function as intellectuals in all its affective ambivalence and implies that we are all ideologues in this sense. Indeed, the example of Burke shows us that the production of an ideology can have a certain grandeur about it, even where it must ultimately be refused; such is, it seems to me, the status of his desperate and ambitious attempt, in the *Grammar* and *Rhetoric of Motives*, to endow the American capitalism of the thirties and early forties with its appropriate cultural and political ideology. We are here, after all, in the thick of a New Deal and Deweyan rhetoric of liberal democracy and pluralism, federalism, the "Human Barnyard," the "competitive use of the coöperative,"[8] and the celebration of political conflict in terms of what the motto to *A Grammar of Motives* calls the "purification of war." From the nostalgic perspective of the present day, the perspective of a social system in full moral and civic dissolution, what seemed at the time a shrewd diagnosis of the cultural and ideological conflicts of the capitalist public sphere and an often damaging critique of the latter's strategies of legitimation must now come to have implications of a somewhat different kind. The very forms of legitimation have been dialectically transformed, and consumer capitalism no longer has to depend on conceptual systems and abstract values and beliefs to the same degree as its predecessors in the social forms of the immediate past; thus, what tends to strike us today about the *Grammar* and *Rhetoric of Motives* is less their critical force than Burke's implicit faith in the harmonizing claims of liberal democracy and in the capacity of the system to reform itself from within.

I turn, finally, to the concept of the self or the subject in Burke's criticism, a problem that will also serve as a transition to a very brief concluding assessment of the dramatistic system itself. Nowhere do the continental and the Anglo-American critical traditions diverge more dramatically than on this whole issue of the subject, or the ego, or the self, and the value and reality to be accorded to it. We do not have to go all the way with the current French repudiation of ego psychology and what they call the "philosophies of the subject" to recognize in the American myths of the self and of its identity crises and ultimate reintegration some final trace and survival of that old ideology of bourgeois individualism whose basic features—juridical equality, autonomy, freedom to sell your own labor power—had crucial functions to fulfill in the establishment and organization of the market system. To repudiate that ideological tradition, to valorize the decentering of the subject with its optical illusion of centrality, does not, I would argue, have to lead to anarchism or to that glorification of the schizophrenic hero and the schizophrenic text that has become one of the latest French fashions and exports; on the contrary, it should signal a transcendence of the older individualism and the appearance of new collective structures and of ways of mapping our own decentered place with respect to them.

However this may be, it is clear that the rhetoric of the self in American criticism will no longer do, any more than its accompanying interpretative codes of identity crisis and mythic reintegration, and that a postindividualistic age needs new and postindividualistic categories for grasping both the production and the evolution of literary form as well as the semantic content of the literary text and the latter's relationship to collective experience and to ideological contradiction. What is paradoxical about Burke's own critical practice in this respect is that he has anticipated many of the fundamental objections to such a rhetoric of self and identity at the same time that he may be counted among its founding fathers. This last and most important of what we have called his "strategies of containment" provides insights that testify against his own official practice. Witness, for example, the following exchange, in which Burke attributes this imaginary objection to his Marxist critics: "Identity is itself a 'mystification.' Hence, resenting its many labyrinthine aspects, we tend to call even the *study* of it a 'mystification.' " To this proposition, which is something of a caricature of the point of view of the present essay, Burke gives himself a reply that we may also endorse: "The response would be analogous to the response of those who, suffering from an illness, get 'relief' by quarreling with their doctors. Unless Marxists are ready to deny Marx by attacking his term 'alienation' itself, they must permit of research into the nature of alienation and into the nature of attempts, adequate and inadequate, to combat alienation.[9]

I have quoted this passage mainly to document Burke's strange reluctance to pronounce the word "ideology" itself as well as his fundamental hesitation to identify his own study of symbolic forms with any of the available strategies of demystification, or of what we today have come to call, following Ricoeur, negative hermeneutics, or the hermeneutics of suspicion. For the issue at stake in the imagined exchange from which I have just quoted is not the need, quite appropriately stressed by Burke, for inquiry into the cultural forms of alienation ("the analysis of the 'strategies' by which men respond to the factor of alienation and by which they attempt to repossess their world")[10] so much as it is the status of the category of identity and of the self, which is itself ideological and which can hardly be properly evaluated if we remain locked into the very ideological system, the ideological closure or double-bind, that generates such concepts in the first place.

This is therefore the moment to characterize the ultimate structural distance between Burkean dramatism and ideological analysis proper: Burke's system has no place for an unconscious, it makes no room for genuine mystification, let alone for the latter's analysis or for the task of decoding and hermeneutic demystification that is increasingly the mission of culture workers in a society as reified and as opaque as our own. The dramatistic modes, if I may put it that way, are all categories of consciousness, open to the light of day in classical, well-nigh Aristotelian fashion; the Burkean symbolic act is thus always serenely transparent to itself, in lucid blindness to the dark underside of language, to the ruses of history or of desire. Characteristically enough, confronted with the great forerunners of ideological analysis, the great explorers of the unconscious proper, with Marx or Freud or Nietzsche, Burke's inclination is simply to apply to their own insights the sorting mechanism of his modal typology.[11]

But now, after our digression on the ego or the subject, we may be in a better position to understand why this is so. The very figure of the drama is itself in this respect infinitely revealing and infinitely suspect: the theatrical spectacle, theatrical space, indeed furnishes the first and basic model of the mimetic illusion, just as it is the privileged form in which the spectator-subject finds itself assigned a place and a center. Drama is then not so much the archetype of praxis as it is the very source of the ideology of representation and, with it, of the optical illusion of the subject, of that vanishing point from which spectacles—whether of culture, of everyday life, or of history itself—fall into place as metaphysically coherent meanings and organic forms.

With the critique of the dramatistic paradigm and of its anthropomorphism, we return to the fundamental equivocality of the symbolic itself, at one and the same time the accomplishment of an act and the latter's substitute, a way of acting on the world and of compensating for the impossibility of such action all at once. It is this kind of ambiguity that Burke will himself articulate by shifting italics from substantive to qualifier; much depends, indeed, on whether you think of art as a symbolic *act* or merely as an act that is *symbolic*. Sebastiano Timpanaro has underscored the structural instability of the analogous Gramscian of Sartrean notion of praxis in much the same terms:

> It is necessary first of all to show that a reference to praxis can have quite different meanings, according to whether one is declaring the inability of pure thought to make man happy and free ("The philosophers have only *interpreted* the world differently, the point is to *change* it"), or declaring that knowledge itself is praxis *tout court*. In the latter case, since *to know reality is already to transform it*, one retrogresses from Marxism to idealism—i.e., to a philosophy of *thought as praxis* [or in our present context, of symbolic form as real action], which makes action seem superfluous.[12]

At the beginning of the present essay, I proposed a checklist of the great contemporary critics, the great readers of an age that has discovered the symbolic; what I then neglected to add was that the art and practice of virtuoso reading does not seem to me to be the noblest function, the most urgent mission, of the literary and cultural critic in our time. In a society like ours, not stricken with aphasia so much as with amnesia, there is a higher priority than reading and that is history itself: so the very greatest critics of our time—Lukács, for example, and to a lesser degree, Leavis—are those who have construed their role as the teaching of history, as the telling of the tale of the tribe, the most important story any of us will ever have to listen to, the narrative of that implacable yet also emancipatory logic whereby the human community has evolved into its present form and developed the sign systems by which we live and explain our lives to ourselves. So urgently do we need these history lessons, indeed, that they outweigh the palpable fact that neither critic just mentioned is a good, let alone a virtuoso, reader, that each could justly be reproached for his tin ear and his puritanical impatience with the various *jouissances* of the literary text.

I will therefore regret that Burke finally did not want to teach us history, even though he wanted to teach us how to grapple with it; but I will argue, for the proper use of his work, that it be used to learn history, even against his own inclination. We have, indeed, in recent American criticism, a canonical example of how this can be done, in a confrontation between Burke and one of the few, rare, and neglected American avatars of the Lukácsean or Leavisite preceptor of history—I am referring to Yvor Winters, whose rewriting, in his "Experimental School in American Poetry,"[13] of Burke's already classic "Lexicon Rhetoricae"[14] is a model of how productively to historicize a powerful but nonhistorical set of aesthetic observations, and of the transformation of the purely formal Burkean interpretative scheme into a powerful historical statement. To prolong the symbolic inference until it intersects with history itself—this is, it seems to me, the only way properly to pay homage to the incomparable critical and theoretical energy of which Kenneth Burke gives us the example.

Spring 1978

Chapter 6
Figural Relativism; or,
The Poetics of Historiography

Certain great verbal hulks there are, vast narrative carcasses stranded in the wastes, infrequently raided by a few daring predators who draw the mammoth tusks or carve off frozen bits of blubber. These are the great narrative histories, of which in our time only a bleeding chunk of Gibbon or Michelet now and again is set before our students, legendary names inferring the vast enormities of text that lie beyond our narrow purview. They seem, indeed, on the point of being followed into extinction by the great three-decker realistic novels on the same period, coaches of the same laborious tempo, whose leisurely rhetoric awakens all the anxiety of the great meals and of conspicuous consumption. In telling us something about the first of these archaic narrative phenomena,[1] Hayden White emboldens us to return to these last in the hopes of surprising those of its secrets still extant; and not the least heartening feature of his example is a refurbished critical machinery, borrowed from literary study in the first place, yet in the process demonstrating unexpected—maybe even, for literary scholars, undesirable—resources and analytic capabilities.

Before we show what these are, however, it is best to say what White does not do in his work on the great narrative historians. For one thing, he is not interested in the narrativity of historical discourse, thereby distinguishing himself from approaches like that of Barthes.[2] Nor can we look to his chapters for what I want to call, in contrast to the relatively surface stylistic probe of Barthes, a narrative analysis proper of any one of the histories that are his objects (in other words, an analysis that follows Propp and Lévi-Strauss, and to a certain extent Greimas as well, in focusing on the ordering of the "events" themselves, on *histoire* rather than *discours*). Finally, we must not forget that White's book engages a polemic in several directions, only some of which are relevant to those of us in literary or cultural studies. For the historians themselves it has a lesson we are supposed to have learned by now, namely, that even empiricism is a theory and the exercise of a model, and that in the present context even the plainest unreflective history—the sheerest, most "mindless" enumeration of "facts" of an annals or a chronicle—implies a whole metaphysics and constitutes through its mere enunciation a whole philosophy of history in its own right. By a similar token, all "philosophies of history" may be assumed to be narratives *in potentia;* such is at any rate his intent—to efface a meaningless distinction and with it a false problem—in ranging the great theorists and philosophers of history (Hegel, Marx, Nietzsche, Croce) alongside the great narrative historians themselves.

White's program—a kind of deep-figural analysis of historical narrative—may perhaps be viewed as most attractive by those still laboring among the so-called realistic novels of the nineteenth century, of which we have been told scornfully by structuralists that they are not very *scriptible,* and by Marxists, strengthened by the authority of Brecht, that we do not have to take Lukács' old-fashioned and maybe even Stalinist taste for them very seriously any longer. White's work makes the conclusion inescapable that the active and practical, *cognitive* force of his histories is a function, not of their "factuality," but rather precisely of their narrative *form;* and this is enough to restore its dignity to the study of so-called fiction as well, and to that otherwise belletristic activity of articulating the master form of the realistic (but not only the realistic) novelists in which many of us are engaged without quite knowing what difference it makes.

The shock is even greater when we draw closer to the critical instruments that have become so strangely unrecognizable in White's hands: so Northrop Frye's old archetypes—romance, tragedy, comedy, and satire, here much more satisfactorily termed "emplotments"—seem familiar enough until we suddenly realize that they have been coordinated with Stephen Pepper's "world hypotheses" (formism, organicism, mechanism, and contextualism), and, as if that were not enough, further with Mannheim's political "ideal types" (White retains only anarchism, conservatism, radicalism, and liberalism). It is, of course, this last that is the most alarming novelty: there was never any problem with weltanschauungen just as long as they remained suitably metaphysical and modestly restricted to a purely aesthetic type of apprehension. Indeed, for a long time the term "world" has been available to the literary critic to soak up all the possible *philosophical* projections of a given form, all the while avoiding a more basely cognitive (and historical) treatment of what thereby remains some relatively eternal "tragic sense of life," "comic spirit," "satiric vision of a fallen or a degraded world," and so forth. Now suddenly the forbidden word has been pronounced, appropriately enough by someone from another discipline who was presumably unaware of the properly literary amenities, and it becomes distressingly difficult to avoid consideration of the *ideological* implications of the various forms or archetypes.

It is only at this price—understanding literature not only as a way of organizing and forming experience but as a process of form-giving that is destined to fulfill a historical, ideological, even protopolitical *function*—that literary study today can recover its urgency or sense of mission. Still, the wholesale borrowings from us by other fields (psychoanalysis and structural anthropology yesterday, ethnomethodology today) may serve to revive our spirits; and *Metahistory* in particular strikes me as having three lessons for us, over and beyond what it has to teach in general about its own subject.

The first springs essentially from a reflection on the old distinction between real and fictive narratives, in other words, between history and the novel. The form-giving power of historiography would appear to be enhanced, rather than diminished, by the "factuality" of its content: that is, it is the independent existence of something like a raw material, something like the historical "facts" (*histoire*), that underscores the shaping power of the historical discourse as it imposes on the content what must in the nature of things be only one possible version of those facts. The aesthetics of historiography rests, therefore, on a preliminary hypothesis about the separation, rather than the identification, of form and content; and if such an idea seems scandalous to us, it is because the new-critical attempt to exorcise the distinction was supported mainly by readings of lyrical texts (and even here, primarily of modernistic rather than traditional rhetorical poems). We must therefore explore the possibility that realism in the novel also is a type of discourse in which form and content are precisely not unified, in which—through its very structure—the content of the text is maintained at a certain determinate distance from its form.

Such a distinction would then permit us to emulate *Metahistory* in two further areas: namely, that of a history of forms and that of ideological as well as aesthetic judgments. For if White's treatment of the nineteenth-century historians is not exactly a history of histories in the diachronic sense (it is something more closely approximating a *combinatoire*, as we will see), nonetheless it offers a suggestive paradigm for dealing with a whole group of variants of a basic narrative structure and thus provides one possible escape from the dead end of the monograph, which has so long dominated the study of the nineteenth-century novel.

Moreover, it is precisely this perspective—in which the various histories are juxtaposed as so many structural variations of each other—that permits judgment, that indeed makes it inevitable. In spite of the "relativism" with which we will wish to reproach him, then, White is only too willing to pass a series of refreshingly hard-nosed judgments on his objects of study, whose ideological strategies his own method makes visible. Thus, "at any place in the historical record where such entities as states, churches, peoples and nations constituted 'problems' rather than 'data,' [Ranke's] method could not possibly work" (p. 175). "Out of his disillusionment [Burckhardt] forged a theory of society and history which was as accurate in predicting the crises of the future as it was symptomatic of the illnesses that would bring them on. Burckhardt regarded his own withdrawal from the world as an act which absolved him from any further responsibility for the coming chaos" (pp. 235-36). "Any attempt to interpret Nietzsche's thought as a purer and more consistent form of the conventional ideological positions—Conservative, Liberal, Reactionary, or even Anarchist—must face the fact that, in his conception of history, the prospects of any *community* whatsoever are sternly rejected" (p. 372). "Croce was trying to do for classical Liberalism what Ranke had done for classical Conservatism a half-century earlier—that is, hedge it around with arguments against Radicalism in any form" (p. 422). Only his skeptical attitude toward what he sees as Michelet's characteristic emplotment—romance as a form—will disappoint those for whom the historian of the French Revolution is the closest prose equivalent to the Jacobin heroics of Beethoven or the grand and manic hysteria of Berlioz in the music of the period. The other chapters—in particular those of Hegel, Marx, and Tocqueville—can be read with profit by readers interested in any of these thinkers, on condition they are willing to take the time to learn White's combination of codes.

But it is a big condition, and we turn now to this bristling conceptual apparatus, which, like all complicated theoretical machinery, tends in the slower passages to provoke the annoyance we feel when heavy artillery is rolled out to dispatch a few (admittedly choice) specimens of game. It is true that White's synthesis—coordinating, as we have indicated, the classificatory schemes of previous theoreticians like Frye, Pepper, and Mannheim—does not suffer from the hubris of his great predecessor and model Kenneth Burke, whose work strikes us in retrospect as a kind of monstrous bricolage designed for the production of nothing less than the philosopher's stone itself. Above and beyond the manner of the two writers, the basic difference between them would seem to lie in the nature of the deep structure in which each grounds his analyses: Burke's "dramatistic" method (measuring the specificity of a given text by its commitment to and emphasis on Act, Scene, Agent, Agency, or Purpose, respectively), although no less time-honored, with its Aristotelian origins, than White's use of an ancient rhetorical tradition, seems somehow far more anthropomorphic to us today, and oddly, anachronistically, resistant to the kinds of hermeneutic "second" or "symptomal" readings to which we have become accustomed since the general diffusion of Marxian, Nietzschean, and Freudian versions of an unconscious.

White's "ultimately determining instance," however, the fourfold system of the tropes, may be said to constitute something like a linguistic infrastructure and thereby to demand less justification than Burke's hypothesis, or at any rate to be more congenial to the spirit of the age.[3]

For *Metahistory* is something more than a study of philosophies of history (although it is that too, and no doubt the most important work in the field since Collingwood); it is also a methodological manifesto, a more sustained argument for a *deep-figural* hermeneutic than has been worked out anywhere before now, in spite of the prestige of the Jakobsonian rediscovery of metonymy and the renewal of interest in rhetoric generally, and in spite of the occasional practice of a kind of ad hoc figural analysis by a number of critics here and in Europe. Unfortunately, access to White's methodological thesis is encumbered by the presence of his substantive application of it to his texts, so that we are never really certain whether figuralism is supposed to be a useful aid in analyzing historiography, or whether, on the contrary, historiography and its structures are simply the most convenient objects on which to demonstrate the method. It is rather as though Frye had tried to convey the essentials of his *Anatomy* through the practical criticism of his Blake book.

This double focus probably accounts for White's failure to clear up a number of purely theoretical ambiguities. When we try, for instance, to determine the exact relationship between the four "master tropes" (metaphor, metonymy, synecdoche, and irony) and the other groups of variables (the Frye emplotments, the Pepperian world hypotheses, and Mannheim's ideological types), it remains an open question whether the tropes add yet another system of variables to this already complicated typology, or whether, on the contrary, they express on some deeper level something like the basic spirit or underlying form of those more surface combinations.

The ambiguity was already present in the surface combinations themselves, where the connection between world hypotheses and ideological types seemed a good deal closer than that of either to the choice of emplotment (and here, with the best will in the world, the old distinction between concept and narrative, cognition and fiction, seems again to rear its head). Clearly, there are at work between these various possibilities what White will call "elective affinities," a conservative ideology tending, for instance, to project an organicist weltanschauung or mode of argument, an anarchist or millenarian "mode of ideological implication" tending to find its fulfillment in romance as a form, and so forth. The appended tabulation of these structural affinities or concordances (from *Metahistory* [p. 29] and to which I have added the appropriate tropes as well) will clarify White's method but also the problems it raises.

Mode of Emplotment	Mode of Argument	Mode of Ideological Implication	Trope
Romantic	Formist	Anarchist	Metaphoric
Tragic	Mechanistic	Radical	Metonymic
Comic	Organicist	Conservative	Synecdochic
Satirical	Contextualist	Liberal	Ironic

For, as a matter of empirical critical practice, a model that distinguishes different levels in a text yields interesting results only when these levels are understood as contradicting each other. This is the practical objection to Greimas' (rather than Goldmann's) notion of homology: if the levels are really structurally homologous, they tend to fold back into each other and not much has been gained by the initial analytical distinction. In fact, this is precisely the conclusion White himself reaches (without, however, feeling the need to readjust his model): "the dialectical tension which characterizes the work of every master historian usually arises from an effort to wed a mode of emplotment with a note of argument or of ideological implication which is inconsonant with it" (p. 29). And it is certain that White's method celebrates its triumph in the object lessons in such a demonstration: the brilliant chapter on Tocqueville, for example, suggests that our contemporary fascination with such a writer is a function of his inner cross-purposes, the complexity of his philosophical aims (in Tocqueville's case, "to mediate not only between alternate concepts of society and between the past and present, but between the present and the future as well" [p. 206]), a complexity that realizes itself in the combination of a *tragic* mode of emplotment with a *liberal* ideology and an ultimately *ironic* figural structure. In a similar way, Hegel is seen as having attempted to coordinate a tragic emplotment of the individual episodes of human history with an essentially comic vision of its overall movement; he achieved this by bracketing "the Metonymical (causal) and Metaphorical (formalist) strategies for reducing phenomena to order within the modalities of Synecdochic characterizations on the one hand and the self-dissolving certitudes of Irony on the other" (p. 121). Finally, in his most idiosyncratic chapter, White sees Marx as combining a diachronic view of the base with a synchronic view of the superstructure (a resolution, perhaps, to the Althusserian controversy about the structuralism of *Capital*!), or, in other words, as coordinating a metonymic, mechanistic view of socioeconomic causality with an organicist reading of culture and human action, the dominant trope of which—synecdoche—projects an ideal of reunification and a renewal of community beyond the broken fragments of a metonymic present.

These are useful insights, but they leave unresolved what we may characterize as a restricted and a generalized objection to White's conceptual machinery. The first may perhaps be conveyed by way of scoring debating points, as Todorov does when, on a similar occasion,[4] he points out that Frye's system of slots provides for thirteen places of which only five are considered by the critic as having any empirical existence in real literary history. As far as *Metahistory* is concerned, even if we amalgamate the two related "levels" of weltanschauung and ideology, there remain sixteen different logical possibilities of combining that set of variables with the archetypal one; if we keep the three sets separate from one another, the number of possibilities rises to sixty-four; and if (God forfend!) the four tropes be seen as yet a fourth set of variables (rather than some underlying structure of their combinations), the ultimate possibilities are so staggering as to suggest that something in the machinery has gone haywire.

Now from a practical point of view, White is quite right to ignore such an objection. On the one hand, as we have seen, he suggests that the merely homologous or "univocal" realizations of his typological scheme (in other words, the four baseline possibilities exemplified in the tabulation) are uninteresting and thus without literary or historiographic value. The axiological hypothesis at work here reminds us of the identification by the New Critics of poetic "greatness" with the greatest possible verbal tension or inner complexity. At the other end of the spectrum, he offers what amounts to an empirical observation, namely, that certain combinations simply do not come into being because of basic logical and structural *incompatibilities* between certain of the variables; thus, "a Comic emplotment is not compatible with a Mechanistic argument, just as a Radical ideology is not compatible with a Satirical emplotment," and so on (p. 29).

Yet one wonders whether texts, and cultural or superstructural phenomena in general, can be thought of in the same terms as, say, biological organisms that, lacking certain vital organs, cannot survive. In particular, it seems most improbable to me—given the immense explosion in cultural production since the eighteenth century—that there should *not* exist, somewhere, examples of all the structural combinations that White here feels to be unviable. On the contrary, nothing seems more likely than that of little research in the archives should turn up a universal history of some eccentric British civil servant or retired French postman that would constitute precisely that ultimate and unimaginable combination of terms we needed to fill the last vacant slot of our Mendelian table.

Such an eventuality of course raises the whole issue of selective accreditation: if Ranke has been recognized as a cultural object, if, in other words, his particular mode of historical discourse has come to be identified as a subcode in its own right while that of the postman remains the sheerest idiolect, like Swift's baby talk or Fourier's private spelling, then what must be explained are the social and cultural reasons for the reception of one private language rather than the other into the public realm. (This is not to suggest that the postman will not some day also have his due: weirder private hobbies—think of Vico or Sorel!—have found their way, with time, into the broad daylight of the cultural "mainstream.")

I have indulged this lengthy imaginary exception, not in order to prove White *wrong* (it would not seem to make much sense to pass such a judgment on a method), but rather to show that his critical procedure has been left incomplete, and that precisely at the point at which it might have become genuinely historical. I would want to argue, indeed, that an operation of this kind—technically called a *combinatoire*—requires three components for its functioning, of which White has given us two alone, namely, the two (or more) sets of variables whose combinations give this piece of machinery its name. What is missing is that mechanism of historical selection—that infrastructural limiting situation—to which it falls, out of the complete range of purely *logical* possibilities, to reject those that cannot empirically come into being in that determinant historical conjuncture. Thus, to use Greimas' dramatic example, a variant of a given folktale provides for an *actant* who unites both paternal and sacerdotal functions: this particular variant, therefore—while it remains a logical possibility—cannot be empirically realized in Roman Catholic Lithuania owing to the celibacy of priests (what happens is that a new variant is generated in which an older brother who happens to be a priest assumes paternal responsibility for the hero).[5]

Obviously, the missing mechanism is essential, for it alone provides the conceptual link between a purely logical play of variables and resultant forms, and the concrete historical situation in which those possibilities flourish or find themselves excluded from the outset. Its absence goes a long way toward justifying the characterization of *idealism* with which we will want to reproach *Metahistory*—not, indeed, that there is not a wealth of social and political detail here, nor a sense of those historically strategic situations in which White's historians invent their ideological choices, but that content constitutes an infrastructure only in the context of some older "realistic" or "referential" historiography. To the new, properly "structural" history of histories Hayden White has set out to compose here must surely correspond some new and equally structural conception of the historical rock bottom, and it is difficult to see how the latter could be anything but that limiting situation described above.

Without it, in the best of circumstances, we are left with nothing but a typology, and it is to this, and to the more generalized version of our basic objection, that we now turn. This is not the place to argue our thesis that typology "is always the sign of historical thinking arrested halfway, a thought which, on the road to concrete history, takes fright and attempts to convert its insights into eternal human essences, into attributes between which the human spirit oscillates."[6] Typological operations bear within themselves their own reward, in the form of that frustrating sense of sterility with which we drop the final object into the approximate box in the classification scheme and then wonder what to do next. Yet it will not be too difficult to show that wherever White's typological or classificatory operation is most interesting, in reality something rather different is at work beneath the surface.

What is abundantly clear from the outset is the advantage White's fourfold set of tropes gives him over the old dualisms of the Jakobsonian metaphor/metonymy types: compare for instance Barthes' threefold classification of historical narrativity (metaphoric, metonymic, and reflexive);[7] compare Lotman's fourfold classification of cultures into semantic (predominance of relationship symbol/thing, or *grosso modo* metaphorical, in White's sense), syntactic (or metonymic), and the synthesis or exclusion of both types, respectively.[8] It is clear that both are locked fatally into a rigid set of alternatives, which just as rigidly generate something that looks like a synthesis or transcendence of them. Less obviously, it is clear that Pepper's fourfold scheme of world hypotheses allows White to skirt definitive oppositions like those of idealism and materialism, in the name of more complex and purely descriptive accounts of his objects.

The multiplicity of his tropes thus allows him to lend each a relative autonomy that they could not have in a dualistic system (where the two terms are so intimately linked that, as has often been pointed out, a moment of analysis is always reached when metaphor and metonymy turn into each other and become virtually indistinguishable). Each may thus for the purposes of exposition be expressed in terms of something like a meaning (even though the theory of tropes consists precisely in reversing these priorities and in seeing a given "meaning-effect" as a projection of the individual trope in question). So metaphor becomes a kind of naive and inaugural stage of thinking in which the simplest verbal act (word = thing) restores or founds a belief in the referent. Paradoxically, metaphor is the moment of *literality* in speech; metonymy, then, clearly enough designates the breakdown of this initial (and perhaps illusory) metaphorical unity, its fragmentation into a segmented kind of thinking that can only move, mechanistically and contiguously, from one part to the next.

The assimilation of synecdoche to metonymy seems to have been a relatively recent development (Genette attributes it to Dumarsias[9]); to restore the distinction between them as it obtained in the traditional fourfold tropological scheme of the Renaissance rhetoricians is a strategic feature of White's method. For him, the differentiation is based on the view that metonymy governs a relationship of part to part, whereas synecdoche tends to focus on the relationship between a part and its whole; synecdoche thus becomes a reintegrative moment and the sign of an attempt to project a new unification as against the fragments of sheer metonymic fission.

Irony, finally—an uneasily different animal from any of the above—marks the coming of the whole tropological system to a stage of consciousness or self-consciousness in which the problematical nature of language itself has been recognized. . . . . In Irony, figurative language folds back upon itself and brings its own potentialities for distorting perception under question. . . . The trope of Irony, then, provides a linguistic paradigm of a mode of thought which is radically self-critical with respect not only to a given characterization of the world of experience but also to the very effort to capture adequately the truth of things in language. It is, in short, a model of the linguistic protocol in which skepticism in thought and relativism in ethics are conventionally expressed. (pp. 37–38)

Such a development, in which it proves possible to effect a qualitative transformation of the inner logic of discourse through a kind of reflection of language upon itself, inevitably suggests affinities with dialectical thinking; and in fact White explicitly identifies the two: "in my view, dialectic is nothing but a formalization of an insight into the tropological nature of all the forms of discourse which are not formally committed to the articulation of a world view within the confines of a single modality of linguistic unity" (p. 428; this last phrase alludes to the various subcodes of the sciences).

So both Hegel and Marx may be enlisted in support of a figural method; and indeed a figural reading of the Hegelian philosophy of history suggests convincingly enough that Hegel's four moments of world history "corresponds to the four modes of consciousness represented by the modalities of tropological projection itself" (p. 125). Thus, the first great archaic civilizations of the Orient and the Near East embody "the awakening of consciousness to the possibility of Metaphorical apprehension" (p. 125) and are followed in turn by the metonymical reduction of Greek individualism, the abstract and then the concrete synecdochic reconstructions of Rome and Christianity, respectively, and finally the ironic self-consciousness of modern post-theological times.

In White's reading of Marx, this tropological logic of world history (the Marxian moments of social evolution from primitive communism through slave and feudal economies to capitalism[10]) is reexpressed on another level in Marx's theory of the four stages in the evolution of economic value and in the emergence of currency:

the Elementary (Isolated, or Accidental) form of value, the Total (or Extended) form, the Generalized form, and the Money form *(Geldform)*. In the first form, the value of a commodity is *equated* with the value presumed to exist in some other commodity. In the second, the value of a commodity is, as Marx put it, "expressed in terms of numberless other elements in the world of commodities," such that the value of a commodity can be expressed in an "interminable series" of different commodities. In the third form, the value of *all* commodities may be expressed in terms of *one commodity* in the series, as when a coat, specific amounts of tea, coffee, wheat, gold, iron and so on, are considered to be "worth" a certain amount of some other commodity, such as linen, so that the common value of all, the amount of labor necessary for their production, can be equated in terms of only *one other commodity*. And, in the fourth form, value comes into being when the specific commodity, gold, is hit upon as the standard by which the presumed value of every com- modity can be set and specified. (p. 288)

White's ingenious tropological reading of the Marxian stages of value can be taken as a contribution to a more general current meditation on the applica- bility of this scheme to other areas, the most notable of these attempts being that of Jean-Joseph Goux, in his *Economie et symbolique* (Paris: Seuil, 1973), where the emergence of gold is homologically accompanied by the emergence of political power, of the authoritarian father, of phallocentric sexuality, and of language (which Goux deals with according to the Derridean coordinates of writing and oral plenitude). It is clear that such a scheme is immediately assimilable, *tel quel*, to White's tropological system, whose adequacy it now remains for us to assess.

We must first observe that the meaning of the individual tropes, if it is not dependent on a static opposition of the metaphor/metonymy type, nonethe- less derives from the relationship of each one to the other three: each trope is read *through* its position in the fourfold scheme, and it should be clear by now that that scheme is diachronic, in other words, that each trope is understood as a *moment* within the intelligibility of some larger ongoing process in which it is subsumed. Perhaps this process may be most strikingly dramatized, and *Metahistory* itself placed in perspective, by quoting Hayden White against himself on the occasion of a similar critique he addressed to Michel Foucault.[11] The essence of this remarkable critique is to discredit Foucault's own ideological view of his research (the latter was offered as a programmatic substitution, for diachronic and dialectical theories of history, of Foucault's own view of history as a series of discontinuous synchronic systems) and to show that "there *is* a transformational system built into Foucault's concep- tion of the succession of forms of the human sciences, even though Foucault appears not to know that it is there" (p. 45). The reader of the present article, or of *Metahistory*, will have already guessed the nature of that deeper struc- ture—the tropes!—that White finds at work in Foucault's four epistēmēs. In the present context, it is enough to say that after White's reinterpretation we can never read Foucault the same way again. Obviously, however, damaging as it is to Foucault's own position to find itself thus assimilated to a Viconian "linguisitic historicism,"[12] White's tropological system emerges strength- ened from the encounter, which permits it to enlist the works of Foucault (as before him, of Marx and Hegel) as testimony on its own behalf.

Yet there is a lesson here which is not without its relevance for *Metahistory* as well: it is that the refusal of genuinely historical thinking carries its own retribution within itself. "Foucault Decoded" offers us, indeed, something like the spectacle of a veritable "return of the repressed," in which diachronic thinking, repudiated, rises up behind the work as a compensation formation in the form of *myth;* and, in fact, mythic thinking is precisely that, the way in which the mind finds itself obliged to deal with time and change when the conceptual instruments of genuine historical thinking are unavailable to it. Myth can be identified by one telltale feature, present not only in Foucault as White rereads him but also in Hayden White himself: that is, the tendency to view change and time in *cyclical* terms. What is more cyclical, indeed, than Foucault's vision of the fall out of a medieval realm of identity, with its redemptive and prophetic hints of the dawn of some new and transfigured, posthumanist and post-Nietzschean era? Or, if you prefer, the cyclical organization of the historical narrative or myth is itself but the vehicle for those theological overtones that lie fatally in wait for any nonmaterialist version of the historical record.

And it is certain that when we draw back from the details of *Metahistory* and attempt to read the larger historical story which its sequence of historians writes out for us, the cyclical pattern becomes unavoidable. It was already in the tropes themselves, whose movement from the naive freshness of metaphor to the disabused skepticism of the ironic mode foretells a return to origins and a reinvention of the tropological cycle. And this is precisely what we find happening in White's story of the development of historiography as it matures from the naiveté of the chronicles to the corrosive skepticism of Enlightenment historians like Hume and Voltaire, thereupon reemerging invigorated and *aufgehoben* into the new and more all-embracing realism of Romantic historiography, only, as the century wanes on, to grow once more aweary of itself and at length to taste the doubt of a new ironic stage, in the attacks of Nietzsche and the skepticism of Croce—the supreme defender of historicism being at one and the same time the thinker who "denied that men could judge with any certitude the nature of their own age" (p. 398).

This should not be taken as an objection to some underlying (and profoundly ideological) pessimism inherent in the cyclical view of history: on the contrary, the cycle is, for White, even while he identifies his own metahistorical stance with ironic self-consciousness, the occasion for an ultimate appeal to some imminent overturning of irony itself:

> I maintain that the recognition of this Ironic perspective [that of
> *Metahistory* as well as of "most of modern academic historiography"]
> provides the grounds for a transcendence of it. If it can be shown
> that Irony is only one of a number of possible perspectives on
> history, each of which has its own good reasons for existence on a
> poetic and moral level of awareness, the Ironic attitude will have
> begun to be deprived of its status as the necessary perspective from

which to view the historical process. Historians and philosophers of history will then be freed to conceptualize history, to perceive its contents, and to construct narrative accounts of its processes in whatever modality of consciousness is most consistent with their own moral and aesthetic aspirations. (p. 434)

Like the original version of Sartrean commitment, such a reduction of the forms of self-justification to the unjustified and unjustifiable choices that underlie them cannot but arouse a therapeutic anxiety. White's own choice may perhaps be detected as the echo, in such passages, of the mountainous wave of the Viconian *ricorso* as, towering, it prepares in its crash to sweep all furiously before it into a new cycle of time. More than Foucault, more than the structural rhetoricians, it is Vico who is the great *absent* from Hayden White's pages, and with whom he now owes it to us (and to himself) to reach some definitive understanding.

Still, for ourselves we must refuse to admit that history repeats itself, and we must patiently insist that the cyclical vision of *Metahistory* as a whole is an optical illusion generated by the autonomization of a set of phenomena—historiography and theories of history—which is not complete in itself and is intelligible concretely only at the price of its reintegration into the social history of culture as a whole. This is the moment for the reader once again to ponder the crucial warning of Marx and Engels in *The German Ideology:* "Morality, religion, metaphysics, all the rest of ideology and their corresponding forms of consciousness, thus no longer retain the semblance of independence. They have no history, no development; but men, developing their material production and their material intercourse, alter, along with this their real existence, their thinking and the products of their thinking."[13]

Even the final "leap of faith" proposed by White does not solve all the problems raised by his treatment of history as narrative. For those groups, indeed, who, like the Marxists, still "believe in the referent," not only is the issue that of relativism versus some form of absolute conviction; it is also that of the validity of narrative analysis, and implies a good deal of anxiety about the status of a historical reality about which we would be willing to agree that its historiography is "nothing but" a narrative, "nothing but" a text. *Metahistory* is, however, not the best occasion on which to raise this particular issue, which it presupposes resolved in advance.

Spring 1976

Chapter 7
Modernism and Its Repressed; or, Robbe-Grillet as Anti-Colonialist

> *The language which provides most of the material for the*
> *analysis is a purged language, purged . . . of the means for ex-*
> *pressing any other contents than those furnished to the individuals*
> *by their society. The linguistic analyst finds this purged language*
> *an accomplished fact, and he takes the impoverished language as*
> *he finds it, insulating it from that which is not expressed in*
> *it. . . . Linguistic philosophy [thereby] suppresses once more*
> *what is continually suppressed in this universe of discourse and*
> *behavior.*
> —Herbert Marcuse, *One-Dimensional Man*

During the current lull in American literary studies, when the rhetoric of the New Criticism is as discredited as the ideology of liberalism itself, when archetypal criticism has turned out to be a merely typological or classificatory operation, and the comfortable old pursuits of image-counting and thematics have settled back down in possession of the field, two more recent European models have seemed to have something new to offer. They are, on the one hand, Franco-Italian structuralism, with its methodological codification in semiotics, and on the other, the streamlined Hegelianism of the Frankfurt School, not the least attractive feature of which—for American intellectuals—lies in its capacity to provide a Marxist theory without a Marxist practice.

The trouble is—as ever more numerous translations of these two tendencies have begun to make clear—that the two approaches appear to be mutually exclusive, both in their basic philosophical presuppositions and in their day-to-day critical operations. It is not very difficult to provide a checklist of these incompatibilities: synchronic versus diachronic thought, scientism versus the critique of positivism, the primacy of language versus the primacy of society, the building of small-scale models versus the intuitive, totalizing, transcultural or transhistorical generalization, and so on. What is harder is to find some field or object over which these two "methods" can meet in such a way that their respective explanatory powers can be concretely compared.

Jacques Leenhardt's book on Robbe-Grillet[1] may serve to give us a glimpse of the form such a confrontation might take. A Marxist study of Robbe-Grillet, its dedication reminds us that it was conceived as a prolongation of the work of the late Lucien Goldmann on the *nouveau roman;* yet its language and diagrams are those, linguistics-oriented, of a more recent semiotic research and thus invite the kind of comparison we have proposed when they do not always articulate it. Yet the very framework of the book, already a strategic choice, dramatizes the structural dilemmas involved in the attempt to use both methods at the same time: for its conception as an immense, in-depth exegesis of a single text at once excludes the comparative study of a whole corpus of works that gave Goldmann's literary analyses their scope and authority, at the same time making it impossible to measure the expressive capacity of *Jealousy* against that of the artworks of other historical periods or social configurations, as Adorno himself was inveterately inclined to do, with results so often luminous. Thus—and this from the very outset, owing to the plan of the work itself—we must not expect to find in Leenhardt's study a treatment of the specificity of the *nouveau roman* as a whole, nor an evaluation of its significance as one moment in the development of modernism. Yet these are not, as we will see later, simply additional topics which it is a critic's privilege to ignore or to postpone for some more general consideration, but rather fundamental limitations which return to take their toll of the study's inherent strengths. The latter, however, and in particular the rock-drill constituted by so systematic a depth-sociological reading of this particular novel, have enough explosive potential to make some fairly consequent inroads of their own on the formalistic landscape.

Leenhardt's book suggests yet a further inconsistency between semiotics and critical theory which is perhaps more fundamental than any of those enumerated above and which I would characterize as the attitude toward, and the role played by, the *negative* in both systems. The importance of negation and of the valorization of contradiction or absence in dialectical thinking is well known; while the reduction of negation to what it used to be in predialectical philosophy, namely a mere logical category or the marking of quasi-mathematical valences, is probably also familiar to anyone who has worked with Lévi-Strauss or Greimas. What is perhaps only now becoming clear, in the writings of so-called poststructuralist thinkers like Deleuze or J.-F. Lyotard, is the ideological significance of the refusal of the negative and the profound vocation of the new philosophy to seek a model made up of nothing but positivities: this repudiation of the dialectic, with its valorization of absence and contradiction, now draws renewed authority for its exaltation of the present from a revival of Nietzschean vitalism. Meanwhile, an analogous "positivism" (did not Lévi-Strauss, on a memorable occasion, describe himself as a "mechanical materialist"?) informs the scientific claims of semiotics itself to banish all traces of the subject, along with the negative from its account of the object itself. The implications of which may quickly be suggested in terms of literary analysis: semiotics is the implicit development of a program explicitly announced in the work of the poststructuralists, namely the attempt to continue to talk of a given phenomenon *without interpretation*, whether it be that of the psychoanalytic diagnosis of a symptom, or of the dialectical reading of a culture in history. Science or schizophrenia, *intensités*, structures or the Freudian death wish—strange bedfellows all temporarily allied against Marx or Freud themselves!

The inextricable relationship of interpretation to the negative may now be concretely measured by what Leenhardt has and has not been able to do with his reading of *Jealousy*. Its superiority to other readings, its incommensurability with them, what is properly scandalous for the orthodoxy of *nouveau roman* scholarship, lies in his demonstration that Robbe-Grillet's novel has content, that it is "about" something and possesses a genuine "referent": in the occurrence Africa, the colonial situation, imperialism and neo-imperialism, racism, wars of national liberation—realities it seems incongruous enough to mention in the same breath as the *nouveau roman*, much as though we were to be told that James Joyce was the greatest novelist of the IRA! Yet the complexity of Leenhardt's critical procedure here may be suggested by a distinction between "referent" and "meaning": insofar, in other words, as the aesthetic of *Jealousy* proposes something like a pure play of signifiers, a combination and variation of relatively free-floating sentences, this insistence on the book's "signified," this search for something like its meaning or message might fairly enough be taken as a way of refusing to perceive the work altogether. It is just such wrongheaded or misguided quests for "meaning" which have been stigmatized as interpretation by the most articulate spokesmen for modern art. But when we recall that Jakobson's terminology substitutes the word "context" for that of "referent," we glimpse the possibility of an interpretive operation of a wholly different type, whose specificity even the term "semantics"—insofar as it might also apply to the study of the "signified"—tends to blur, and which might better be characterized as a transcendence of the inner, formal experience of the work or of the signifier by a study of its material and referential *preconditions*. This is, it seems to me, what Leenhardt is up to in a work that juxtaposes travel brochures and sociological treatises on the colonial experience with explorations of the novel's imagery and close attention to the patterns of the banana trees; such heterogeneity is indeed deliberate, and the shock in store for the student of *belles lettres* is not only healthy, it is exemplary, and emblematic of that reversal of work and reader alike which any genuinely materialistic criticism ought to effectuate and to which we will return shortly. Suffice it to say that Leenhardt's approach goes a good deal further than Robbe-Grillet's own program, according to which the reality which the *nouveau roman* was "about," and the sense in which it could be considered "realistic,"[2] was simply a shift in the phenomenological experience of the world in our own day, and the subsequent disintegration of categories like those of the subject, of time, of things, and the like; Robbe-

Grillet, indeed, makes a case for some profoundly *critical* value of his own novels in the sense of the Frankfurt School, in their narrative demystification of the very categories of the ideology of everyday life. This suggests a rather peculiar reading of *Jealousy* as standing somewhere between Gide's *Voyage au Congo* and Voltaire's *Contes philosophiques.* But if it cannot be stressed enough that a project like that outlined by Robbe-Grillet is an essentially *idealistic* one, in that it takes as its object our thoughts about and experiences of reality rather than the latter's material origins and causes, its real ambiguity lies, as Leenhardt shows and as we will see shortly, in that concept of a "newer" reality in the name of which the critique of the older one is undertaken.

At any rate, this kind of description of the overall aims of Robbe-Grillet's narrative technique in general must give way to more specific local traditions in the reading of *Jealousy* itself; and here, it seems to me, Leenhardt's thesis—necessarily metacritical as well as critical—confronts two main formalistic strategies, or, if you prefer, two versions of the canonical formalist position on the novel, something like a weak and a strong version, or a literal and a figurative, a restricted and a generalized approach. The purer of these positions—Ricardou may be taken as its most vigorous representative—refuses interpretation in the name of the text itself, seen as a process by which the combination of metaphoric and descriptive functions ultimately neutralize expression itself. This process has an inner logic of its own:

> In so perfectly closed a set as this book is, a systematic combination of all its elements would ultimately require, along with the disruption of time, the actualization of all their possibilities, which is to say, in particular, of all their contraries. Along with this saturation of relationship, textual space also gives rise to a concept of neutralization: this is indeed the phenomenon in which the cause of the novel's ultimate return to stillness may be found.[3]

I suspect, as I have suggested elsewhere,[4] that even this extreme and rigorously absolute formalism is not really as formalistic as it means to be, and that in reality—far from constituting a repudiation of interpretation—it is itself an allegorical interpretation whose "signified" or allegorical key is simply that of language or *écriture* or the text itself.

Even if such a suspicion proves baseless, however, it is undeniably true that the position of Ricardou is too demanding to be maintained for long, and that it tends imperceptibly to slip into another one which this time is quite openly a hermeneutic with its own specific interpretive content, namely that of psychoanalysis itself. (Derrida may be taken as a textbook illustration of this process, a book like the *Grammatologie* drawing its most fundamental content and persuasive force from that very Freudianism which it was concerned to assimilate to the more formal model of *différance* and trace.) As far as Robbe-Grillet is concerned, this slippage is no doubt facilitated by some deep structural ambiguity within the novels, in which, alongside the endless textual variations of the surface, there rises some more global atmosphere of psychopathology, whether it be child molesting *(Le Voyeur)*, a drop in mental functioning characteristic of brain injuries *(Dans le labyrinthe)*, or the sado-masochism of the later works, whose more conventional alliance with por-nography signals a weakening of some of the more interesting tensions and transgressions of the earlier ones. In the case of *Jealousy*, Leenhardt observes that none of the previous critics have been able to free themselves from the spell of the title and from the immediate first impression that the book must be about a *ménage à trois:*

> One is indeed astonished to observe that all the critics, from the most traditionally psychologizing, like Bruce Morrissette, to those, like Jean Ricardou, most rigorously attentive to narrative mecha-nisms, have discussed this novel in terms of erotic jealousy, of a cuckolded husband, etc. Such wondrous unanimity conveys the power of the myth, none of the critics having been able to transcend it by way of some second-degree recuperation. (p. 209).

His first task will therefore be an assault on this unspoken primacy of psychological and psychoanalytic interpretation, the relative autonomy of which reflects the profound fragmentation of modern social life into private and public sectors of the psyche, at the same time that—as in the present case—it offers a last-ditch strategy for evading any genuinely historical or social approach to literary material. For the most private and solitary fact re-mains a *social* one, and the invention of mediations between the psychoana-lytic and the political simply demands the enlargement of the frame of reference in such a way that the social character of the psychic phenomenon in question becomes visible. This is, I suppose, why Leenhardt begins his restructuration of the classic psychoanalytic reading of *Jealousy* with what is perhaps its most generalizable version, namely the diagnosis of this novel (and others by the same writer) as an obsessional construction. Such a reading,[5] in contrast to some of the other Freudian codes available (Oedipus complex, phallic symbols, allegory of the psyche, etc.), is already in itself mediatory by virtue of the phenomenological description inherent in it of the movement of the text: that rhythm according to which the sentences begin to live a compulsive life of their own ("in *Jealousy*, indeed, what is sick or jealous is simply language itself, as a whole" [p. 131]), suddenly and obsessively beginning to count all the banana trees in the plantation, to describe the geometrical arrangement of the fields, to enumerate even the most minor deviations from the overall plan of the cultivated area.[6] The depersonalized autonomy of these sentences thus comes to figure something like those mechanical rituals by which hysterical patients distract themselves from the pressure of anxiety forcing at the conscious mind; yet in itself the account of Anzieu is not inconsistent either with that of Ricardou above—it simply lends it nascent content. And in a more general way, this characterization of the *écriture* of *Jealousy* corrects the abstractness of the two standard views of the *nouveau roman*, as the novel of things (objective version), or of the *école du regard* (subjective version, not only by insisting that both these poles are part of a process, but also and above all by suggesting that this process itself needs explanation as to a determinate phenomenon in its own right.

To describe the process as obsession is indeed to bracket both subject and object and to evoke an operation through which external surroundings are somehow neutralized by a look that is itself wholly depersonalized from the outset; it is therefore not a question of reintroducing a psychopathology of the subject at this point, but rather of making a phenomenological analysis of the Look as a social phenomenon whose meaning is independent of individual psychology. Here Leenhardt uses Sartre against Robbe-Grillet's own critique of *La Nausée*, of which the later novelist perspicaciously observes that "the first three perceptions recorded at the beginning of the book are all gained by the sense of touch, not that of sight. . . . The sense of touch constitutes, in everyday life, a much more *intimate* sensation than that of sight" (*For a New Novel*, p. 65). In what is a *locus classicus* of modern polemics, indeed, by underscoring the crucial role of smell and tactility and color perception in Sartre's novel, Robbe-Grillet went on to denounce the tragic humanism—the unconscious anthropomorphism, if you like—implicit in Sartre's presentation of a world and of its objects, in which human beings remain, in spite of themselves, inextricably entangled:

> Drowned in the depth of things, man ultimately no longer even perceives them: his role is soon limited to experiencing, in their name, totally humanized impressions and desires. . . . The sense of sight immediately appears, in this perspective, as the privileged sense. . . . Optical description is, in effect, the kind which most readily establishes distances: the sense of sight, if it seeks to remain simply that, leaves things in their respective place. (*For a New Novel*, pp. 68, 73)

This demystification of the several senses is of course a fundamental component of Robbe-Grillet's aesthetic program and a key strategic operation in that narrative critique of the ideology of everyday life and perception of which we spoke above. But what if one could evaluate all this in a wholly different way? What if the pure look, indeed, were rather the vehicle for something like a *will* to power over the external world? What if the very refusal of anthropomorphism and of its tragic spirit (of which we may well agree that it continues to lead an underground life in the classical moment of

French existentialism) were itself not altogether innocent and expressed a longing to free one's self from the world and from things that had a pro-topolitical content of its own? We thus return to Sartre's own analyses of the Look, and in particular that outlined in "Orphée noir" (his preface to Senghor's historic anthology of the *négritude* poets), in which the Look, and the position of the subject which it affords ("the right to look without being looked at"), is denounced as the very element of white supremacy and of the colonial situation. The symbolic significance, or, in other words, the social content, of the act of looking is simply the reaffirmation of my own white skin: an interpretation corroborated by the commanding situation of the manor in the novel, dominating the slope from which, across a protective distance, the objects of the surrounding world can be effectively mastered and visually enumerated to the last detail.

We need a better term than that of mere phenomenological analysis to designate the way in which the historical origins and the repressed situational content of an activity like this one—the special kind of inspection inherent in the obsessive visual survey—are restored to the phenomenon itself, thereby constituting its interpretation and revealing the social significance of what had hitherto seemed a psychological comportment or a mode of perception. This is in fact a sociological version of the Nietzschean genealogy, in which the trace of older concrete situations is revealed through the demystification of a kind of X-ray process within modern "civilized" phenomena that no longer seem to have anything in common with them; so Nietzsche showed how an older aristocratic insolence lives on within the etymology of the im-poverished vocabulary of modern value judgments, while the classes of the heroic age itself—conquerors and conquered—continue to live out their disguised struggle, transfigured beyond all recognition by *ressentiment*, in the shabby white collars of the industrial city. This process is now to be understood, however, in a concrete and sociological sense, rather than in that of the Nietzschean myth of history. We would expect as genealogy of the gaze in *Jealousy* to reveal its distant origins in the rationalization and quantifica-tion of that first commercial world of the primitive accumulation of capital, and to bear scars of that transformation of the whole world into one immense bookkeeping system which resulted from the spread of money and the expan-sion of the market economy. By the mid-twentieth century, however, this type of visual inspection has already entered a late and pathological stage, and Leenhardt rightly points out that what psychoanalysis calls obsession in this respect has its exact social and historical equivalent in what he describes as the "morbid geometralization" of the whole colonial system, that deper-sonalized fascination with numbers and geometrical arrangements rather than with human beings so characteristic of the pacification strategies of the various colonial and counterinsurgency operations (pp. 54-55). So the ap-parently purely formal disembodied compulsion of the gaze across the fields has genuine political and economic content which goes far beyond even that of the ideological significance attributed by Robbe-Grillet to his own mode of composition, and this despite the fact that we are never given to witness any overtly oppressive act committed by the "narrator" against the native population, and, indeed, in the virtual absence of the field-workers themselves.

Such a phenomenological or genealogical reading of the act of looking now provides a transition to the more purely thematic content of the novel, and in particular to the omnipresent effect of light and darkness, with their privileged alternation cast by the slats of the jalousie itself. Yet the preceding discussion has put us in a position to understand these "images" (and it would be well for us to admit that the concept of the image as it is used in current literary criticism is deeply problematical) in something other than the standard "symbolic" sense. Leenhardt's splendid analysis of these materials strikes me as offering a model that may be generalizable to other kinds of literature as well: for him, the thematic imagery of *Jealousy* may be said to be a compensation and a substitution for precisely those more basic realities of the colonial situation and the native population, which, as we have indicated above, have been systematically repressed and excluded in the strict Freudian sense of neurotic denial or *Verneinung* (the Lacanian *dénégation*). In such a replacement sign-system, *light* will clearly continue to be the element of the *colon* himself and the medium of his domination, while its privative, darkness, is as indeterminate and inchoate as the surrounding population itself and expresses fear of the menacing absence through the very vulnerability of the masters and of their mansion in a henceforth invisible world.

Leenhardt's analysis also suggests, at this point, the relevance and indeed the fruitfulness of semiotic instruments and methodology. He points out, indeed, that what organizes these elements into a complete sign system cannot really be something so banal as an opposition between light and darkness. Rather, the latter is reorganized into a new artificial, and therefore *foregrounded*, sign-system in which the opposite of light is not so much darkness as rather *nature* itself: "Light and nature are thus complementary yet mutually exclusive. We may observe a constant alternation of the two from one end of the novel to the other, in a kind of Manichaean struggle" (p. 70.) The content of this new sign or thematic unity may then be resolved into a number of constituent elements, among which we can enumerate: the natives themselves and their songs, but also organic life in general, which is itself significantly "repressed," the larger animals associated with Africa, and the various emblematic wild flora and fauna all here represented by something like their most disembodied manifestation, namely insects (the *mille-pattes!*), and finally refined out of existence in the form of sounds, so that the final opposition of light and sound knows a rich genealogical content of its own. Here, if anywhere, it would seem to me that the analytic machinery worked out by A. J. Greimas finds its proper place and would have much to offer a sociological enterprise of this kind in the way of new insights and corroborative data.

Yet the basic objection to this section seems to me to lie elsewhere, in what might be called the insufficient radicalization of Leenhardt's approach to these thematic materials. For it seems to me possible that the hasty reader may well ignore the fairly complicated model that supports this work, and rather conclude—quite against its whole spirit—that the images of light, sound, nature, and the like are for Leenhardt precisely nothing but those "symbols" of some degraded and transparent allegorical meaning. We thus return, in a misreading of this kind, to a confusion between the "interpretation" of a work's signified and that deduction or deconstruction of its referential preconditions of which we spoke above. Before suggesting how this kind of misunderstanding might be avoided, however, let us follow Leenhardt's account of *Jealousy* on to the point at which it seems to open itself most fully to such objections.

This is, of course, the "political reading" which gives the work its title and which bears essentially on the central triangle itself: the moment, in other words, when the critic must fulfill his promise to transform the apparently psychological material to the novel's plot (the trip to the city of the wife and her lover Franck, the husband-narrator's unnamed fantasies of vengeance and depersonalized waves of jealousy) into phenomena of a sociological order. It is here, perhaps, that the legacy of Lucien Goldmann can most strongly be felt; here also that Leenhardt's reading is most liable to one of the classical objections made to the Marxist criticism in general, namely that it is essentially *allegorical* (the "typical" figures standing for the various social classes). For Leenhardt, the two male rivals undoubtedly "represent" two distinct moments of the colonial mentality, in its historical evolution from the stage of classical Western imperialism to that evolved during the decolonization process after World War II, or, in other words, what is henceforth termed neocolonialism. He marshalls a good deal of detail to support this reading: the disagreements between the narrator and Franck on the skills of the native population, Franck's table manners (repugnant to the narrator, as is in general the former's physicality and his erotic/aggressive vitality), Franck's own mechanical ability (repairing the truck), finally, the various opinions of and positions taken on the so-called African novel, the discussion of which thus serves to place the characters ideologically. In this connection, the key passage is the long plot *résumé* of the "novel within the novel" toward the end of the book, in which the "facts" rewrite themselves in a bewildering and comical series of reversals and contradictions whose inner logic the above hypothesis now clarifies:

The main character of the book is a customs official. This character is not an official but a high-ranking employee of an old commercial company. This company's business is going badly, rapidly turning shady. This company's business is going extremely well. The chief character—one learns—is dishonest. He is honest, he is trying to re-establish a situation comprised by his predecessor, who died in an automobile accident. But he had no predecessor, for the company was only recently formed; and it was not an accident, etc. (*Two Novels*, p. 137).

The alternatives, in their most extreme form, are clearly the new entre-preneurial-type private corporation and the older government-protected family firm, often assimilated into the colonial administration itself; while from the point of view of emotional investment and dramatic prognosis, the passage hesitates significantly between the death of Franck (the truck in flames, a fantasy already elaborated earlier in the novel) and the historical supercession of the narrator's own way of life. It is in this sense that the nar-rative of *Jealousy* ultimately, for Leenhardt, dramatizes the values of the new technological elite which will come to power in the Fifth Republic, marking an attempt to evolve "an ideology corresponding to the technocratic group or class subdivision on the level of production, whose fundamental mission is to overcome both those class antagonisms symbolized by socialist thought as well as the individualism associated with the traditional novel and with right-wing political thought" (p. 36).

So at length—and in spite of Leenhardt's evident attempt to sidestep the terms of the canonical realism/modernism debate—the classical dilemma of Marxist aesthetics, that of *evaluation*, comes once more slowly into view. The situation, as he states it, is not terribly different from that of the romantic culture into which Marxism itself emerged: a literature "progressive" in its aristocratic critique of capitalism and the nascent business civilization, "reac-tionary" in its defense of the privileges of a limited group or class. What makes this solution less suitable for the *nouveau roman* is precisely the qualitative transformation of modernism itself, in other words, the need to come to terms not only with the ideology of content, but with that of *form*, of the message inherent in the medium, of the connotative value of experiments with aesthetic perception itself. The older Marxism, that of the thirties, felt itself strong enough to reject the modernistic culture out of hand; yet its strength depended upon the presence of some genuine mass and working-class movement to which it could look for real cultural alternatives, and also upon a cultural field less saturated then than it is today by that palpable prac-tice of modernism which is at one with consumer society itself. For in that second "Great Transformation" which followed World War II (and which, for the U.S., we can perhaps conveniently date from the introduction of television and the simultaneous beginning of the Cold War in 1947), the aesthetic of modernism has triumphantly penetrated every corner of our psychic space and come to seem as unavoidable as cellophane, pollution, or paperback books. What is perhaps less widely understood is the degree to which the very economics of the consumer society, with its emphasis on planned obsolescence and ever more rapid styling and model changes, is intimately dependent on modernism and the new or modernistic sensibility as a laboratory and source of new shapes and patterns.

The ultimate evaluation of "modernism" is thus at one with the diagnosis of the new "société de consommation" itself, and we must surely reject—albeit with regret—the confidence of the Frankfurt School in the continuing negativity and subversive effect of the great modern works of art, voiced as recently as the following statement of Habermas: "Modern art is as little suited to fulfill the political system's need for legitimation as universalistic value systems. . . . The critical potentials of art and the powers which it frees for subversive countercultures are unmistakable."[7] This illusion may still be possible in Europe, but from the American vantage point surely it is rather Professor Trilling's distress which reflects the more realistic assessment, when, in *Beyond Culture*, he deplores the waning power of those great and explosively antisocial monuments of the first generation of modernism, when assimilated to the curriculum and transformed into cultural institutions in their own right.

To insist upon the effortlessness with which the consumer society is able to absorb and co-opt even the negativity of formalistic works like those of Beckett and Robbe-Grillet is not necessarily to suggest that a different type of aesthetic would have some easier situation to face. On the contrary, I would myself tend to go even further and to claim that *all* forms of art, when taken as objects in themselves, are co-optable today, and this holds for art of a revolutionary intent—posters, songs, novels—just as much as for the modernistic ones. Witness, if proof be needed, the burgeoning Brecht-Industrie, which, busily psychologizing those models of political propaganda, transforming them into the objects of scholarly scrutiny and thereby turning the whole corpus itself into some kind of grisly cultural "institution" in its own right, has triumphantly recuperated everything dangerous in Brecht's plays. (One thinks of the moment in Godard's *La Chinoise*—its director another prime target for just such cooptation—when the "revolutionary" heroes, effacing one after another the host of theatrical names on their blackboard from Sophocles to Strindberg, at length sadly run an eraser through the lone surviving one of Brecht himself.)

Yet this is so, not because there is no difference between a formalistic and a revolutionary literature, but rather because the very concept of the work of art *qua* aesthetic object is itself a fetishization and an abstraction. What is real is precisely not the isolated script or text itself but rather the work-in-situation, the work-in-performance, in which for a brief moment the gap between producer and consumer, between *destinataire* and *destinateur*, is momentarily bridged, and the twin crisis of a missing public and an artist without social function is temporarily overcome. We need something like a speech act theory on the level of aesthetics itself to shatter the academic reification of the "work of art" and to convince us that the concrete work of art—in other words, Brecht in performance, and by a revolutionary theater group to a politically conscious public—can never be coopted or shorn of its subversive elements.

This is, of course, why performance arts like the theater are more easily adaptable to a revolutionary aesthetic than is a form like the novel, itself already a reified product of the twin crisis to which we have just alluded. Yet it is precisely this inherent reification of the novel as a thing and a portable object which gives radical criticism its reason for being; and if there is a profound ambiguity about a Robbe-Grillet novel all by itself, that ambiguity may surely be reduced, either in that approximation to a concrete situation of performance which is the academic seminar, or in conjunction with a critical work like that of Leenhardt, which addresses itself to reducing just those ambiguities and to offering precise instructions for the "bon usage" of the modernistic object in question.

What, then, ought those instructions to be, and can we invent a new way of reading in which the requirements of political and historical consciousness and the specific demands of this particular aesthetic form are reconciled, albeit in some new and complex, second-degree mental operation? For it is clear that there can be no question of simply turning *Jealousy* back into one more novelistic presentation—whether naturalistic or revolutionary—of the colonial situation. We have shown, indeed, that while in the sense of the "referent" the novel is surely "about"colonialism, it must immediately be added that it is also trying *not* to be, and that its formal structure must be described precisely as an effort to *repress* that referential content and to defuse the implications of its raw material. Perhaps it would be more adequate to think of this operation in terms of the intentional act of Sartrean *mauvaise foi* rather than the unconscious of classical psychoanalysis: for every reader knows, when reading sentences about banana trees and native servants, insects and tropical drinks on cool verandas, that the narrative "intends" Africa as its ultimate object or referent; the real problem remains that of the use to which that "knowledge" is put.

Here perhaps Cubist painting may furnish a convenient analogy, inasmuch as Cubism also entertains complicated relations with representation and representationality: the viewer is in the same fashion well aware that his or her gaze "intends" bottles of wine, banjoes, flower vases, tables and bread knives; and yet the paintings demand that in some fashion we bracket or suspend that knowledge and attempt to "see" all those objects in some new and utterly unreferential way. They are in other words no longer meant to be stared at as elements of an object-world in their own right, as in Chardin or

the great Dutch still lifes; rather, they stand as the last inexpungeable vestiges of reality that must persist as a pretext for the viewer's pure absorption
in the painterly surface. Yet—and it is this critical reversal that Leenhardt's
book seeks to accomplish for *Jealousy*—yet the fact remains that Cubist paintings also have content, and that content is, if you will, simply the painter's
garret, the *bateau lavoir*, "ma jolie," Paris 1900, and the situation of the
artist himself in it, his patrons among intellectuals and aristocracy, the collec-
tors and the dealers, the Americans, the Third Republic, and ultimately the
entire cultural and historical moment itself as it leaves its concentrated trace
in the round stain of a wine glass on a deal table.

What we are now in a position to see is that modernistic works are not, as
the older Marxism would have it, simply ways of distracting us from reality,
and of substituting trivial concerns and encouraging "decadent" values and
activities (values we can today recognize as simply those—universally programmed in all of us—of the consumer society itself). Such works are (also?)
ways of distorting and repressing reality: they do not speak about something
essentially different from the content and raw material of revolutionary art;
rather, the same fears and concerns, the same historical perceptions and
political anxieties pass through them also, only what they attempt to do is not
to express, but rather to *manage* those fears, to disguise them, and drive them
underground. Thus, in *Jealousy* itself, the conflict between colonist and colonized is repressed, and its determinant underground reality masked by a
more local conflict among the colonists themselves; in classical Marxist
theory, we would describe the operation as the substitution, for the conflict
between classes, of a secondary or nonantagonistic contradiction within the
hegemonic class itself, between two of its tendencies, the older colonial mentality and the newer technocratic one of postindependent neocolonialism.

I would argue that to repudiate these modernistic works of art, or, even
more, to exercise, upon the silent and terroristic objects of the museum of
modern culture, the dramatic option of iconoclasm, is simply to reconfirm
the reified prestige, and as it were the sacred aura, of these fetishized names
and reputations. What is needed is rather something on the order of the
psychoanalytic *working through*, yet now on the level of political and ideological content. Such a process can be expected to dissolve the reification of the
great modernistic works, and to return these artistic and academic
"monuments" to their original reality as the private languages of isolated individuals in a reified society. This is no doubt in many cases to destroy the
works themselves in the process: only as a dream is destroyed by analysis,
through exhausting its content along with its fascination and leaving a shell or
husk to be discarded. It must no doubt also make us more uncomfortably
aware of our own vested interest, as academic scholars, in preserving precisely these scholarly "objects of specialization" to which our own professional
status is necessarily linked. Yet only through such a process of dereification

and of working-through can we restore something of the fragility and the pathos of aesthetic play as it stirs feebly and intermittently within the massive solidification of contemporary culture and media language. "Every master-piece," Gertrude Stein once said, "came into the world with a measure of ugliness in it . . . the sign of the creator's struggle to say a new thing in a new way. . . . It's our business as critics to stand in front of [Raphael's Sistine Madonna] and recover its ugliness."[8] Ugliness, but also clumsiness, amateurishness, indecision . . . all so many sloppy brushstrokes that signal the dissolution of the reified artwork back into its original *praxis*, that, free-ing us from the spell of the artistic commodity, once more permit a just and fraternal evaluation of the real achievement, as well as of the dilemma, of the solitary and subjectivized artist in a capitalist world.

Summer 1976

Chapter 8
Morality versus Ethical Substance; or, Aristotelian Marxism in Alasdair MacIntyre

Not unsurprisingly, this Hegelian distinction is underscored in Alasdair MacIntyre's recent *After Virtue*,[1] in such remarks as the following: "A moral philosophy . . . characteristically presupposes a sociology. For every moral philosophy offers explicitly or implicitly at least a partial conceptual analysis of the relationship of an agent to his or her reasons, motives, intentions and actions, and in so doing generally presupposes some claim that these concepts are embodied or at least can be in the real social world" (p. 22). MacIntyre's is far and away the most important and the most brilliant reformulation of the question of the ethical in recent years, a book with which any statement on the subject must necessarily come to terms. It proposes a return to the classical Aristotelian conception of the virtues, which he understands as being inseparable from a realized community, or polis, in which those virtues correspond to real social practices and not to either unrealizable imperatives or rules or to Stoic repressions. The move is therefore the Hegelian one in which individual conceptions of morality are dissolved in a vision of collective ethical substance; and indeed for MacIntyre the one great deficiency of Aristotle from any modern standpoint is the absence from classical thought of historicity as such, of the concept of the historical. This is not some personal weakness of Aristotle himself, however, but an inevitable consequence of the social formation or mode of production within which Aristotle did his thinking, and in this MacIntyre's designation of the structural limits of Aristotle's philosophy is at one with Marx's analogous remarks in the first volume of *Capital*. MacIntyre's is therefore a Hegelian Aristotelianism, and finally a Marxian one, insofar as Marx everywhere in this book constitutes the richest ultimate source for MacIntyre's vision of history and of social life.

Indeed, were one to wish to appropriate *After Virtue* for the Marxian tradition, it would be enough to point out that the first section of this book offers the most probing and devastating analysis of the reification of moral categories under capital that we possess. The conceptual adversaries addressed by MacIntyre—most notably, utilitarianism—are by him explicitly linked to the liberal individualism of the market system (as are a number of his seeming allies in the whole neoconservative or radical Right "return to virtue").

We can also learn something from MacIntyre's discussion of the collective or social basis of Aristotelian ethics in the polis itself; I am thinking in particular of his demonstration that for the Greeks generally and for Aristotle in particular, the virtues are not rules, commandments, or taboos that one enforces on one's self by violence. Rather, it is the other way around. The absence of virtue, or the enactment of some active form of evil or vice, constitutes a form of violence done to the community, a failure of one's commitment to that ongoing collective *project* that essentially defines community: "an offense against the laws destroys those relationships which make common pursuit of the good possible. . . . The response to such offenses would have to be that of taking the person who committed them to have thereby excluded himself or herself from the community" (p. 142). There is then a conception here of the group as a collective project, which already begins to suggest some of the newer ways of thinking about group formation toward which our contemporaries seem to be feeling their way—namely, the notion of Utopia as a state of siege, as a permanently beleaguered community, something as vivid in Ursula Le Guin's idea of a Utopia of scarcity (in *The Dispossessed*) as it is in Sartre's notion of the "group in fusion" (in the *Critique of Dialectical Reason*).

Yet it is precisely from the standpoint of anti-Utopianism that MacIntyre renounces the active part of his Marxian heritage—as well as repudiating the Nietzschean Utopia of the *Ubermensch* and indeed all overtly political movements and causes generally. Here the argument is at first linguistic and Wittgensteinian: "Both [Nietzsche and Sartre] saw their own task as in part that of founding a new morality, but in the writings of both it is at this point that their rhetoric—very different as each is from the other—becomes cloudy and opaque, and metaphorical assertion replaces argument. The *Ubermensch* and the Sartrean Existentialist-cum-Marxist belong in the pages of a philosophical bestiary rather than in serious discussion. Both by contrast are at their philosophically most powerful and cogent in the negative part of their critiques" (p. 21). Much the same is implied in his intermittent discussion of Marxism itself, where the projections of future socialist or communist societies are dismissed as empty of content and thus as nonphilosophical, on the grounds that what one cannot *say* is not to be considered thinking.

Two features of this rejection of the Utopian and the prophetic seem worth noting. The first has to do with the Popperian overtones of the judgment, which would imply that Marxism's vision of the future wanted somehow to be predictive in some "scientific" sense. MacIntyre reasserts the Renaissance and Machiavellian notion of *fortuna* as the predictably unpredictable, the necessarily unforeseeable form of future events, but this in a very different context, a context of the greatest interest to people in the field of cultural studies. For it is a striking feature of MacIntyre's book that it also rehearses one of the newest and most profound tendencies of contemporary thought in general, namely, the increasing foregrounding of narrative itself as a fundamental instance of human understanding (something also dramatically argued in Paul Ricoeur's recent *Time and Narrative*).[2] The insistence on storytelling is of course a significant component of MacIntyre's Aristotelianism, implying as it does a fundamental relationship between the intelligibility of a life and its social roles and possibilities; but it is also a crucial move in his critique of the increasing reification—that is, denarrativization—of contemporary ethical categories.

The other point to be made about MacIntyre's anti-Utopianism is that it recapitulates one of the great debates within Marxism itself, namely, the critique of Utopian socialism. "They have no *ideals* to realize," cried Marx of the workers at the climactic moment of his address on the Paris Commune; rather, he insisted that we should grasp them at work uncovering and revealing the new forms of cooperative and collective social relationships that had already begun to emerge within the interstices of the capitalist mode of production. For Marx also, then, socialism is a matter of already existent tendencies within our world, rather than of empty visions of the future to be realized on some mode of an ethical imperative (a Kantian position into which, as is well known, the Second International tended to lapse).

MacIntyre's call for a return to the Aristotelian virtues can thus, as he is only too keenly aware, be subjected to the same objections he raises to Marxism as a political movement: namely, whether from within capital it is possible to regenerate a life of social groups, a concrete social fabric, which on his own account is inseparable from the practice of those virtues.

His response, paradoxically and even ironically (given the tone and stance of his book as a whole), entails a kind of enclave theory very consistent with the increasing preoccupation with small-group or micro-politics characteristic of the late 60s and beyond. "Within the culture of bureaucratic individualism conceptions of the virtues become marginal and the tradition of the virtues remains central only in the lives of social groups whose existence is on the margins of the central culture" (p. 209). Even to the rhetoric of "marginality," this is a rather astonishing statement to find in a work whose thrust will generally be identified as conservative. It is, however, altogether logical in MacIntyre's framework, since he must be able to identify still surviving social groups approximating the polis sufficiently for their practice of the virtues to be concrete rather than projecting ideal and empty moral imperatives. The basic difference between MacIntyre's enclaves and those of 60s radicalism lies not in the concept, but in the content of those enclaves themselves. Although ethnic and religious communities are noted (see p. 234), it is significant that MacIntyre's central symbolic illustration is drawn from the work of the "last Aristotelian," namely, Jane Austen, in whose novels marriage comes to figure the last space of the older polis: "the restricted households of Highbury and Mansfield Park have to serve as surrogates for the Greek city-states and the medieval kingdom" (p. 224).

The entire complex argument of *After Virtue* would have to be ignored or misread for us to see in this emblematic evocation of the hearth yet another symptom of bourgeois "privatization." That it is a symptom of depolitization, however, is surely undeniable. The other argument mustered against historical materialism is not, indeed, the latter's empty Utopianism, but rather its increasing lack of any kind of Utopian politics: "as Marxists organize and move towards power they always do and have become Weberians in substance, even if they remain Marxists in rhetoric" (p. 103)—it is a telling reproach, but one that assumes that Marxism has in itself no further possibilities of development. But Marxism is here merely the marker for *all* contemporary political movements, a sign for the more general absence of any "tolerable alternative set of political and economic structures which could be brought into place to replace the structures of advanced capitalism. For I . . . not only take it that Marxism is exhausted as a *political* tradition, a claim borne out by the almost indefinitely numerous and conflicting range of political allegiances which now carry Marxist banners—this does not at all imply that Marxism is not still one of the richest sources of ideas about modern society—but I believe that this exhaustion is shared by every other political tradition within our culture" (p. 244). It would be a mistake to think that such discouragement does not also characterize the Left today, with its flirtations with various post-Marxisms and its return to a whole variety of Utopian speculations (in this sense, the whole so-called crisis of Marxism is in reality a crisis of Leninism, and it is not a crisis in Marxian "science" but rather in Marxist "ideology," which has everywhere singularly abandoned any attempt to project politically and socially gripping visions of a radically different future).

Jane Austen aside, however, MacIntyre also turns out to be just as Utopian as the rest of us. For in his closing lines yet another vision of the future is offered, one of a new dark age during which groups of people set about to construct "new forms of community within which the moral life could be sustained so that both morality and civility might survive the coming ages of barbarism and darkness. . . . This time however the barbarians are not waiting beyond the frontiers; they have already been governing us for some time. And it is our lack of consciousness of this that constitutes part of our predicament. We are waiting not for a Godot, but for another—doubtless very different—St. Benedict'' (p. 245). To which one is tempted to add, however, that such a St. Benedict, who will undoubtedly have studied the first stammering premonition and prophecy of his role in an ancient text called *After Virtue,* will necessarily by that book be sent back to read Marx fully as much as Aristotle.

Winter 1983-84

Notes

Notes

Unless otherwise indicated, all translations of foreign-language quotations are the author's.

Foreword: Fredric Jameson
and the Fate of Dialectical Criticism

1. James H. Kavanagh and Fredric Jameson, "The Weakest Link: Marxism and Literary Studies," *The Left Academy; Marxist Scholarship on American Campuses*, 2 vols. (New York, 1984), vol. 2, pp. 1-24.

2. Perry Anderson, *Considerations on Western Marxism* (London, 1976).

3. In an interview appearing in *Diacritics* (vol. 12 [1982], pp. 72-91) Jameson professes to see in his own potential leftward influence on intellectuals a modest form of practical engagement.

4. Fredric Jameson, *Marxism and Form* (Princeton, N.J., 1971), p. xviii.

5. Eugene Lunn, *Marxism and Modernism; an Historical Study of Lukács, Brecht, Benjamin and Adorno* (Berkeley, 1982), p. 130.

6. See Georg Lukács, "Expressionism: Its Significance and Decline," in *Essays on Realism*, ed. Rodney Livingstone, trans. David Fernbach (Cambridge, Mass., 1980), pp. 76-113.

7. This volume, p. 165.

8. See "Conclusion: The Dialectic of Utopia and Ideology," in *The Political Unconscious* (Princeton, N.J., 1981), pp. 281-99.

9. Jean-Paul Sartre, *Search for a Method*, trans. Hazel Barnes (New York, 1968), p. 7.

10. Samuel Weber, "Capitalizing History: *The Political Unconscious*," in *Institution and Interpretation* (Minneapolis, 1986), pp. 41-59.

11. Ibid., p. 46.

12. The suspicion that Jameson has rather too easily and hastily made his peace with rival, "bourgeois" theory through a premature appeal to a dialectical suspension of difference has been echoed elsewhere. Thus, for example, Terry Eagleton, in a review of *The Political Unconscious* (see "Fredric Jameson: The Politics of Style" in *Diacritics*, 12 [1982], pp. 14-22) more sympathetic than Weber's, has remarked in Jameson "a mode of absorption [of bourgeois theory] that leaves everything just as it was" (p. 18). Jameson's dialectical, metacritical stance astride non-Marxist theories allows the latter to be appropriated "at once too much and too little" (p. 17), a phenomenon which Eagleton discerns even on the level of the Jamesonian sentence itself, "at once both political message and play of signifier" (p. 16), and which he attributes, in a curious deviation from Weber's French take on Jameson's North American ex-

oticism, to Jameson's simultaneously un-American and yet not quite *European* intellectual affinities. In the end this Hegelian "too much, too little" is to be understood as perhaps a reflection of "the intractable problems of class-struggle in the contemporary US" (p. 21).

13. Weber, "Capitalizing History," p. 49.

14. Ibid., p. 51.

15. Ibid., p. 54.

16. Karl Marx, "Toward the Critique of Hegel's Philosophy of Law: Introduction," *Writings of the Young Marx on Philosophy and Society*, ed. and trans. Loyd D. Easton and Kurt H. Guddat (New York, 1967), p. 263.

17. Georg Lukács, *History and Class Consciousness: Studies in Marxist Dialectics*, trans. Rodney Livingstone (Cambridge, Mass., 1971), p. 169.

18. Jameson, *Marxism and Form*, pp. 372-73.

19. Fredric Jameson, "Third World Literature in the Era of Multinational Capitalism," *Social Text*, 15 (Fall 1986), p. 85.

20. Aijaz Ahmad, "'Jameson's Rhetoric of otherness and the 'National Allegory'," *Social Text*, 17 (Fall 1987), pp. 3-25.

21. Jameson, "Periodizing the 60s," *The Ideology of Theory*, vol. 2, p. 208.

22. Jameson, *The Political Unconscious*, p. 48.

23. See Jorge Larrain, *The Concept of Ideology* (Athens, Ga., 1979) and *Marxism and Ideology* (London, 1983).

24. See Jameson, "The Politics of Theory," *The Ideologies of Theory*, vol. 2, p. 111.

25. Ibid. p. 111.

26. Jameson, "Periodizing the 60s," *The Ideologies of Theory*, vol. 2, p. 207.

27. *Intellectual and Manual Labour: A Critique of Bourgeois Epistemology*, trans. Martin Sohn-Rethel (Atlantic Highlands, N.J., 1978), contains the essential arguments, although it excludes much of the more interesting political material included in the second German edition of Sohn-Rethel's work, *Geistige und körperliche Arbeit: Zur Theorie der gesellschaftlichen Synthesis* (Frankfurt, 1973).

28. See Sohn-Rethel, *Intellectual and Manual Labour*, pp. 170-72.

29. Sohn-Rethel, *Geistige und körperliche Arbeit*, pp. 212-13.

30. Ibid., p. 185.

31. Sohn-Rethel, *Intellectual and Manual Labour*, p. 158.

32. Ibid.

33. Perry Anderson, *In the Tracks of Historical Materialism* (London, 1983), p. 54.

Chapter 1. Metacommentary

1. Thus E. D. Hirsch, Jr.'s *Validity in Interpretation* (New Haven, Conn., 1967) strikes me as a victim of its own Anglo-American, "analytic" method: the most interesting idea in the book, indeed—that of a "generic" dimension to every reading, a preconception as to the type and nature of the text or Whole that conditions our apprehension of the various parts—is on the contrary a speculative and dialectical one.

2. *Théorie de la littérature*, ed. Tzvetan Todorov (Paris, 1965). Compare Shklovsky on the predominance of a particular authorial mode of being-in-the-world such as sentimentality: "Sentimentality cannot serve as the content of art, if only because art has no separate contents in the first place. The presentation of things 'from a sentimental point of view' is a special method of presentation, like the presentation of them from the point of view of a horse (as in Tolstoy's *Kholstomer*) or of a giant (as in Swift's *Gulliver's Travels*). Art is essentially trans-emotional . . . unsympathetic—or beyond sympathy—except where the feeling of compassion is evoked as material for the artistic structure" (Lee T. Lemon and Marian J. Reis, *Russian Formalist Criticism: Four Essays*, Lincoln, Neb., 1965; translation modified).

3. In *Forme et signification* (Paris, 1965).

4. The model derives from the *Cours de linguistique générale* of Ferdinand de Saussure, its wider relevance having been suggested by Marcel Mauss' *Essai sur le don* (The Gift), where various behavior patterns are analyzed in terms of presentation or exchange, thus making them easily assimilable to the exchange of information in the linguistic circuit.

5. *Anthropologie structurale* (Paris, 1958), "La Structure des mythes," esp. pp. 235–42; in English, *Structural Anthropology*, trans. C. Jacobson and B. G. Schoepf (New York, 1963).

6. See A. G. Wilden, *The Language of the Self* (Baltimore, Md., 1968), particularly pp. 30–31: "Ellipse and pleonasm, hyperbaton or syllepsis, regression, repetition, apposition—these are the syntactical displacements; metaphor, catachresis, antonomasis, allegory, metonymy, and synecdoche—these are the semantic condensations in which Freud teaches us to read the intentions—ostentatious or demonstrative, dissimulating or persuasive, retaliatory or seductive—out of which the subject modulates his oneiric discourse."

7. *Anthropologie structurale*, p. 239; *Structural Anthropology*, p. 215 (translation modified).

8. *Le Cru et le cuit* (Paris, 1964), p. 346; in English, *The Raw and the Cooked*, trans. Don and Doreen Weightman (New York, 1969), p. 341 (translation modified).

9. *Validity in Interpretation*, pp. 8, 211. Cf. Barthes' analogous distinction between literary *science* and literary *criticism* in *Critique et vérité* (Paris, 1966), p. 56.

10. *Against Interpretation* (New York, 1966), p. 220.

Chapter 2. The Ideology of the Text

1. "The central recommendation [of ethnomethodological study] is that the activities whereby members [of a given social group] produce and manage settings of organized everyday affairs are identical with members' procedures for making those settings 'account-able.' . . . I mean observable-and-reportable, i.e., available to members as situated practices of looking-and-telling." Harold Garfinkel, *Studies in Ethnomethodology* (Englewood Cliffs, N.J., 1967), p. 1. "To treat the cockfight as a text is to bring out a feature of it . . . that treating it as a rite or a pastime, the two most obvious alternatives, would tend to obscure: its use of emotion for cognitive ends." Clifford Geertz, *The Interpretation of Cultures* (New York, 1973), p. 449.

2. Page references to *S/Z* throughout this essay are to the English translation by Richard Miller (New York, 1974), with frequent modifications. The second numeral refers to the page number in the French original (Paris, 1970).

3. *Barthes par lui-même* (Paris, 1975), p. 120.

4. "L'Effet de réel," *Communications*, 11 (1968), p. 88.

5. "Texte," article on the theory of, in *Encyclopaedia universalis*, vol. 15 (1973), p. 1016. The word "semiosis," derived from Peirce, designates that process of the interpretations of signs whereby, in a properly infinite series, a new sign is proffered as an explanation, interpretation, or translation, of the older one. For an approach to semiotics based on this notion, one that successfully surmounts the strictures made on classical semiotics in the present essay, see Umberto Eco's *Introduction to Semiotics* (Bloomington, Ind., 1975). And see, for an earlier statement of Barthes on the nature of textuality, "De l'oevure au texte," *Revue d'esthetique*, 25, 3 (1971), pp. 225–32.

6. The number of codes is not immutable, and Barthes introduces somewhat different ones in "Analyse textuelle d'un conte d'Edgar Poe," in *Semiotique narrative et textuelle*, ed. Claude Chabrol (Paris: Larousse, 1973), pp. 29–54. The concept of a code has also been widely developed in film theory, particularly in the early work of Christian Metz, where, however, we find the same general hesitation shortly to be noted in *S/Z* between "narrative codes" or generic conventions and cultural languages, stereotypes, and "meanings."

7. See "Vraisemblance et motivation," *Communications*, 11 (1968), pp. 5–21.

8. See *Art and Illusion* (Princeton, 1960), chap. 1, pp. 33–62.

9. Jean Paul Sartre, Qu'est-ce que la littérature?" *Situations*, vol. 2 (Paris, 1948), p. 181.

10. Jonathan Culler, *The Uses of Uncertainty* (Ithaca, 1974).

11. Wayne Booth, *The Rhetoric of Fiction* (Chicago, 1961), p. 85; and see, for further strictures on Flaubert, n. 27, p. 373.

12. Booth, *Rhetoric of Irony* (Chicago, 1974), p. 172.

13. Veronica Forrest-Thomson, "The Ritual of Reading *Salammbo*," *Modern Language Review*, 67, 4 (1972), quoted by Culler, p. 223. And see, for a related study, her "Levels in Poetic Convention," *Journal of European Studies*, 2, 1 (1971), pp. 35–51.

14. Fredric Jameson, *The Prison-House of Language* (Princeton, 1972), p. 148.

15. Sigmund Freud, "Creative Writers and Day-Dreaming," Standard Edition (London, 1959), vol. 9, p. 252.

16. Ibid., p. 249.

17. "Vraisemblance et motivation," p. 13.

18. Barthes, *Mythologies* (Paris, 1957), n.7, p. 212; and compare his triumphant description of an ideological analysis capable of "despatching codes, one by one, along the strand of the text, their bellies in the air" (p. 100).

19. Michel Foucault, *The Order of Things* (New York, 1973), p. 16.

20. "Historical Discourse," in *Introduction to Structuralism*, ed. Michael Lane (New York, 1970), p. 151. The strongest literary statement of such a diagnosis has been made by Françoise Gaillard, who explicitly assimilates the structure of representationality to that of voyeurisme (see "La Représentation comme mise en scène du voyeurisme," in *Revue des Sciences Humaines*, 154, 2 (1974), pp. 267–82). Her arguments are, however, weakened by the choice of an example, *Les Diaboliques* of Barbey d'Aurevilly, which like the "Sarrasine" of Barthes, may scarcely be considered an example of nineteenth-century realism at all, but rather a pastiche of older storytelling.

21. See "Galileo and Plato," in A. Koyre, *Metaphysics and Measurement* (Cambridge, 1968).

22. Harold Weinrich, *Tempus* (Stuttgart, 1964).

23. Gilles Deleuze and Félix Guattari, *Anti-Oedipus: Capitalism and Schizophrenia*, trans. Robert Hurley, Mark Seem, and Helen R. Lane (Minneapolis, 1983).

24. Descartes, *Discourse on Method*, part 3 (New York, 1960), p. 20.

Chapter 3. Imaginary and Symbolic in Lacan

1. See Hegel, *Phenomenology of Mind*, chap. 1 ("Certainty at the Level of Sense Experience"), for the classic description of the way in which the unique experience of the individual subject (sense-perception, the feeling of the here-and-now, the consciousness of some incomparable individuality) turns around into its opposite, into what is most empty and abstract, as it emerges into the universal medium of language. And see, for a demonstration of the social nature of the object of linguistic study, V. N. Voloshinov, *Marxism and the Philosophy of Language* (New York, 1973).

2. Emile Durkheim, *Les Règles de méthode sociologique* (Paris, 1901), p. 128.

3. Sigmund Freud, *Standard Edition*, vol. 9 (London, 1959), p. 152.

4. It is true that the taboo on biographical criticism ought to make statements of this kind inadmissible; yet, particularly in a period when literary biography is flourishing as never before, it is perhaps time to have a closer look at the ideological function of that taboo. It should be observed that where the older biographical criticism understood the author's life as a context, or as a cause, as that which could explain the text, the newer kind understands that "life," or rather its reconstruction, precisely as one further text in its turn, a text on the level with the other literary texts of the writer in question and susceptible of forming a larger corpus of study with them. In any case, we need a semiotic account of the status of what are here designated as

"autobiographical" passages, and of the specificity of those registers of a text in which authorial wish-fulfillment—in the form of complacency, self-pity, and the like—is deliberately foregrounded.

5. Freud, p. 153. The mechanisms outlined here are much closer to the model of *Jokes and the Unconscious*—its object a message and a communication situation—than to that of *The Interpretation of Dreams*.

6. For good and for ill, Sartre's theory of language has much in common with that of Dilthey.

7. So, for example, in his discussion of the sacrificial dance in Stravinsky's *Sacre du printemps*, Adorno observes: "The pleasure in a condition that is void of subject and harnessed by music is sadomasochistic. If the liquidation of the young girl is not simplistically enjoyed by the individual in the audience, he feels his way into the collective, thinking (as the potential victim of the collective) to participate thereby in collective power in a state of magical regression" (*Philosophy of Modern Music*, New York, 1973, p. 159). I am tempted to add that recourse to the hypothesis of a sadomasochistic or aggressive impulse is always a sign of an unmediated and psychologizing ideology (on the other hand, Adorno's use of the concept of "regression" is generally mediated by the history of form, so that regression to archaic instincts tends to be expressed by or to result in regression to earlier and cruder formal techniques, etc.).

8. See "Authority and the Family," in Max Horkheimer, *Critical Theory* (New York, 1972), pp. 47–128; and also Martin Jay, *The Dialectical Imagination* (Boston, 1973), chaps. 3–5. The appeal to the institution of the family as the primary mediation between childhood psychic formation and class realities is also an important feature of Sartre's program for a reform of Marxist methodology in *Search for a Method* (New York, 1968), pp. 60–65.

9. Marie-Cécile and Edmond Ortigues, *Œdipe africain* (Paris, 1966), pp. 301–3.

10. Ibid., p. 304.

11. Serge Leclaire, "A la recherche des principes d'une psychothérapie des psychoses," *La Solution psychiatrique*, 1958, p. 383. A selection of the *Ecrits* (Paris, 1966) is now available in English, translated by Alan Sheridan (New York, 1977); meanwhile, of the five seminars thus far published in French (I, II, III, XI, and XX), only Volume XI *(The Four Fundamental Concepts of Psychoanalysis)* has been translated, also by Alan Sheridan (New York, 1978). An "authorized" guide to Lacan's thought, by Anika Rifflet-Lemaire *(Jacques Lacan,* Brussels, 1970), now also exists in English *(Jacques Lacan,* trans. David Macey, London, Boston, and Henley, 1977), and A. G. Wilden's pioneering *Language of the Self* (Baltimore, Md., 1968) has been reissued. The present essay also draws on Louis Althusser's "Freud and Lacan," in *Lenin and Philosophy* (New York, 1971). The newer literature on Lacan is too voluminous to list here; of the more personal and biographical accounts that have appeared since Lacan's death in 1981, Catherine Clément's *Lives and Legends of Jacques Lacan,* trans. A. Goldhammer (New York, 1983) and Stuart Schneiderman's *Death of an Intellectual Hero* (Cambridge, Mass., 1983), can be recommended. The quality and interest of the newer American approaches to Lacan can be measured by Ellie Raglund-Sullivan, *Jacques Lacan and the Philosophy of Psychoanalysis* (Urbana, Ill., 1984), and Jane Gallop, *Reading Lacan* (Ithaca, N.Y., 1986).

12. Rifflet-Lemaire, *Jacques Lacan,* p. 364.

13. A. Vergote, quoted in ibid., p. 138.

14. The fundamental text here is Ernest Jones, "The Theory of Symbolism," in *Papers on Psychoanalysis* (Boston, 1961); to juxtapose this essay, one of the most painfully orthodox in the Freudian canon, with the Lacanian doctrine of the signifier, which appeals to it for authority, is to have a vivid and paradoxical sense of the meaning of Lacan's "return to the original Freud." This is also the place to observe that American feminist attacks on Lacan, and on the Lacanian doctrine of the signifier, which seem largely inspired by A. G. Wilden, "The Critique of Phallocentrism" in *System and Structure* (London, 1972), tend to be vitiated by their confusion of the penis as an organ of the body with the phallus as a signifier.

15. "Le Stade du miroir," *Ecrits,* p. 94.

16. Insofar as this insistence becomes the basis for an anthropology or a psychology proper— that is, for a theory of human nature on which a political or a social theory may then be built—it is ideological in the strict sense of the term; we are thus entitled to find Lacan's stress on the "prepolitical" nature of the phenomenon of aggressivity (see *Le Séminaire*, Livre I, p. 202) somewhat defensive.

17. "L'Aggressivité en psychanalyse," *Ecrits*, p. 113.

18. Hans-Georg Gadamer, "Der Begriff des Spiels," in *Wahrheit und Methode* (Tübingen, 1965), pp. 97-105.

19. Freud, *Standard Edition*, vol. 17, pp. 179-204; and compare Jean-Louis Baudry's discussion of the 1911 essay, "On the Mechanism of Paranoia," in his "Ecriture, fiction, idéologie" in *Tel Quel: Théorie d'ensemble* (Paris, 1968), pp. 145-46.

20. *Le Séminaire*, I, p. 98.

21. Rifflet-Lemaire, *Jacques Lacan*, p. 219; and for an analysis of schizophrenic language in terms of part-objects, see Gilles Deleuze, "Préface" to Louis Wolfson, *Le Schizo et les langues* (Paris, 1970).

22. The archetypal realization of these fantasies must surely be Philip Jose Farmer's classic story "Mother," in *Strange Relations* (London, 1966), which has the additional interest of being a historic document of the psychological or vulgar Freudian weltanschauung of the 1950s, and in particular of the ideology of "momism" elaborated by writers like Philip Wylie.

23. St. Augustine, *Confessions*, Book I, part 7, quoted in *Ecrits*, p. 114.

24. See in particular *The Genealogy of Morals* and *Saint Genêt*. Neither fully realizes his intent to transcend the categories of "good and evil": Sartre for reasons more fully developed below, Nietzsche insofar as his philosophy of history aims at reviving the more archaic forms of rivalry rather than dissolving them.

25. "Le Stade du miroir," *Ecrits*, p. 97.

26. Melanie Klein, *Contributions to Psychoanalysis, 1921-1945* (London, 1950), p. 238.

27. *Le Séminaire*, I, p. 81.

28. Melanie Klein, *Contributions to Psychoanalysis*, p. 242.

29. See "L'Instance de la lettre dans l'inconscient," *Ecrits*, p. 515; or, in translation, "The Insistence of the Letter in the Unconscious," *Yale French Studies*, 36/37 (1966), p. 133. But for a powerful critique of the Lacanian figural mechanism, see Tzvetan Todorov, *Théories du symbole* (Paris, 1977), chap. 8, esp. pp. 302-5; and for a more general analysis of Lacan's linguistic philosophy, Henri Meschonnic, *Le Signe et le poème* (Paris, 1975), pp. 314-22.

30. *Le Séminaire*, I, p. 178.

31. Rifflet-Lemaire, *Jacques Lacan*, p. 129.

32. "Subversion du sujet et dialectique du désir dans l'inconscient freudien," *Ecrits*, p. 819.

33. *The Prison-House of Language* (Princeton, N.J., 1972), p. 205. This is the place to add that, while I would maintain my position on the other thinkers there discussed, I no longer consider the accounts of Lacan and of Althusser given in that book to be adequate: let this chapter and the next serve as their replacements.

34. Its fundamental texts are now available in English: "The Function of Language in Psychoanalysis" or so-called "Discours de Rome" (translated in Wilden, *The Language of the Self*); "The Insistence of the Letter" (see note 29 above) and the "Seminar on 'The Purloined Letter,' " in *Yale French Studies*, 48 (1972), pp. 39-72.

35. "La Direction de la cure et les principes de son pouvoir," *Ecrits*, p. 593.

36. As, e.g., in "Subversion du sujet et dialectique du désir," *Ecrits*, p. 814.

37. Freud, *Standard Edition*, vol. 14, pp. 152-53. This is the term Lacan translates as "le tenant lieu de la représentation."

38. *Ecrits*, p. 53.

39. *Ecrits*, pp. 805-17; but see also J. B. Pontalis' account of the 1957 and 1958 seminars, *Bulletin de psychologie*, 11, nos. 4-5, p. 293, and 13, no. 5, pp. 264-65.

40. Wilden, "The Function of Language in Psychoanalysis," p. 44, translation modified.

41. Ibid., p. 61ff. (or *Ecrits*, p. 297); here and elsewhere, Lacan bases a whole phenomenology of Imaginary space on ethological data. It would be suggestive, but not altogether accurate, to claim that the Imaginary and animal or "natural" languages alike are governed by *analog* rather than *digital logic*. See Thomas A. Sebeok, *Perspectives in Zoosemiotics* (The Hague, 1972), esp. pp. 63–83, and also A. G. Wilden, "Analog and Digital Communication," in *System and Structure*, pp. 155–90.

42. "Kant avec Sade," *Ecrits*, p. 780.

43. "Subversion du sujet et dialectique du désir," *Ecrits*, p. 820.

44. The aesthetic chapters of Guy Rosolato, *Essais sur le symbolique* (Paris, 1969), may serve to document this proposition: they also suggest that our frequent discomfort with psychoanalytic criticism may spring just as much from those ahistorical and systematizing categories of an older philosophical aesthetics in which it remains locked, as from its Freudian interpretative scheme itself. It will indeed have become clear that in the perspective of the present essay all of that more conventional Freudian criticism—a criticism that, above and beyond some "vision" of human nature, offers the critic a privileged interpretive code and the ontological security of some ultimate content—must for this very reason be understood as profoundly ideological. What now becomes clearer is that the structural oscillation here referred to in Lacanian conceptuality itself—the strategic alternation between linguistic and "orthodox Freudian" codes—often determines a slippage in the literary or cultural analyses of its practitioners whereby the properly Lacanian tension (or "heterogeneity") tends to relax into more conventional Freudian interpretations.

45. But see the chapter on Michel Leiris in Jeffrey Mehlman, *A Structural Study of Autobiography* (Ithaca, N.Y., 1974), as well as chap. 3 of Fredric Jameson, *The Political Unconscious* (Ithaca, N.Y., 1981), pp. 151–84; and see also Christian Metz, "The Imaginary Signifier," *Screen*, 16, no. 2 (Summer 1975); pp. 14–76. With respect to this last, not strictly speaking an analysis of an individual work, it may be observed that the structural discontinuity, in film, between the visual plenitude of the filmic image and its "diegetic" use in the narrative of a given film makes it a privileged object for the exercise of the Lacanian dual registers.

46. *Ecrits*, pp. 11-41 (for English translation, see note 34).

47. See Jacques Derrida, "The Purveyor of Truth," in *Yale French Studies*, 52 (1975), esp. pp. 45–47. But it might be argued against Derrida that it was Poe himself who first opened up this gap between the abstract concept and its narrative illustration in the lengthy reflections on detection and ratiocination with which the tale is interlarded.

48. "Présentation de la suite," *Ecrits*, p. 42.

49. See *The Prison-House of Language*, pp. 182–83, 197–201.

50. "Seminar on 'The Purloined Letter,' " p. 39 (or *Ecrits*, p. 11). Derrida's reading (see note 47), which emphasizes the moment of "dissemination" in the Poe story (in particular, the generation of doubles ad infinitum: the narrator as the double of Dupin, Dupin as the double of the Minister, the story itself as the double of the two other Dupin stories, etc.), thus in opposition to the Lacanian seminar foregrounds what we have learned to identify as the Imaginary, rather than the Symbolic, elements of Poe's text. Whatever the merits of the polemic here engaged with Lacan, as far as the tale itself is concerned, there emerges a sense of the tension between these two kinds of elements which suggests that it is not so much Lacan as rather Poe's text itself that tends toward a suppression of the traces of just this Imaginary "drift" of which Derrida here reminds us; and that is precisely the "work" of the text itself to transform those Imaginary elements into the closed Symbolic circuit that is Lacan's own object of commentary. This is why it does not seem quite right to conclude, from such a reemphasis on the Imaginary and "disseminatory," that "the opposition of the imaginary and symbolic, and above all its implicit hierarchy, seem to be of very limited relevance" (Derrida, pp. 108–9). On the contrary, it is precisely from this opposition that the exegetical polemic here launched by Derrida draws its interest.

51. Reread from this perspective, Walter Benjamin's seminal essay on *Elective Affinities,* "Goethe's *Wahlverwandtschaften,*" in *Schriften,* vol. 1 (Frankfurt, 1955, pp. 55–140), takes on a suggestively Lacanian ring.

52. Leclaire, "A la recherche," p. 382.

53. Edmond Ortigues, *Le Discours et le symbole,* p. 194.

54. Ibid., p. 205. The difference between an Imaginary study of the image and a Symbolic one may be dramatized by juxtaposing properly Imaginary works like Gaston Bachelard's *L'Eau et les rêves* (or its equivalent in the Anglo-American criticism of writers like G. Wilson Knight), with the new iconographic studies of the same image patterns, as in Alistair Fowler, "Emblems of Temperance in *The Faerie Queene,* Book II," *Review of English Studies,* n.s., 2 (1960), pp. 143–49.

55. It does not follow that as literary critics and theorists we have any business idly perpetuating the Lacanian polemic in the field of psychoanalytic criticism proper. Rigorous work like that of Ernst Kris or Norman Holland deserves to be studied in its own terms and not in those of some (properly Imaginary) feud between rival standard-bearers.

56. Mehlman, *Structural Study,* p. 182. Mehlman's critique of the limits of Sartre's Hegelianizing conceptual instruments in *Saint Genêt* (and most notably of the concept of synthesis) might well have been extended to Hegel himself, whose system in this respect constitutes a veritable *Summa* of the Imaginary.

57. See, for example, Roland Barthes, "An Introduction to the Structural Analysis of Narrative," *New Literary History,* 6, no. 2 (Winter 1975), pp. 256–60; and François Rastier,"Un Concept dans le discours des études littéraires," *Essais de sémiotique discursive* (Paris, 1973), pp. 185–206.

58. I have tried to explore the possibility of such an approach in two essays: "After Armageddon: Character Systems in Philip K. Dick's *Dr. Bloodmoney,*" *Science-Fiction Studies,* 5 (March 1975), pp. 31–42; and chap. 3 of *The Political Unconscious,* esp. pp. 161–69.

59. F. Jameson, "On Goffman's *Frame Analysis,*" *Theory and Society,* 3, no. 1 (Spring 1976), pp. 130–31.

60. On seriality, see *Marxism and Form* (Princeton, N.J. 1971), pp. 247–50. The concept of the dialogical is most fully developed in Mikhail Bakhtin, *Problems of Dostoevski's Poetics* (Ann Arbor, Mich., 1973), pp. 150–69.

61. Derrida, "The Purveyor of Truth," pp. 81–94.

62. *Le Séminaire,* I, p. 80.

63. "La Science et la vérité," *Ecrits,* p. 876; and see also the remarks on historiography in the "Discours de Rome" (Wilden, pp. 22ff, p. 50; or *Ecrits,* pp. 260ff, p. 287). The problem of the function of a genetic or evolutionary set of stages within a more genuinely dialectical conception of historical time is common to both psychoanalysis and Marxism. Lacan's insistence on the purely schematic or operational nature of the Freudian stages (oral, anal, genital) may be compared with Etienne Balibar's reflections on the proper uses of the Marxian evolutionary schema (savage, barbarian, civilized) in *Lire le capital,* vol. 2 (Paris, 1968), pp. 79–226.

64. "Seminar on 'The Purloined Letter,' " p. 61, or *Ecrits,* pp. 30–31.

65. The reproach that patients in analysis do not so much rediscover as rather "rewrite" their pasts is a familiar one, argued, however, most rigorously by Jürgen Habermas, in *Knowledge and Human Interests* (Boston, 1971), pp. 246–73.

66. Jacques Lacan, "Radiophonie," *Scilicet,* (1970), p. 75: "Some formulations are not just made up. At least for a time, they fellow-travel with the Real."

67. For the most powerful of recent attempts to reinvent this older kind of materialism, see Sebastiano Timpanaro, "Considerations on Materialism," *New Left Review,* 85 (May–June 1974), pp. 3–22. The reckoning on Timpanaro's attempt to replace human history within the "history" of nature comes due, not in his politics, nor even in his epistemology, but rather in his aesthetics, which, proposing that Marxism now "do justice" to the natural elements of the

human condition—to death, sickness, old age, and the like—turns out to be nothing more than a replay of existentialism. It is a significant paradox that at the other end of the Marxist spectrum—that of the Frankfurt School—an analogous development may be observed in Herbert Marcuse's late aesthetics.

68. For the most part, these developments on the subject of science have not yet been published; but see *Le Séminaire*, 20: *Encore* (Paris, 1975), pp. 20-21.

69. See Mark Poster, *Existential Marxism in Postwar France* (Princeton, N.J., 1975), chap. 2.

70. As outlined, for instance, in "Sur la dialectique matérialiste," in *Pour Marx* (Paris, 1965), pp. 161-224.

71. Louis Althusser, *Réponse à John Lewis* (Paris, 1973), pp. 91-98.

72. But it would be possible to show that Lukács' critique of bourgeois philosophy in *History and Class Consciousness* turns precisely on the distinction between referent and signified outlined above, particularly in the systematic demonstration of the inner structural limits of that philosophy which takes the place of a more conventional denunciation of the latter's "errors" of content.

73. Jacques Lacan et al., *Feminine Sexuality*, ed. Juliet Mitchell and Jacqueline Rose (New York, 1985), pp. 160-61, n. 6.

Chapter 4. Criticism in History

1. Serge Doubrovsky, *Corneille et la dialectique du heros* (Paris, 1963), p. 15.

2. George Eliot, *Middlemarch* (Boston, 1956), p. 613.

3. Northrop Frye, *Fables of Identity* (New York, 1963), pp. 33-34.

4. Ibid., p. 12.

5. See Mikhail Bakhtin, *Rabelais and His World* (Cambridge, 1968) and *Problems of Dostoevsky's Poetics* (Ann Arbor, 1973). A revised version of the latter work is now available, ed. and trans. Caryl Emerson (Minneapolis, 1984).

6. Jacques Ehrmann, "The Structures of Exchange in Corneille's *Cinna*," trans. Joseph H. McMahon, *Yale French Studies*, 36/37 (Fall 1966), 169-99.

7. Ibid., p. 198.

8. See "The Structural Study of Myth," in *Structural Anthropology* (New York, 1967), pp. 202-28.

9. See, for example, his *Philosophy of New Music* (New York, 1974).

10. Ehrmann, "Structures," p. 198.

11. Translated as *Man and Ethics: Studies in French Classicism* trans. E. Hughes (New York, 1971).

Chapter 5. Symbolic Inference; or, Kenneth Burke and Ideological Analysis

1. Frank Lentricchia's *Criticism and Social Change* (Chicago, 1983) proposes a rather different Burke, a genuine American "Western Marxist" whose stress on the political significance of culture and consciousness anticipates many of the reconstructions of Marxism in Europe after World War II (Sartre, Western Maoism, Marcuse, Fanon, the rediscoveries of Gramsci and Reich): this is a precursor and heroic ancestor whom one would be only too grateful to acknowledge. I continue to think, however, that the texts are objectively ambiguous, and that if they can be also read in the ways enumerated in the present chapter, their political function and authority will never be altogether secure.

2. John Berger, *The Look of Things* (1972; New York, 1974), p. 115; Louis Althusser, *Pour Marx* (Paris, 1965), pp. 238-43; and see also Terry Eagleton, *Criticism and Ideology* (London, 1976), p. 69: "Ideology is not just the bad dream of the infrastructure."

3. Kenneth Burke, *The Philosophy of Literary Form* (1941; 3d ed. rev., Berkeley and Los Angeles, 1973), pp. 5-6.

4. Burke, *A Grammar of Motives* (1945; reprinted Berkeley and Los Angeles, 1974), p. 462.

5. Ibid., p. 461.

6. Ibid., p. 289.

7. Ibid., p. 147.

8. Ibid., p. 142.

9. Burke, *The Philosophy of Literary Form*, p. 308. In fact, certain contemporary Marxisms—most notably those of Althusser and of Lucio Coletti—explicitly repudiate the concept of alienation as a Hegelian survival in Marx's early writings.

10. Ibid.

11. The point is not the absence of the terms from Burke's writing, but rather of the type of diagnostic or symptomal analysis to which they correspond. In fact, the concept of the unconscious is discussed at some length in an essay like "Mind, Body, and the Unconscious," *Language as Symbolic Action* (Berkeley and Los Angeles, 1966), pp. 63-80; for Burke's position on demystification and negative hermeneutics, see "The Virtues and Limitations of Debunking," *The Philosophy of Literary Form*, pp. 168-90.

12. Sebastiano Timpanaro, *On Materialism*, trans. Lawrence Garner (London, 1975), p. 56.

13. Yvor Winters, *In Defense of Reason* (Chicago, 1947), pp. 30-74.

14. Burke, *Counter-Statement* (1931; reprinted Berkeley and Los Angeles, 1968), pp. 123-83.

Chapter 6. Figural Relativism; or, The Poetics of Historiography

1. This chapter was originally written as a review of Hayden White, *Metahistory: The Historical Imagination in Nineteenth-Century Europe* (Baltimore, Md., 1973). The interested reader will find some different and more recent thoughts on *Metahistory* in my Foreword to A. J. Greimas, *On Meaning* (Minneapolis, 1987).

2. See Barthes' "Historical Discourse," in *Introduction to Structuralism*, ed. Michael Lane (New York, 1970), pp. 145-55.

3. An instructive comparison between the two is afforded by Burke's pathbreaking "Four Master Tropes," reprinted in the appendix to *Grammar of Motives* (Englewood Cliffs, N.J., 1954).

4. *Introduction à la littérature fantastique* (Paris, 1970), p. 18.

5. *Du Sens* (Paris, 1970), pp. 254-57. For a fuller description of a *combinatoire*, see my "Magical Narratives: Romance as Genre," chap. 2 of *The Political Unconscious* (Ithaca, N.Y., 1981), pp. 103-50.

6. Fredric Jameson, *Marxism and Form* (Princeton, N.J., 1971), pp. 93-94.

7. Barthes, "Historical Discourse," p. 52.

8. Lotman, *Statii po tipologii cultury* (Tartu, 1970).

9. Genette, "La Rhétorique restreinte," *Communications*, 16 (Fall 1970), p. 161.

10. It should be pointed out that the *Grundrisse* show that Marx by no means thought of this as an invariable sequence, but that he envisaged the emergence of capitalism precisely in terms of what Julian Steward calls "multilinear evolution." The myth of Marx as a unilinear evolutionist was developed as part of a general attack on Marxism by anthropologists of the school of Boas, assisted by the relatively simplistic positions of Engels in *The Origins of Private Property, the Family and the State*: see Marvin Harris, *Rise of Anthropological Theory* (New York, 1968), chaps. 9 and 10, pp. 250-300. For a convenient selection of Marx's own writings on the subject, see *Pre-Capitalist Economic Formations*, ed. E. Hobsbawm (New York, 1965).

11. "Foucault Decoded: Notes from Underground," *History and Theory*, 12 (1973), pp. 23-54.

12. Ibid., p. 48.

13. Marx and Engels, *The German Ideology* (New York, 1972), p. 47.

Chapter 7. Modernism and Its Repressed; or, Robbe-Grillet as Anti-Colonialist

1. This chapter was originally written as a review of Jacques Leenhardt, *Lecture politique du roman:* La Jalousie *d'Alain Robbe-Grillet* (Paris, 1973).
2. Alain Robbe-Grillet, *For a New Novel* (New York, 1965), "From Realism to Reality," pp. 157-68.
3. Jean Ricardou, *Problèmes du nouveau roman* (Paris, 1967), p. 143.
4. Fredric Jameson, *The Prison-House of Language* (Princeton, N.J., 1972), pp. 182-83.
5. See Didier Anzieu, "Le Discours de L'obsessionnel dans les romans de Robbe-Grillet," *Temps Modernes*, 233 (Oct. 1965), pp. 608-37.
6. See, for example, Alain Robbe-Grillet, *Two Novels* (New York, 1965), pp. 50-54.
7. Jürgen Habermas, "The Place of Philosophy in Marxism," *The Insurgent Sociologist*, 2 (Winter 1975), pp. 44-45.
8. Gertrude Stein, *Four in America* (New Haven, 1947), p. vii.

Chapter 8. Morality versus Ethical Substance; or, Aristotelian Marxism in Alasdair MacIntyre

1. Alasdair MacIntyre, *After Virtue: A Study in Moral Theory* (Notre Dame, Ind., 1981).
2. Paul Ricoeur, *Time and Narrative*, trans. K. McLaughlin and D. Pellaner (Chicago, 1984).

Index

Index

(Compiled by Joel Reed)

RITTER LIBRARY
BALDWIN-WALLACE COLLEGE

Fredric Jameson is the William A. Lane, Jr., Professor of Comparative Literature and director of the Graduate Program in Literature and Theory at Duke University. He previously taught at Harvard University, the University of California (San Diego and Santa Cruz) and Yale University. Jameson's books include *The Political Unconscious, Sartre: The Origins of a Style, Marxism and Form,* and *The Prison-House of Language.* He is also a co-editor of the journal *Social Text.* Three other forthcoming books will deal with film, dialectical aesthetics, and postmodernism.

Neil Larsen is an assistant professor of Spanish, comparative and Latin American literature at Northeastern University. He received his Ph.D. in comparative literature from the University of Minnesota in 1983. Larsen contributes to *Ideologies and Literature* and *Hispamérica.*